UNITED STATES

NAVAL AIR STATIONS

OF

WORLD WAR II

VOLUME 2: WESTERN STATES

UNITED STATES

NAVAL AIR STATIONS

OF

WORLD WAR II

VOLUME 2: WESTERN STATES

BY

M. L. SHETTLE, JR.

Library of Congress Catalog Card Number : 96-070565

ISBN: 0-9643388-1-5

Schaertel Publishing Co.
P.O. Box 66
Bowersville, Georgia 30516

Printed in Hong Kong

DEDICATION

This book is dedicated to LCdr. James H. Morrow, USN - MC retired.
For his service as a Navy corpsman during World War II, he received a Purple Heart and a Bronze Star.
As a Naval Flight Surgeon during Korea, he was awarded the Purple Heart, a Bronze Star, the Silver Star,
and the Prisoner of War Medal for two years as a guest of the North Koreans.
He contributed much of his time researching the Corpus Christi area for this book.

Table of Contents

Introduction

Prior to 1938, Naval Aviation was rather sparse in the Western States. The Western Naval Aviation establishment consisted of NASs at North Island, Seattle, Sitka, and Ford Island, plus small Naval Reserve Aviation Bases (NRAB) at Minneapolis, St. Louis, Oakland, Long Beach and a Fleet Operational Base under construction at Terminal Island. Due to the deteriorating world political situation, Congress passed the Vinson Navy Bill in May 1938 to support 3,000 Naval aircraft. During 1939, construction began at Alameda and Kaneohe Bay plus expansion of existing stations. In June 1940, Congress increased the useful ceiling of Naval aircraft to 10,000, only to raise it one month later to 15,000. That year, construction started at Corpus Christi, Tongue Point, Kodiak, and Dutch Harbor. NRABs were added at Dallas and New Orleans. The next year saw the start of Los Alamitos, Barbers Pt., Puunene, and Midway.

Before WW II, airports in the United States were very primitive and the vast majority consisted of grass or gravel runways. The introduction of larger and heavier military aircraft had made most airports obsolete. Congress funded the Civil Aeronautic Act of 1938 to improve the nation's airport system for national defense. A January 1939 CAA survey of the 1,907 civil airports in the U.S. showed 882 with refueling facilities, 230 with adequate lighting, and only 231 with hard-surfaced runways. Initially, the Army cooperated with the CAA in selecting sites to be developed or improved for military use that would benefit civilian aviation after the war. Beginning in 1941, the Navy, as a member of the Interdepartmental Air Traffic Control Board, participated in the selection process. The CAA also improved existing airports or approached local governments and offered to build an airport if the land were provided. The Navy took over several of these civilian developed airports and only had to add

buildings and other facilities. In addition, the CAA built 28 Flight Strips for Army defense purposes in remote areas adjacent to highways. Most of these Flight Strips were located in coastal areas. State highway departments were consulted in the selection of these sites, since highway crews were to provide maintenance. During 1942, 21 Flight Strips were constructed at an average cost of $394,000. The program was halted after 1942, because the government felt that the resources could be better spent elsewhere. The Navy eventually took over several Flight Strips that included Half Moon Bay, Lomita, and Oxnard California; Battle Mountain and Lahontan, Nevada; and Aurora, Oregon. Most of the United States' modern hard-surfaced airports were built or improved from 1939 to 1945 with the majority remaining in use today.

One month after Pearl Harbor, President Roosevelt approved a total of 27,500 aircraft for the Navy. An appropriate number of additional air stations west of the Mississippi were begun. These included primary training, fleet operational, fleet training, plus development and testing stations. Naval aviation's build-up was slow, since around two years were required to build and put an Essex Class aircraft carrier into combat operations. Most of the new construction reached completion by the end of 1943. On June 15, 1943, President Roosevelt approved a total of 31,447 planes. The final wartime ceiling of 37,735 Naval aircraft was set on February 2, 1944.

The one group of stations yielding the least amount of return were the new blimp bases. Two stations were added on the Gulf of Mexico to counter the U-boat threat there; however, by the time the stations reached completion in 1943, the U-boats had been driven out of the Gulf. The mission could have easily been accomplished with landplanes and the money spent elsewhere. On the Pacific Coast, the

Navy's LTA program called for the establishment of three blimp stations. The Navy reclaimed Moffett, transferred to the Army in 1935, and built two new stations at Tillamook and Santa Ana. Japanese submarines never became a serious factor on the Pacific Coast. Blimp hangars cost approximately $2.5 million each and, in retrospect, the ones built west of the Mississippi were superfluous at best.

Meanwhile, the Army was engaged in a very ambitious base building program. Inevitably, conflict broke out with the Navy. In the Author's opinion, the primary cause was the Army's lack of appreciation for Naval aviation -- an attitude that persists to this day in the Air Force. The Army believed aviation was its exclusive domain and considered the Navy an intruder. In addition, elements in the Army still resented the agreement in the 1930s, whereby the Army was forced to turn over its holdings at Ford Island, North Island, and Bolling Field to the Navy in exchange for Moffett Field. This agreement, ordered by President Roosevelt, caused the Army to feel short-changed. As a result, the Army derisively referred to FDR as "an old Navy man" -- in fact, Roosevelt served as Assistant Secretary of the Navy from 1913 to 1921. Army Chief of Staff General George C. Marshall, repeatedly frustrated at Roosevelt's wartime favoritism toward the Navy, once blurted out: "At least Mr. President, stop speaking of the Army as "they" and the Navy as "us."

As early as April 1941, an Interdepartmental Air Traffic Control Board, consisting of the Army, Navy, and CAA formed to resolve conflicts. Most disagreements occurred during the base build-up by both services during 1942-43. One of the chief antagonists was BGen. Robert Olds, at that time, commander of the Second Air Force. Although he had almost exclusive use of the entire state of Kansas, Olds, nevertheless, objected to the Navy's plan to develop a base at Hutchinson in 1943. Olds wanted to develop an airbase at Hutchinson and was nonplused when he learned the Navy had previously received permission from the Board. Additionally, the Navy objected to the Army's planned nearby bases at McPherson, Newton, and Lyons. The Board sided with the Navy, but in return, the Navy had to abandon plans to develop a station at Grand Island, Nebraska. Later in the year, another disagreement involving Olds developed over air space around Pasco, Washington. After receiving what he considered to be "an extremely arrogant letter" from the Commandant of the 13th Naval District, Olds threatened to patrol the disputed airspace area with fighters and fire in front of Navy primary trainers. Hostilities were avoided when the Board agreed with Olds. Navy aircraft were restricted to an altitude of less than 3000 ft. within 20 miles of Pasco. Following the war, Secretary of War, Henry L. Stimson wrote: "The Air Forces considered the Navy a backward service with no proper understanding of air power; the Navy considered the Air Forces a loud-mouthed and ignorant branch which had not even mastered its own element... What too often came to Army and Navy headquarters in Washington were emotionally embroidered reports of the incompetence of the other service. "

Generally, cooperation between the services was good. As early as May 1942, the Navy used the Army airfields at Little Rock, Arkansas; Tuscon, Arizona; Wichita, Kansas; Shreveport, Louisiana; Jackson and Meridian, Mississippi; Oklahoma City, and Tulsa, Oklahoma; Medford and Portland, Oregon; and Abilene and El Paso, Texas, to service Navy transient aircraft. In return, the Navy allowed the Army to station interceptor aircraft at Navy airfields. Case in point is the San Diego area, where no Army airfields existed and the Army stationed fighters at the Navy's Ream, Camp Kearny, and Brown Fields. Let there be no doubt about it, the majority of airfields in the West were built by the Army or for

Army interests by the CAA. Being charged with the air defense and antisubmarine mission of the country, the Army began its base building program earlier and more aggressively than the Navy. In the Pacific coastal regions, the Army improved the airfields for air defense on Navy fields at Arlington, Mt. Vernon, Quilliyute, and Shelton, Washington, as well as Navy-owned San Nicolas Island, California. In addition, in 1942, a Japanese invasion of the West Coast was a serious threat. To counter this, additional airfields were built or improved inland to repulse a possible Japanese landing. Future Navy fields built or improved under this program included Inyokern, California; Klamath Falls, and Lakeview, Oregon; and Fallon, Nevada.

Due to lack of available land in Hawaii and Alaska, cooperation was by necessity extremely good. Most of the airfields in Alaska were built by the Army for joint use by the Navy. The Army stationed its interceptor fighters at many of the Navy fields in Hawaii. The Navy built an NAS at the Army developed airfield at Hilo. In early 1944, the Army also allowed the Navy to use Barking Sands for six months.

Most of the Army Air Force's expansion had taken place during 1942. By the end of 1943, the large training push by the Army had ended and many unused bases were on hand. The base surplus was further aggravated by the fact that the Army's antisubmarine mission had been turned over to the Navy in the fall of 1943 and the threat of a Japanese invasion or carrier raid had evaporated. Such was the over-build, that in early 1944, General Hap Arnold ordered there would be no additional construction without his personal approval. At the Navy's request for additional airfields, Army commanders identified 84 surplus airfields available for transfer. During 1944 and 1945 in the west, the Army transferred to the Navy the former airbases at King City, Thermal, Twenty Nine Palms, Ventura, California; and Corvallis, Oregon plus many auxiliary fields. Some

transfers were conditional and others on a permanent basis. While the Army had reduced its main and sub-bases from a high of approximately 460 in December 1943 to 400 by VJ-Day, the Navy continued to add stations almost to the end of the war. Of the 69 WW II Naval air stations west of the Mississippi (excluding Alaska and Hawaii) with airfields, only 29 were built from scratch by the Navy.

In 1942, Naval planners established a need to train 30,000 new pilots a year. After combat losses, combat fatigue, and flight training failures fell way below expectations, a proposal surfaced in August 1943 to reduce the pilots in training by 50%. Morale in the Training Command dropped to an all-time low. At the Great Lakes Training Center, an Admiral, trying to address a group of ex-cadets on their place in the Navy, was summarily booed off the podium. The 50% reduction was later revised downward, but by then an increase in pilot training time had taken place. Incredibly, a cadet who began training in mid-1943 could remain in the pipeline for over two years and never reach combat. Primary trainers had been reduced from a high of 3857 to 2000 aircraft by the end of 1944. As the demand for primary training lessened, some of those stations were converted for the training of fleet units and other uses. All of the former primary training stations on the West Coast, Pasco, Los Alamitos, and Livermore, went this route as well as St. Louis, Minneapolis, Hutchinson, and Olathe. Intermediate training diminished as well with operational training being added at Corpus Christi and Kingsville.

The West saw the greatest growth of Naval aviation during the war. With vast un-populated land areas, the Western States were suited to the establishment of gunnery and bombing ranges. On the other hand, in the East, gunnery ranges had to be established over water. Most importantly, the Western States were the closest to the Pacific Ocean and the United States Navy's prime adversary, the Japanese.

UNITED STATES

NAVAL AIR STATIONS

OF

WORLD WAR II

VOLUME 2: WESTERN STATES

MAY 1943 NATIONAL ARCHIVES

NAS Adak, Alaska

Prior to the Japanese invasion of the Aleutians, Navy PBYs operated from seaplane tenders at Adak. The Navy temporarily retreated to the east, following the Japanese occupation of Attu and Kiska on June 7. The seaplane tender *Gillis* and the destroyer *Kane* returned to Adak on July 19 and were attacked shortly thereafter by three Japanese seaplanes from Kiska. After two unsuccessful attacks on Adak, two of the seaplanes were shot down by Army P-38s over Atka on August 4. The Japanese withdrew the remaining seaplane to Japan.

U.S. forces needed a base closer to Attu and Kiska. The Army wanted to develop Tanaga Island -- its terrain allowed for a better airfield, but it had no harbor. On the other hand, the Navy opted for Adak which had the best harbor in the Western Aleutians. After the local Army and Navy commanders reached an impasse, the decision was sent to Washington. The Joint Chiefs of Staff chose Adak.

On August 30, 1942, U.S. forces landed on Adak and began construction. A seaplane tender, the USS *Teal*, set up an advanced seaplane base the same day. Army engineers filled in a tidal basin and completed an airfield in ten days, while Seabees set about to construct the Navy's facilities. The first operation of Army aircraft on September 14, sunk two ships and killed 200 Japanese in an attack on Kiska. The Navy's presence on Adak grew rapidly. A PT boat base and other ship facilities were developed as Adak became the major Naval base in the Aleutians. The headquarters of the Alaskan Sector of the 13th Naval District and Fleet Air Wing 4 moved to Adak from Kodiak in March 1943. VB-135 with Lockheed PV-1 Venturas arrived in April and began operations against the Japanese. The radar equipped PV-1s also acted as pathfinders for Army B-24s in bombing raids. On May 1, the Navy commissioned Adak an NAS. On May 11, U.S. forces invaded

Attu and by May 30, had wiped out the Japanese garrison. Naval aircraft then moved forward to Attu after completion of the base there. Operations continued against the island of Kiska, still occupied by the Japanese. One year after construction started at Adak, the island's Army and Navy military population totaled 90,000.

During 1944, Adak grew in size and importance, although most operational flights had moved forward to Attu. When the 17th Naval District was created in 1944, its headquarters were at Adak. The Navy further developed the base as a communications and supply center for possible attacks of Japan through the Kuriles Islands.

The Naval reservation on Adak totaled 2613 acres. Naval aviation had three seaplane ramps, the use of the Army's 6,000 and 5200 ft. runways, and nine hangars. The base supported two 12-plane amphibian squadrons, one 12-plane PV squadron, and one 12-plane observation squadron. Barracks were available for 331 officers and 3320 enlisted men. NATS and Pan American provided transport service to the island. Adak also had the command of the auxiliary air facility at Kiska.

After the war, the Navy remained at Adak although the headquarters of the 17th Naval District moved to Kodiak. When the Air Force left Adak in 1950, the Navy took over all military facilities on the island. In the next 40 years, Adak became the center for U.S. Naval antisubmarine operations against the Russians. Naval patrol aircraft, first P2Vs and later P-3s, maintained a constant presence on the island as the base's population reached 5,000 persons. Adak was recommended for closure by the Navy to the 1995 Base Realignment and Closure Commission. The station is scheduled for complete shutdown by January 1, 1998. The U.S. Fish and Wildlife Service, which manages the southern end of the island, the American fishing industry, and the Aleut Indians are presently lobbying for control of the Navy's $1.5 billion facility.

Navy area at the Adak Army Airfield in June 1943 with PV-1s and a lone PBY-5A.   *NATIONAL ARCHIVES*

NAS Alameda, California

Alameda is located on the eastern shore of San Francisco Bay, adjacent to Oakland. The first local aircraft flight occurred in 1911 to entertain the visiting President Taft. During WW I, the City's fathers proposed Alameda for a Naval base, but no action was taken. In 1927, an airport was built with one east/west runway, an administration building, three hangars, and a yacht harbor. Three years later, the Army established an air base at the airport, now known as Benton Field. Over the next few years, the City continued to expand the airport's area by filling land into the bay. In 1935, Pan American Airways took over the yacht basin and inaugurated flying boat service to Hawaii and the Orient. On June 1, 1936, Alameda deeded the entire property to the government for the nominal fee of $1. Four months later, the Army abandoned Benton Field and turned over its facilities to the Navy. Due to budget constraints, no construction would take place by the Navy for another two years.

In 1938, Congress finally appropriated $10 million to develop a Naval Air Station at the site. The next year, Pan American moved to a new base at Treasure Island. Construction at Alameda proceeded at a leisurely pace. The station commissioned on November 1, 1940, with a minimum of facilities.

Initial construction provided for two carrier air groups, five seaplane squadrons, two utility squadrons, and an Assembly and Repair Department. In July 1940, additional funds were appropriated to enlarge the station with two seaplane hangars and a carrier berthing pier, as well as other facilities. With the start of the war, patrol and scouting squadrons began operations commanded by Fleet Air Wing 8. Carrier squadrons also were formed and commenced combat training. CASU 6 commissioned to support the carrier units. Construction resumed once again and proceeded rapidly with hydraulic fill operations

adding more land. A 345-man Army antiaircraft unit moved aboard after Pearl Harbor to provide air defense. On April 1, 1942, the Navy's second Naval Air Transport Squadron, VR-2, formed at the station and operated its first flight to Hawaii on May 15.

The same day VR-2 commissioned, LCol. Jimmy Doolittle's 16 B-25s arrived at Alameda and were loaded aboard the USS *Hornet*. The next day, the *Hornet* departed in broad daylight -- destination unknown with the exception of three men: Doolittle; Adm. Mitscher, commander of the Task Force; and Navy Lt. Henry Miller, who had instructed the Army pilots in short-takeoff procedures. Sixteen days later, Doolittle and his men bombed Tokyo. Of the 80 crewmen, five died in crash landings and three were executed by the Japanese. Doolittle received the Medal of Honor for leading the raid.

San Francisco Bay area was the major Naval surface and supply base on the West Coast -- Alameda provided aviation support for these activities. Scout and Observation Service Unit 3 (SOSU 3) commissioned at Alameda and supported the various aircraft assigned to the battleships and cruisers in San Francisco Bay. SOSU 3 functioned similar to a CASU, but serviced and trained personnel in the operation of catapult and scouting aircraft. During the remainder of 1942, Alameda began building several auxiliary air stations in the central California area. In January 1943, station personnel stood at 100 officers and 3,543 enlisted men. In April, Alameda opened an auxiliary at Oakland, followed in May by Crows Landing and Monterey. The next month, additional auxiliaries commissioned at Vernalis, Santa Rosa, and Hollister -- Arcata opened in July and Watsonville in October. In addition, Pan American Airways' Pacific operation had been placed under contract to the Navy and Pan Am's base at Treasure Island was made an NAAF. The

Navy designated Alameda as a Naval Air Center with overall command of these auxiliaries. The Commander Fleet Air Alameda was vested with command of the aviation activities of these stations and held the rank of Commodore. By year's end, personnel aboard reached over 10,000.

In June 1944, Alameda opened an additional auxiliary at Fallon, Nevada for an aerial gunnery school. When Pan Am moved its operation from Treasure Island to Mills Field, San Francisco's municipal airport, the Navy established an NAAF at that location. When primary training ended at Livermore in 1944, that station was also placed under the command of Alameda. Various patrol squadrons of PBMs, PVs, and PB4Ys also passed through Alameda during the war and were supported by Patrol Aircraft Service Unit 8 (PATSU 8). By the end of 1944, almost 1400 aircraft were on board, although over 1000 were in various stages of overhaul or repair by the Assembly and Repair Department -- the largest activity on the station. VR-2 ultimately operated 54 aircraft that included transport versions of the Consolidated PB2Y Coronado and the PBM Mariner plus the lone Martin PB2M-1R Mars. On April 6, 1945, Alameda opened the last of its auxiliaries at King City, formerly used for Army primary training. By the end of the war, Alameda's personnel totaled 29,000 servicemen and civilians with almost 2,000 aircraft present. The Navy investment in the station reached a total of $75 million.

Alameda's 2327 acres had five 500-ft. wide asphalt runways -- the longest 5,000 ft. Initially, the airfield was painted in a camouflage pattern to guard against possible air attack. The station had twelve auxiliaries and one OLF at Concord, California. Aircraft assigned to the station totaled 18, plus the 12th Naval District Commandant's JRB. Barracks existed for 979 officers and 14,417 enlisted men.

Following the war, Alameda continued to provide services and support to the aviation activities of the Pacific Fleet. All of Alameda's auxiliaries eventually closed with the exception of Fallon, Nevada, that became an NAS and Crows Landing that became an OLF. With the arrival of jet aircraft, one of the base's runways was extended to 7,200 ft. and a new 8,000-ft. runway added. The seaplane transport squadron, VR-2, continued to operate from Alameda with JRM Mars and R3Y Tradewinds until that squadron decommissioned in April 1958. With the closing of Oakland in 1961, Reserve activities moved to Alameda. In the last 30 years, the primary activities of the station have been homeport of aircraft carriers, aircraft overhaul and repair, and Reserve activities.

In 1994, Alameda was homeport to the nuclear-powered aircraft carriers, the USS *Carl Vinson* and the USS *Abraham Lincoln,* as well as two guided missile cruisers and a destroyer tender. The Naval Aviation Depot (former Assembly and Repair Department) is the largest activity on the base and employs over 3,500 civilians that overhaul, repair, and modify Naval aircraft. Five Reserve squadrons are also based at the station. Alameda, after 50 years of service to the fleet, has been selected for closure by the 1993 Base Realignment and Closure Commission. The planned date is set for 1997.

UPPER RIGHT: Naval Air Transport Service office at Alameda in August 1943. Alameda was home to VR-2, an all seaplane operation after March 1943 when its landplanes were transferred to Oakland's VR-11.   *NATIONAL ARCHIVES*

RIGHT: The lone Martin PB2M-1R served with VR-2 during 1944 and early 1945. Early in 1944, the Mars set a world record when it flew the 4700 miles to Hawaii and back in 27 hours and 26 minutes, delivering 20,500 lbs. of cargo to Hawaii in the process. Six additional single-tail Mars were delivered after the war as the JRM. In 1996, one Mars was still flying as a forest fire water-bomber in Canada.   *MAY 1944 NATIONAL ARCHIVES*

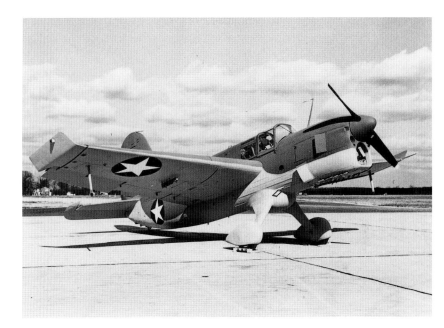

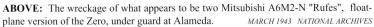

ABOVE: The wreckage of what appears to be two Mitsubishi A6M2-N "Rufes", float-plane version of the Zero, under guard at Alameda. *MARCH 1943 NATIONAL ARCHIVES*

ABOVE RIGHT: The Curtiss SO3C Seamew was designed to replace the biplane SOC Seagull. The Seamew was plagued with instability problems that led to the upturned wing tips and a larger vertical stabilizer. The powerplant was a Ranger V-770 inline, a rarity for U.S. Navy aircraft. Unsatisfactory performance caused the aircraft to be withdrawn from fleet use in early 1944. As a result, the biplane SOC remained in frontline service to the end of the war. Many of the Seamews were modified as radio controlled drones. A total of 459 was produced with 250 of that number going to the British.

NATIONAL ARCHIVES

RIGHT: Problems with the SO3C, prompted Curtiss to propose the SC Seahawk. Ordered in June 1943, the first of 577 Seahawks was delivered in October 1944. All the Navy's floatplanes were delivered with fixed landing gear. The Navy ordered float kits separately and installed them when needed. *NATIONAL ARCHIVES*

NAAS Arcata, California

In 1939, the U.S. government sent a survey team north from San Francisco to find sites within one mile of the coast that could accommodate a 5,000-ft. runway. In the 400 miles to the Oregon border, only two sites were found -- Arcata and Crescent City. In early 1943, the Navy leased 442 acres, seven miles north of Arcata, to build an auxiliary air station. The area, known as Dows Prairie, had a grass air strip. During construction, the coast highway, U.S. 101, had to be relocated to accommodate the runways. The station's commissioning took place on July 7, 1943, as an auxiliary of Alameda.

Unfortunately, after the Navy opened the station, it discovered that Arcata had the third foggiest weather in the world. On occasion, fog would set in for weeks at a time. As a result, the Navy failed to achieve the maximum intended utilization of the station, but did take advantage of the situation by conducting fog dispersal experiments. Arcata was initially planned as a base for 24 Ventura patrol bombers. The first operational unit on board, however, was the utility squadron VJ-2 that arrived in December 1943. VJ-2's complement consisted of five Avengers, six JMs, one J2F Duck, and one R5O. In the summer of 1944, VS-71 with 11 SBDs was on board. For the remainder of the war, Arcata served as a rocket training facility for squadrons and air groups from Santa Rosa. The training was conducted by a detachment of Santa Rosa's CASU 36. In September 1944, CASU 36 had 15 F6F Hellcats. Four months later, CASU 36's aircraft consisted of 11 FM-2s, one SBD, and 12 Avengers. CASU 36's activities diminished and ended before VJ-Day.

Located 290 miles north of San Francisco, Arcata had one 6,000-ft. and one 4,500-ft. asphalt runway. An additional runway, previously planned, was cancelled. In March 1944, station personnel numbered 153 officers and 532 enlisted men with barracks for 180 officers and 732 men. The station had a 128 x 160-ft. Kodiak hangar plus gun emplacements around the airfield. Arcata's station planes consisted of two GH Howard ambulance planes and one GB Staggerwing Beech.

Following the war, the area's bad weather served some useful purpose with the establishment of the Landing Aids Experiment Station. This unit was a joint project of the Army, the Navy, and the CAA that experimented with low visibility landings. United Airlines served as the prime contractor of the project. The most novel method was the "Fog Intensity Dispersal Of" or FIDO that involved the burning of gasoline along the sides of the runway to lift the fog. The British first used FIDO during the war when 157 Lancaster bombers landed at Heathrow during zero/zero weather. The simplest method consisted of burning the fuel in open trenches alongside the runway. The best results were obtained by burning from pressurized nozzles positioned every 50 ft. down the runway edge. Unfortunately, it took 20,000 gals. to sufficiently raise the fog for each landing. Gasoline cost alone was $15,000 per landing -- plus an additional $10,000 per landing for the system's maintenance. Not only was the cost prohibitive, but the system only worked on 150-ft. wide runways. When used on 200-ft. wide runways, the fog merely lifted from the sides and settled onto the center. Finally, the effort concentrated on the electronic-guided ILS. Arcata had the first ILS system in California that was eventually certified down to zero/zero. The government closed the experimental station in 1950 and deeded the property to the County.

In 1977, the Coast Guard opened an air station at the airport -- today, known as Arcata Eureka Municipal. Several Navy structures have survived. The foggy weather has lessened over the years.

Ordnance men load Avenger with 3.5" and 5" AR rockets. *NATIONAL ARCHIVES*

AUGUST 1945 NATIONAL ARCHIVES

NAAS Arlington, Washington

The City of Arlington, 40 miles north of Seattle, first developed an airport in 1934. The City leased a 200-acre tract and cleared a 4000 x 400-ft. area with the help of the WPA. Burnt-over stumps were removed before the laying of a light asphalt airstrip. During the next seven years, local aviators, flying circuses, and the Forest Service used the airport. With the increase of elimination training by NRAB Seattle in August 1940, the Navy purchased the airport for an OLF and erected a small building. Following the beginning of the war, the Army obtained the Navy's permission to develop the airfield for defense of the West Coast. The Army purchased additional land and built two 5000 x 150-ft. runways, taxiways, with a couple of dozen dispersal hardstands, plus a well and water storage tank. The Army's facilities, of temporary wartime construction, also included a small shop, operations building, and control tower, with barracks and mess for 450 officers and men. By the time the Army's construction reached completion in March 1943, the Japanese threat had lessened and the Army no longer had an immediate need for the base. The Army and the Navy then reached an agreement where the Navy paid the Army for its investment in the additional land and construction costs. The Army retained the right to use the airfield if necessary for defensive purposes.

The Navy immediately let a contract of $917,000 for additional buildings including a hangar. The commissioning of Arlington occurred on June 26, 1943. Limited berthing and messing were available when the first squadron, VB-139, arrived one week later. VB-139 and its PV-1 Venturas were supported by a detachment of Headquarters Squadron Six from Whidbey Island. VB-139 departed on July 22 and the station was then designated for carrier squadrons. VC-55 arrived in August and conducted intense night flying for a week and a half. VC squadrons continued to be based at Arlington for the next year.

Along with the VC squadrons of Avengers and Wildcats came a detachment of NAS Seattle's CASU 7. The Navy added a synthetic trainer building as well as a new firehouse and munition magazines. VC-3, VC-4, VC-77, VC-78, VC-87, and VC-90 all passed through the station during this time. Fog and rain hampered flight operations during the fall and heavy frost during the winter. Another problem arose with strong crosswinds during certain weather conditions, especially with the Wildcats and their narrow landing gear. This resulted in a recommendation to build an additional crosswind runway in the fall of 1943.

Beginning in June 1944, the VC squadrons departed for a while as light carrier air groups of a VT and a VF squadron were posted to the station for several months. CVLG 38 remained on the base until August when replaced by CVLG 49. The light carrier air group's fighter squadrons operated Hellcats and the torpedo squadrons Avengers.

In early 1945, VC squadrons returned to the base and included VC-4, VC-14, VC-79 plus CVLG 51.

Construction of the crosswind runway and the installation of flush runway lighting reached completion by the end of the war. One patrol, 12 composite squadrons, and six light carrier air groups had passed through Arlington with personnel numbering 732 officers and 2,229 men.

Arlington, at completion, had three 5,000 x 150-ft. runways on 1162 heavily wooded acres, owned by the Navy. The nearest gunnery range was only five minutes flying time away. In March 1944, personnel stood at 150 officers and 954 enlisted men with billeting for 113 officers and 714 enlisted men. The strength of CASU 7 peaked at 12 officers and 500 enlisted men. Station aircraft usually consisted of two GH Howard ambulance planes, a GB transport and an NE Piper Cub.

The Navy closed Arlington in July 1946, returning the airfield to the City at the end of the year. In 1997, the former base is a general aviation airport as well as location of light industry. Among the buildings that have survived are the hangar, parachute loft, link trainer building, and fire house.

F6F-3 Hellcat
NATIONAL ARCHIVES

MAY 1944 NATIONAL ARCHIVES

NAS Astoria, Oregon

During WW II, the Naval aviation establishment at Astoria originally consisted of NAS Tongue Pt., a seaplane base, and NAAS Clatsop County, a land-plane base. On May 31, 1944, the stations were combined as NAS Astoria.

Clatsop County

The Clatsop County Airport was first established in 1936 by a local WPA project. In May 1942, the Army's 406th Bombardment Squadron used the airfield for antisubmarine patrols. Satisfactory terrain for an airport is difficult to find in this part of Oregon. The original facility was quite small and in July 1942, the CAA and the WPA allocated $1 million to hydraulically fill an area to build three runways. The next month, the Navy received permission to construct an air station on the property provided the Army could also use the airfield if needed. Clatsop County leased the airport to the Navy at $1 a year for the duration of the war plus six months. The Navy initially allocated $2.5 million for the station commissioning it on January 5, 1943, as an auxiliary of NAS Tongue Pt.

On March 27, 1943, the first squadron, VC-55, reported on board with CASU 55 present for support. On May 31, 1944, Clatsop County and NAS Tongue Pt. were combined as NAS Astoria. VS-50 and a detachment of VJ-10 used Clatsop County on practically a permanent basis. An additional 12 VC squadrons trained at the station until July 1944. That month, CAG 12's three squadrons were sent to the base for four months training. Starting in November, three torpedo squadrons, VT-24, VT-25, and VT-49 also spent time at the field. In January 1945, CAG 18 arrived as improvements and a new hangar were added to the Clatsop County airfield. VC-65 also visited for a short time in March. CAG 7 arrived after the departure of CAG 18 in April.

CAG 7 remained on board until the end of the war. The Navy had its share of accidents at Clatsop County, suffering seven fatalities during the course of the base's existence. The most bizarre accident happened on October 15, 1944, when an SB2C of VB-12 collided with a portable blimp mooring mast on landing, killing the Ensign pilot.

The Navy facilities at the Clatsop County airfield were generally considered quite primitive. When billeting was available, the squadron's officers were housed at the Tongue Pt. BOQ. Most married and single officers found good accommodations, as well as other diversions, at the summer resort town of Seaside, 18 miles away on the coast.

Clatsop County had three concrete runways -- the longest 5745 ft. The station also had two blimp mooring masts and a seaplane ramp into the adjacent Columbia River. Available barracks could house 200 officers and 1476 enlisted men. The station had one OLF, the Moon Island Airport at Hoquiam, Washington, 55 miles to the north. Built by the CAA, Moon Island had been used by the Army in 1942 for antisubmarine patrols. The Navy acquired control of the airport in December 1943 -- the CAA spent an additional $158,000 adding a taxiway and a parking apron for Navy use. Carrier aircraft from Clatsop County used the airfield for practice landings. Tow planes from Shelton's utility squadrons also used Moon Island in support of the Naval anti-aircraft school at Pacific Beach, Washington.

After closing in June 1946, the Clatsop airport was returned to the County. In August 1964, the Coast Guard established an air station. The Coast Guard has operated three HH-65A Dolphin helicopters and three HU-25A Guardian jets from the facility. A few of the temporary wartime buildings, including hangars, have survived.

Tongue Point

Tongue Point is a small peninsula in the Columbia River, east of the town of Astoria and 100 miles northwest of Portland. Tongue Pt. was first proposed as a Naval base during WW I. In 1919, the Columbia Land Improvement Company offered the Navy 240 acres for $75,000, but Congress failed to appropriate the funds. The Navy announced that if a Naval base was to be built, the City would have to provide the property. In 1921, the City issued $100,000 in bonds to purchase 371 acres and presented the land to the Navy. Some land was cleared and four wooden piers built. The Washington Treaty of 1922, limiting naval armament, ended further development. Although the Coast Guard built a small lifeboat station on the point, no other Naval activity took place for another 18 years and the site became a local picnic ground. The Naval Expansion Act of 1938 finally brought some action. In 1939, $1.5 million was first approved for dredging, four piers, and wharfs. Funds followed to provide a seaplane base for two 12-plane VP squadrons and 18 observation floatplanes. NAS Tongue Pt. commissioned on December 21, 1940, with three hangars and two seaplane ramps.

For the next year and a half, several PBY patrol squadrons made Tongue Pt. their homeport including VP-41, VP-42, VP-43, and VP-62. With logging operations upriver, the Columbia was not the most desirable seaplane operating area. On March 8, 1942, a PBY-5 of VP-41 hit an escaped log and immediately sank. Only one of the nine-man crew survived. After the last VP squadron departed for Alaska in July 1942, the station was used very little for air operations with the exception of VS-50 plus a few aircraft of VJ-7 and HEDRON FAW 6. No further VP squadrons would be based here for the next two years. Beginning in May 1943, the station's mission became the assembly point and training base for pre-commissioning crews of CVE escort carriers and APA assault transports being built at Portland, Oregon by the Oregon Ship Building Corporation and at Vancouver, Washington by Henry J. Kaiser Co. Each CVE team consisted of 50 officers and 500 men that trained in Combat Information Center operations and other work at Tongue Pt. The first ship, the CVE USS *Casablanca*, commissioned on July 8, 1943. The program ended on June 8, 1944, with the CVE USS *Munda* -- a total of 50 CVE and 61 APA pre-commissioning crews had been trained. VP-41 and nine PBY-4s were at the station in May. The next month, the Navy suspended regular seaplane operations due to hazardous operating conditions on the river.

During the summer of 1944, CAG 12 pilots from the airfield were billeted at Tongue Pt. until a certain incident. One group of pilots arrived late from night flying, tired and hungry, only to find the BOQ mess secured for the night. Fortified with beer, the pilots broke into the locked mess refrigerator and acquired several pieces of meat. Back at their rooms, the pilots set up a makeshift barbeque grill in a sink and the resulting smoke caused someone to call the fire department. The BOQs were situated on a cul-de-sac. One fire truck approached the BOQ clockwise and the other fire truck counterclockwise -- abruptly meeting in the middle. The base C.O. did not find this episode very amusing and kicked CAG 12's pilots out of the Tongue Pt. BOQ. So while the pre-war, relatively luxurious, brick quarters remained unoccupied, the CAG 12 pilots had to live in the ramshackle temporary barracks amongst the sand dunes at the Clatsop County airfield. After an appropriate banishment, CAG 12's pilots were allowed to return to Tongue Pt.

On November 25, 1944, the Navy established a PBM line maintenance training school at Tongue Pt. The school had a complement of 70 officers and 1000 enlisted men with eight early model PBMs used for maintenance instruction. Although flying operations were minimal, the station's Assembly and Repair Department remained in full operation. Severely damaged landplanes from Clatsop County airfield were towed through the town of Astoria or barged to Tongue Pt. for repair. Rather than risk damaging the aircraft on the return trip, the station came up with a novel idea. As early as March 1943, an OS2U Kingfisher had taken off from the seaplane parking apron. A 2400-ft. takeoff strip was laid out across the seaplane apron and repaired aircraft flown off. In January 1945, the station's XO took off a Beech Staggerwing from the seaplane ramp and an FM-2, a week later. Several more takeoffs from the apron were conducted during the remainder of the war without incident.

The Navy's holdings at Tongue Pt. totaled 673 acres with barracks for 200 officers and 1766 enlisted men. Following the war, the station became a storage site for LSTs of the Reserve Fleet. Over 500 ships were placed into mothballs by the facility.

In 1997, Tongue Pt. remains in government service. The former base is used by the Coast Guard, the Job Corps, the State of Oregon, and the Government Service Agency. Most of the permanent buildings, including hangars, have survived and are in use.

LEFT: The Tongue Pt. seaplane base.　　*NATIONAL ARCHIVES*

ABOVE: An SBD of VS-50 with the former Mt. St. Helens in the background.

JULY 1944   NATIONAL ARCHIVES

ABOVE RIGHT AND RIGHT: Clatsop County's ramp in September 1945 with CAG 7 present.

NATIONAL ARCHIVES

NAS Attu, Alaska

Attu is the western most of the Aleutian Islands, measuring 14 by 38 miles. In June 1942, the Japanese invaded the island, occupied at the time by 39 Aleut Indians plus a 60-year-old American teacher and his wife. The teacher tried to flee and was killed. The remaining inhabitants were evacuated to Japan. The Japanese abandoned Attu in September and sent the troops to Kiska. The next month, Tokyo decided to remain in Alaska to block a possible invasion of Japan from the Aleutians and sent troops back to Attu to build an airfield. All the heavy construction equipment had been sunk en route so work on the airfield was done by hand.

The U.S., slow to respond, spent almost another year building up bases and forces. The American command did not feel strong enough to invade Kiska and chose Attu instead. Japanese strength was estimated at 500, while in fact it was 2650. On May 11, 1943, the Army invaded the island expecting to conquer Attu in three days -- it took 18. The Japanese force was wiped out with exception of only 28 prisoners. The cost was high for the Americans with 3829 casualties -- including 500 deaths. The Army had been supported by Naval aircraft of the CVE USS *Nassau*. This was the first use of an escort carrier for air support in the Pacific. On June 7, Fleet Air Wing 4 established a primitive advanced seaplane base on the island.

Army engineers set to work building an airfield before the Japanese had been overcome and completed a 3,000-ft. strip in just two weeks -- something the Japanese had been unable to accomplish in the previous seven months! In August, VB-135's Venturas transferred aboard from Adak. After a Japanese bomber raid from the Kuriles, VB-136 also moved to the island. The two squadrons then began patrols and on two occasions attacked and turned back Japanese raids. VB-135 and VB-136 were relieved by VB-139 in December. The next month, VB-139 began night photograph and bombing missions against the Kuriles, 750 miles distant. VB-139 completed 78 photo and bombing missions to the Kuriles before being relieved by VB-135 in May 1944. The next month VB-136 also returned to Attu. The PV squadrons continued missions to the Kuriles and shot down several Japanese aircraft. The PV-1 was well armed and could outrun Japanese fighters in level flight. In October 1944, VB-131 relieved VB-135 with rocket-equipped Venturas. On October 13, nine Japanese bombers attacked Attu. The last Japanese raid occurred on October 20. VB-131 continued to attack the Kuriles as well as flying diversionary raids for Army B-24s. Army fighter aircraft on Attu shot down several Japanese balloons.

Attu's Ventura's squadrons suffered heavier losses than any other PV squadrons, although more aircraft were lost to the weather than to the Japanese. Several PVs and Army planes had to make emergency landings in Russian territory. An outrageous situation developed as the Russians treated the Americans as virtual POWs and impounded the aircraft. The Russians eventually returned the Americans through Europe. In the Author's opinion, this was a national disgrace. The U.S. government tolerated this situation while continuing to supply the Russians with untold millions of dollars in aid, paid for by U.S. taxpayers. Russian aid should have been cut off until our men and aircraft were returned!

The Navy reservation at Attu's Casco Bay numbered 2500 acres. Barracks could accommodate 546 officers and 7645 enlisted men. Seaplane facilities of one hangar and one seaplane ramp supported one squadron of PBYs. The Seabees completed a Navy airfield at Casco Bay in 1944. This airfield consisted of pierce steel plank runways of 5000 x 150-ft. and 4200 x 150-ft. dimensions. Construction included seven hangars that supported two PV squadrons and one 12-plane observation squadron. Additional Navy facilities on the island supported submarines, PT boats, and other craft. Attu commanded the NAAF at Sheyma.

Following the war, Attu remained as an air station for a few years. The Navy finally closed the base on November 1, 1948. The facility was used as a Coast Guard Loran station for many years.

A PBY at Attu in June 1943.

SEPTEMBER 1944 NATIONAL ARCHIVES

NAS Barbers Point, Hawaii

Barbers Pt. is located approximately ten miles west of Pearl Harbor on the extreme southwest corner of Oahu. The prominence was named, punctually incorrectly, after Henry Barber, the master of the British brigantine *Arthur*, who struggled ashore here in October 1796 after losing his ship in a storm. In the 1930s, the Navy leased a 3,000 x 3,000-ft. section of land from the estate of James Campbell erecting a mooring mast for the dirigible *Akron* and building an oil-surfaced 1,500 x 150-ft. OLF. The mooring mast was never used as neither the *Akron* nor any other dirigible ever made it to Hawaii. With war on the horizon in September 1940, the Navy acquired 3,500 acres from the same estate and began improving the airfield for the Ewa MCAS. Marine Air Group Two moved to the partially completed Ewa in February 1941. In November 1941, the Navy had started work on an additional air station a few miles to the west of Ewa that would eventually become NAS Barbers Pt. (BP). Although originally conceived as an OLF for Pearl Harbor, BP evolved as the base for two carrier air groups of 90 aircraft. After the attack on Pearl Harbor, construction crews were pulled off the BP site to complete Ewa.

When work resumed at BP, civilian construction crews had been reinforced from the Mainland and work proceeded rapidly. Nevertheless, the station was only partially completed when commissioned on April 15, 1942, with a complement of 14 officers and 242 men. Following the Battle of Midway, the carrier air group of the *Hornet* arrived. Although most of the buildings had been planned as permanent structures, after December 7, temporary frame buildings were substituted to conserve critical materials and time. The operations building, command post, power house, telephone exchange, and other crucial facilities were built of reinforced concrete, while less critical barracks and other buildings were of temporary wood-frame construction. Housing and messing

were initially provided for 2,000 men. Barbers Pt. became one of the stations in Hawaii where squadrons and CAGs fine tuned their operations before shipping out for the combat zone. Along with the arrival of the squadrons came CASU 2 in support. CASU 2 remained at the station for the duration of the war.

BP continued to grow throughout the war. In August 1942, facilities were enlarged to accommodate four carrier air groups, two land patrol squadrons, and 4000 men. British Fleet Air Arm squadrons 882, 896, and 898 were on board during March 1943. The civilian contractors ended work on July 15, 1943, relieved by the 16th Seabees. In 18 months, 19 miles of roads had been built and four million cubic yards of rock and coral moved. Aviation gasoline storage tanks with a capacity of 570,000 gallons had been buried deep in coral. For the various projects, the contractors had used 27 million board feet of lumber, 12,000 tons of steel, and 80,000 cu. ft. of concrete. Around midnight on October 17, 1943, the station was alerted by what was believed to be a Japanese floatplane.

By the end of the war, Barbers Pt. encompassed 3856 acres with barracks for 1199 officers and 11,786 enlisted men. The Assembly and Repair Department, that included most of the station's 733 civilians, overhauled over 2,500 engines in a year's time with a record 345 in one month. The station also had a Combat Aircrew Training Unit with a staff of 22 officers and 186 men that conducted a pilot gunnery training course -- including training with a Gunairstructor, added in May 1944.

Following the war, BP also became a separation center. Up to August 1946, 6,000 personnel were processed to civilian life. A community type college, staffed by 35 instructors, began courses at the

station in various subjects. By the end of 1947, station complement had dropped to 378 as BP settled down to provide a base for two CAGs and four patrol squadrons. In the middle of 1949, a major restructuring of the Navy's bases in Hawaii took place. The Navy decommissioned the NASs at Kaneohe Bay and Honolulu's Rodgers Airport. Honolulu became an OLF of BP for seaplane operations. Ford Island remained open, but in a reduced role as Barbers Pt. became the main activity for all Naval and Coast Guard flight operations in Hawaii (the Coast Guard had established a unit at Kaneohe Bay in 1946). In 1950, VP-6 deployed to Hawaii with the first P2Vs. The Korean War brought a resurgence of activity, with the station serving as a final training base for combat bound units and a logistics support facility. Ewa closed in 1952 and the Marines moved to Kaneohe Bay

During the height of the Cold War, BP played a key role in one of the Navy's contributions to America's defense. In the mid-1950s, the Navy purchased 142 Lockheed WV-2s (later EC-121Ks) radar aircraft. Nicknamed "Willie Victors", the aircraft were formed into two squadrons, Airborne Early Warning Barrier Squadron One and Two. Squadron Two, based at BP beginning in 1956, was more commonly known as BARONPAC. The WVs rotated to Midway Island and provided airborne radar coverage of the Pacific extension of the Distant Early Warning or DEW Line. When BARONPAC ceased operation in June 1965, 58 million nautical miles of radar patrol had been flown. This was equivalent to 121 trips to the moon and back.

When NAS Honolulu closed in 1949, VR-21, the Navy's Pacific Fleet Logistic squadron moved its operations to BP. VR-21 or "Pineapple Airlines" maintained several detachments throughout the Pacific providing freight service, VIP transportation, personnel transportation, and Carrier On board Delivery (COD) to the Pacific Fleet. VR-21's aircraft were distinguished by the "RZ" tail code and their highly polished aluminum surfaces. In September 1964, the squadron and its detachments operated a total of 35 aircraft that included 13 C-118s and two C-130Gs at BP. On March 30, 1977, VR-21 disestablished, after accumulating over 358,000 accident free flight hours to that date.

When the Navy returned the Honolulu airport to civilian control in 1949, the powers that be dropped the John Rodgers name and renamed the airport as Honolulu International. On September 10, 1974, the Navy dedicated the airfield at Barbers Point as John Rodgers Field. Rodgers had attempted the first mainland to Hawaii flight in 1925.

Meanwhile, BP's primary role as a VP support base served as the home for various VP squadrons of P2Vs and later the Lockheed P-3, as well as antisubmarine helicopter squadrons. In mid-1981, VQ-3, the TACAMO (Take Charge and Move Out) squadron arrived at BP. VQ-3 grew to eight EC-130Qs and 650 men that maintained communications with the U.S. ballistic missile submarine fleet. In August 1990, VQ-3 transitioned to the E-6A (Boeing 707 derivative) and two years later transferred to Tinker AFB, Oklahoma. Another long-time resident of the base was Fleet Composite Squadron One. Commissioned as VU-1 in 1951, the squadron redesignated as VC-1 in 1965. VC-1 provided various services for the fleet including target towing and photography missions. VC-1 decommissioned in September 1992.

The 1993 Defense Base Realignment and Closure Commission recommended closing Barbers Point after more than 50 years of service. The base was originally scheduled to be decommissioned in September 1997; however, that date has been postponed to 1999. All Naval and Coast Guard aviation activities will move to Kaneohe to consolidate with the Marine aviation at that facility, although the Navy will retain the base housing at BP. The airfield will probably become a general aviation airport and cargo facility for Oahu, relieving some of the congestion at Honolulu International Airport.

The Navy built concrete revetments throughout its stations in Hawaii. Here an SBD receives some needed maintenance.
NATIONAL ARCHIVES

A VF squadron of F6F-3 Hellcats polish up their skills prior to shipping out for the combat zone.
NATIONAL ARCHIVES

ABOVE: The Curtiss SB2C Helldiver, or <u>S</u>on of a <u>Bitch 2</u>nd <u>C</u>lass, was rushed into production without being thoroughly tested. Stability, carrier handling, and reliability were some of the problems. Such were the Helldivers shortcomings that squadrons of F6F and F4U bomber/fighters formed for the expected invasion of Japan. *NATIONAL ARCHIVES*

ABOVE RIGHT: F8F Bearcat, developed by Grumman in 1943 as a derivative of the F6F, was the Navy's ultimate piston engine carrier fighter. With the same engine, the empty weight of the Bearcat was 1500 lbs. lighter than the Hellcat and out performed the F6F by 30%. The Bearcat got as far as Hawaii, but failed to reach combat before the end of the war. *NATIONAL ARCHIVES*

RIGHT: The sun sets on the ramp after a hard day's work by both ground and flight crews. *NATIONAL ARCHIVES*

NAAS Brown Field, California

In conjunction with the WW I development of San Diego's North Island, the Army established an airfield at Otay Mesa, 16 miles southeast. In 1918, the field was named in honor of Major Killian East, who had been killed in an automobile accident near Mitchell Field, N.Y. The Army invested $17,580 in East Field using it for formation and acrobatic training. During the 1920s and 1930s, military and civilian aviation used the airfield.

Located five miles from the coast, Otay Mesa has an elevation of 500 ft. and is less subject to ocean fog that reduced flying hours at other airfields in San Diego. After the beginning of WW II, the Navy improved the airfield. During the first of 1943, construction began on buildings. Just three months later, the station commissioned on March 17, as NAAS Otay Mesa. By the end of June, VC-20, VC-21, VC-25, and VC-35 had passed though the base, while Air Group 38 and 40 were on board. The squadrons were supported by a detachment of North Island's CASU 5. The same month, two Link trainers were installed and an aircraft recognition training building completed. On August 25, the Navy dedicated the field as NAAS Brown Field in honor of Cdr. Melville S. Brown, who had been killed in an aircraft accident in 1936. Cdr. Brown's sword was hung in the Officer's Mess. During the last six months of 1943, Air Group 35, VC-39, VC-33, VC-36, VC-42, and VC-66 had spent time at Brown.

On New Years Day of 1944, VF-34, VC-68 and VC-12 were on board. In April and May 1944, Army P-38 fighters were present at the field in the air defense mission. During the first half of the year, VC-10, VC-11, VC-20, VF-30X2, VC-27, and VC-79, arrived and departed. October 1944, saw a major change at the station as personnel arrived to form the PB4Y squadron, VPB-122. Whereas most carrier squadrons were on board the station for three to 10

weeks, the VPB squadron was scheduled to be present for four months. The departments of the base changed to support the bomber squadron. The Training Department added various devices including a five turret gunner's trainer. On December 4, 1944, VPB-122 transferred to Camp Kearny; however, Brown Field's Training Department continued to ground train PB4Y replacement crews throughout the remainder of the war. During the six months ending December 1944, VC-84, VC-85, VC-86, VC-87, VC-94, CVLG 30, VC-71, VC-25, and CVEG 24 arrived. All departed by the end of the year except VC-71 and CVEG 24.

In January 1945, CASU 66 commissioned out of the CASU 5 Detachment. During 1945, the station added several improvements including a new BOQ, brig, nose hangars, and a training building. VC-70, VC-49, CAG 38, VT-41, VC-66, VF-50, CVEG 36, VC-68, VC-65, VC-5, VC-4, VC-75, VC-78, VC-76, VC-79, and CAG 152 passed through Brown during 1945.

Brown Field consisted of 805 Navy-owned acres. Barracks existed for 378 officers and 1992 enlisted men. Brown had 6,000-ft., 5,000-ft., and 3,500-ft. runways of asphalt and concrete construction. At the peak, station aircraft consisted of one GB Beech, a GH Howard, an AE hospital plane, and a Stearman. OLF Sweetwater was assigned to and maintained by the station.

Brown closed in 1946 and became a civilian airport. The Korean War necessitated reopening the field as an ALF on November 1, 1951 -- the east/west runway was later extended to 8,000 ft. The station became home base to a utility squadron, two antisubmarine squadrons, and a Regulus air missile unit. In 1954, Brown recommissioned as an NAAS. On November 2, 1954, Convair's XFY-1 Pogo made its first flight from vertical takeoff to horizontal flight and back to vertical for landing. In the last few years of the station's existence, it was home to Douglas AD Skyraiders before the Navy closed Brown for the last time during 1962.

APRIL 1944 NATIONAL ARCHIVES

JANUARY 1943 NATIONAL ARCHIVES

NAAS Cabaniss Field, Texas

Cabaniss Field, initially known as P-2, was part of the original plan for the Corpus Christi Naval Air Training Center. In September 1940, contractors broke ground at P-2, three months after construction began on the main station. Located 6.5 miles south of the City of Corpus Christi and 15 miles west of Mainside, the Navy obtained the station's 1005 acres through condemnation. The Navy officially opened the base on July 9, 1941, naming it in honor of Cdr. Robert W. Cabaniss who lost his life in an aircraft crash in the West Indies in 1927.

When the airfield opened earlier on July 2, 1941, primary training squadron VN-11B moved aboard from Mainside with 54 N3Ns. At the outset, since neither the roads nor the barracks had been completed, cadets and enlisted men commuted by bus from Mainside. On August 27, 1941, an additional primary squadron, VN-11D, commissioned. Late in 1941, the barracks reached completion. In July 1942, VN-11B decommissioned. Two months later, basic training squadron VN-12C moved aboard from Cuddihy with SNVs and OS2U Kingfishers on wheels. An additional basic squadron, VN-12D, commissioned when VN-11D decommissioned on September 21, 1942. Cabaniss's primary squadrons had trained 1305 cadets, completed 1173, and logged 90,000 flying hours with no fatalities. Administrative control of the station remained at Corpus Christi until November 1, 1943, when Cabaniss commissioned as an NAAS.

By early 1943, all construction reached completion at the station and included an administration building, three hangars, a maintenance building, ship's service building, an Assembly and Repair Shop, a storage building, and four barracks. By the end of 1944, every cadet that arrived for intermediate training at Corpus Christi took basic training at Cabaniss. Basic training consisted of a three-week course that transitioned the student from light primary trainers to the heavier and faster SNJ advanced trainer. Until mid-1945, the predominate aircraft used was the Vultee SNV Valiant. Flight time included 15 hours of familiarization, 15 hours of formation, and four hours of night flying. At that time, VN-12B and VN-12C were operating 229 SNVs and 25 SNJs. In addition to American cadets, British and South American students were also present. Cabaniss had an enviable safety record -- one of the best in the entire training command. Between November 1943 and April 1945, the station flew 162,377 hours with no fatalities. By June, the SNVs had all been replaced by SNJs. By this time, VN-12C and VN-12D combined into one squadron.

Cabaniss had four 5,000 x 300-ft. asphalt runways and 10 OLFs. Station complement in March 1944 numbered 231 officers and 1014 enlisted men with barracks for 128 officers and 1050 enlisted men. The base could handle a maximum of 448 students. Station aircraft consisted of an SNB, an NE, an AE ambulance plane, an SNJ and two N2Ss.

Following the war, Cabaniss remained open and in March 1947 participated, along with other stations, in an experimental project of putting cadets through primary training in the SNJ. On December 13, 1947, Cabaniss closed and all aircraft transferred to Mainside. Less than a year later, the station reopened on November 15, 1948, when the Advanced Training Command transferred to Corpus Christi from Jacksonville. Initially, the station conducted fighter training with F4U Corsairs and attack training with TBMs. By 1953, Cabaniss hosted the advance training pipeline for students in the Douglas AD Skyraider. On October 1, 1958, Cabaniss closed, its AD squadron moved to Mainside, and the airfield became an ALF.

In 1997, Cabaniss is owned by the City of Corpus Christi. During the week, aircraft from Mainside use the airfield for touch-and-go landings. On weekends, the field hosts drag races.

One of the more unusual shaped OLFs in the Corpus Christi area.   *NATIONAL ARCHIVES*

JUNE 1943 NATIONAL ARCHIVES

NAAS Camp Kearny, California

In WW I, the U.S. Army purchased the 2,130-acre Miramar Ranch for an infantry training center. The Army named the facility Camp Kearny (frequently misspelled as Kearney), in honor of General S. W. Kearny, former governor of California who also served in the Mexican War. Although Army aircraft occasionally landed on the camp's parade ground, an official airfield was never established. Between the wars, the government retained the property as an airfield for military and civilian use. The Ryan Company weight tested Charles Lindbergh's *The Spirit of St. Louis* here in 1927. During 1929 and 1930, the facility was known as Airtech Field, operated by the San Diego Air Service Corp. The Navy installed a mooring mast on the airport in 1932, first used by the *Akron* on a West Coast flight May 11, 1932. Twenty five thousand spectators watched in horror as the *Akron's* first mooring attempt ended when a gust of wind carried the airship upward, taking four ground handlers with it. One man jumped to the ground before the airship reached too high of an altitude and suffered a broken arm. As the *Akron* continued to ascend, two other men lost their grip and fell to their deaths. One man managed to hold on as a news camera crew, on hand for the event, captured the entire incident. The Navy continued to use the facility and *Macon* moored at Camp Kearny four times during 1934.

In December 1940, the Navy began a series of projects to improve and expand the airfield. On December 21, the First Marine Air Wing arrived and set up a tent city, remaining until August 1942 when it moved to Guadalcanal. Meanwhile, the Navy began the construction of an air station at the camp and commissioned NAAS Camp Kearny on February 20, 1943, an auxiliary of San Diego. The station was also known at times as Kearny Mesa. The Marines occupied an area adjacent to the Navy station where they commissioned the Marine Corps

Air Depot Camp Kearny one month later. The primary Navy mission at Camp Kearny was the training in Consolidated PB4Y Liberators. Training was supervised and conducted by the Transition Liberator Unit. When the asphalt runways began to deteriorate under the PB4Y's weight, two concrete runways were added during 1943. Confusion arose between the Navy and Marine installations at Camp Kearny, so the Marines changed their station name to Marine Corps Air Depot Miramar on September 2, 1943. MCAD Miramar served as the West Coast processing depot for embarkation of Marine squadrons to the South Pacific as well as home base for other squadrons.

British use of the Liberator and other landbased aircraft in antisubmarine and long range patrol missions impressed the Navy. In 1942, the Navy began to negotiate with the Army for some of its aircraft. On the other hand, the Army coveted the Navy-owned Boeing plant at Renton, Washington that was developing the PBB Sea Ranger. In July 1942, an agreement was reached as the Navy cancelled the Sea Ranger. In exchange for the Renton plant, the Army would allow the Navy to purchase B-24s, B-34s (PVs), and B-25s from its production lines. The Navy also agreed to limit orders of Consolidated PBYs at the San Diego plant as to not interfere with B-24 production. Initially, the Navy drew B-24s directly from Army production and modified the aircraft to Navy specifications. Earlier PB4Ys had the glass house nose just like the Army B-24. Later models had the Erco ball turrets installed previously manufactured for the cancelled Boeing PBB Sea Ranger. PB4Ys were flown across the bay from the Consolidated plant at San Diego's Lindbergh Field to North Island for the installation of the ball turret. In addition to patrol bombers, the Navy also converted some PB4Ys to a photographic reconnaissance configuration assigned to VD squadrons. Several of

these squadrons passed through Camp Kearny. In May 1943, work began on a Navy dedicated PB4Y. Three B-24Ds were taken from the production line and converted to the PB4Y-2 Privateer. The Privateer had a lengthened fuselage, a single vertical stabilizer, and non-supercharged engines. The first PB4Y-2s were delivered in March 1944. In the meantime, the Army disbanded its Antisubmarine Command in August 1943, turning its airplanes over to the Navy.

On January 20, 1944, Camp Kearny lost its first PB4Y when an aircraft of VB-101 crashed after takeoff killing its 13-man crew. On May 25, 1944, the Transition Liberator Unit's name changed to Headquarters Squadron 2 Fleet Air Wing 14 (HEDRON 2 FAW 14). In the fall of 1944, the designation of PB4Y squadrons changed from VB to VPB. In less than two weeks in mid-1944, the station reeled from the loss of three PB4Ys and their crews. On May 27, seven crewmen were killed when a PB4Y crashed on approach. Three days later, a PB4Y of VB-102 had a midair collision with an F4F claiming 12 lives. The worst was yet to come. One week later, a PB4Y crashed into a building on the base killing a total of 17 men from the aircraft and on the ground. Thirty six men from Camp Kearny lost their lives in ten days!

When VP-14 returned to the U.S. from combat in the South Pacific, it was recommissioned as VPB-197 on December 1, 1944. Under the command of HEDRON 2 FAW 14, VPB-197 conducted the final phase of operational training that formed replacement crews. After the completion of training, the crew and its aircraft were sent to Kaneohe Bay, Hawaii, for assignment to combat squadrons where needed. Initially, VPB-197 operated 15 PB4Y-1 Liberators. By March 1945, the squadron's aircraft numbered one PB4Y-1 and 44 PB4Y-2s.

Camp Kearny had one 3,000 x 500-ft. asphalt and two 6,000 x 200-ft. concrete runways. The 3,000-ft. runway was mainly used for aircraft parking. In mid-1944, station personnel numbered 611 officers and 4076 enlisted men with accommodations for 688 officers and 4176 enlisted men. After VJ-Day, the Navy used the station as a separation center returning 25,000 men to civilian life.

On May 1, 1946, the Navy departed Camp Kearny and the station became MCAS Miramar. After only a year, the Marines closed the base and moved all units to El Toro. On June 30, 1947, the Navy redesignated Miramar an NAAS. In July 1949, the Navy began a project to improve the runways and establish a Master Jet Base. The station upgraded to an NAS on April 1, 1952. Following the Korean War, the Navy faced a cutback and offered Miramar to the City of San Diego in 1954 for $1. In what will go down in San Diego's history as the most idiotic decision ever made by the City's leaders, the offer was turned down! In the Author's opinion, San Diego's Lindbergh Airport remains today one of the worst commercial airports in the United States -- obstructions, no CAT II or CAT III approaches, noise problems, and a relatively short runway with no overruns. Miramar would have made a wonderful international airport for San Diego!

The Navy decided to keep Miramar open and eventually built the station into one of the Navy's biggest bases. In 1961, the station was designated for fighter squadrons only and was unofficially known as "Fightertown." During the Vietnam War, the famous "Top Gun" school formed. The 1993 Base Realignment and Closure Commission has caused major changes at Miramar. The F-14 squadrons have moved to Oceana, Virginia, while Top Gun is being transferred to Fallon, Nevada. With the closing of El Toro, the Marines are scheduled to assume command of Miramar on October 1, 1997.

ABOVE: Weather reconnaissance PB4Y-2 Privateer at Camp Kearny following the war.

NATIONAL ARCHIVES

UPPER RIGHT: Photographer in PB4Y-1 mans oblique camera.   *CURTISS SILVERNAIL*

RIGHT: Camp Kearny's ramp in April, 1944.   *NATIONAL ARCHIVES*

OPPOSITE PAGE: Bombardier training devices for PB4Ys.   *NATIONAL ARCHIVES*

NAAS Chase Field, Texas

Located 60 miles north of Corpus Christi, an airport for the town of Beeville was built by the CAA during 1942. The City of Beeville offered to lease the airport and 456 acres to the Navy for $1 per annum. The Navy purchased an additional 607 acres and began construction at the site. The first cadets arrived in April 1943. Squadron VN-13, previously operating at Corpus Christi, transferred aboard the station and began operations one month later. On June 1, the Navy commissioned the base as NAAS Chase Field in honor of LCdr. Nathan Brown Chase. LCdr. Chase lost his life in a fighter midair collision in 1925. The station was Corpus Christi's last auxiliary opened during the war.

When cadets arrived at Chase, some felt they had arrived at the end of the earth. The base facilities were considered by many cadets to be the worst in the training command. The barracks were described as large tar paper covered boxes with the barest of essentials. During the dry summer of 1944, the grass that existed was burnt brown. As a result, dust covered everything. In addition, the base was also treeless. On top of all this, Beeville was not much of a liberty town. Fortunately, the course here only lasted four to five weeks.

VN-13 had the distinction of being the largest instrument training squadron in the world. Aircraft in use consisted of 94 SNJs and 100 SNVs. By January 1944, over 8,000 students had gone through the instrument training course. A change of mission occurred in December 1944, when VN-19, commissioned in August at Cuddihy Field, replaced VN-13. Along with Saufley Field at Pensacola, VN-19 conducted a 21-hour, pre-operational training syllabus with over 160 SBDs. The SBDs were weary former combat airplanes and on any given day, 50% could be down for maintenance. On July 1, 1946, the Navy closed Chase Field returning it to the City of Beeville six months later.

Chase's airfield consisted of three 4,500-ft. asphalt runways. In March 1944, complement totaled 222 officers, 588 students, and 1194 enlisted men. Available barracks accommodated 180 officers, 900 students, and 1110 enlisted men. The station operated one each SNJ, AE, GH, and SNB.

The Korean War renewed Navy interest in Chase. The Navy paid the City $100,000 for the airport and initially used the field as an OLF to Corpus Christi. The Navy, intending the station for jet training, constructed three new 8,000-ft. runways. In addition, former Navy buildings were renovated and new ones built. The recommissioning of the field was celebrated on July 1, 1954, with an open-house and a performance by the Blue Angels. Advanced Training Units 203, 204, and 223 initially conducted

training with straight-wing Grumman F9F-2 Panthers and Lockheed TV-2s (T-33). In the following years, Chase became the first training station to receive the F9F-8T Cougar two-seat trainer. In 1959, Chase also received the supersonic single-seat Grumman F11F Tiger, in which students received a check-out prior to winning their wings. Around the same time, the training units were redesignated as VT-24, VT-25, and VT-26. October 1, 1971, saw the creation of Air Training Wing Three to oversee the three squadrons. In the last years of its existence, Chase operated 100 Douglas TA-4J Skyhawks and 60 North American T-2 Buckeyes, turning out 200 new Naval Aviators a year.

The Navy closed Chase in February 1993. A Texas State prison has been established on the property as well as light industry. In 1997, one runway has remained open for general aviation.

Instrument instructor writes up a maintenance gripe on SNJ following a training hop. Instrument trainers had green stripes around the fuselage and wings.
NATIONAL ARCHIVES

APRIL 1946 NATIONAL ARCHIVES

NAS Clinton, Oklahoma

In 1942, the Navy developed plans for an additional Naval Experimental Station and chose a 5,000-acre site, 19 miles southwest of Clinton, Oklahoma at the community of Burns Flat. After paying $75 per acre for the land, construction began on October 1, 1942. VJ-6 arrived on January 1, 1943, and used the Dill City CAA Intermediate Field, five miles south, prior to the completion of the station's runways.

The primary mission of the base was the development of drones, remotely controlled craft, and smart bombs. To mask the true nature of the top-secret work, the Navy chose the innocuous name of the Training Task Force (TTF) for the command that came into being on March 23, 1943. The commissioning of Clinton took place on June 1, with 349 officers, 2210 enlisted men, and 127 aircraft on board. Under the TTF, three equally innocuously named Special Task Air Groups (STAGs) formed on June 1, 1943. The mission of the STAGs included the operation of assault drones, target drones, bomb release drones, remote control landing craft, remote control torpedo boats, and the dropping of assault bombs and target seeking bombs. Clinton's secondary mission involved the modification of aircraft with the station completing 125 per month. A total of 1500 aircraft were modified during this program.

On July 14, 1943, NAS Traverse City, Michigan opened under the command of the TTF. The next month, STAG 1, with two TBM squadrons and a HEDRON, transferred to Traverse City. On September 15, Clinton added an auxiliary at Conroe, Texas -- one month later, another one at Durant, Oklahoma. By October, station strength stood at 487 officers, 3154 enlisted men, and 209 aircraft. The next month, Clinton took over Eagle Mt. Lake, Texas, temporarily abandoned by the Marines. STAG 2 and three squadrons of Lockheed PV Venturas, including VK-13, and VK-14, moved to

that station on November 1. STAG 2 remained at Eagle Mt. Lake until March 1944, when the field transferred back to the Marines.

On April 4, 1944, drone control squadrons VPB-152 and VPB-153 formed at Clinton. By mid-year, developmental work of the TTF and the STAGs was put to an operational test. On June 12, elements of STAG 1 arrived in the Russell Islands to operationally test the TDR assault drone. The TDR could carry a 2,000-lb. bomb 300 miles at a speed of 105 knots. The control aircraft could guide the TDR from a maximum range of 20 miles. On September 27, STAG 1 began a month long demonstration of the TDR. On that date, TBMs guided TDR assault drones against antiaircraft emplacements on South Bougainville with two of the four drones launched hitting the target. One month later, the demonstration ended. STAG 1 launched 46 TDRs and achieved 29 hits.

In Europe, Special Air Unit One, formed from elements of VK-13 and VK-14, arrived on July 6 to attack V-1 and V-2 launch sites with remote controlled PB4Y-1s. Pilots would takeoff the aircraft, set the radio controls, and then bail out. The Liberator would then be guided to its target by a PV control aircraft that utilized a TV camera in the nose of the PB4Y. The operation got off to a tragic start on August 12. Shortly after takeoff, a PB4Y with 21,000 lbs. of high explosives detonated prematurely. One of the two pilots killed was Lt. Joseph P. Kennedy, Jr., brother of John F. Kennedy, who had volunteered for the mission. On September 3, another PB4Y was launched against submarine pens on Helgoland Island. Due to poor weather in the target area, the PB4Y missed the intended target striking a barracks area. This was the Allies only use of a remote controlled bomb in the European theater of operations during WW II.

On November 23, the TTF was decommissioned and its equipment, aircraft, and personnel reallocated. VPB-152 moved to Whidbey Island and VPB-153 to Moffett. The next month, VK-11 and VK-12 decommissioned. Following the disbanding of TTF, the Navy made Clinton an aircraft storage and salvage facility. At the end of March 1945, over 1000 aircraft were on hand.

The Naval Air Navigation School (NANS), located at Shawnee, Oklahoma, needed additional facilities for a proposed expansion of the school. Since adequate space existed at Clinton, the NANS moved aboard during March. With the cutback of the blimp program, many of the additional navigator trainees were former blimp pilots. At that time, NANS was in the process of transitioning from the SNB to the R4D. By the end of June, aircraft assigned to NANS consisted of 43 R4Ds, four SNBs, and one SNJ. At the end of the war, 1762 aircraft were on the station for storage or scrapping.

Clinton had four 6000 x 300-ft. asphalt runways, and auxiliaries at Durant, Oklahoma and Conroe, Texas, plus OLFs at Stillwater and Hobart, Oklahoma. Clinton received Hobart from the Army on October 1, 1943. The Navy's investment in Clinton totaled $10 million and included three hangars, 14 barracks, and 10 BOQs. On December 15, 1945, the Navy transferred Clinton to the Reconstruction Finance Corporation for storage, disposal, and scrapping of aircraft. On April 6, 1946, the number of aircraft present had skyrocketed to almost 9000.

In 1957, the Air Force's Strategic Air Command took over the property establishing Clinton-Sherman AFB. The Air Force utilized some of the former Navy facilities making improvements including a 13,500-ft. north/south runway. The Author shot touch-and-go landings at Clinton-Sherman while a student at the MATS C-118 school at Tinker AFB, Oklahoma in 1963. Following the closure of Clinton-Sherman in 1970, the airfield was taken over by the FAA. Aircraft from the FAA's training center at Oklahoma City uses Clinton-Sherman as a practice landing field to this day.

RIGHT: This section of the disposal area contains 1500 F6Fs; 1000 F4Us and FGs; 1100 SBDs; 250 OS2Us and OS2Ns; and 550 SB2Cs, SBWs, and SBFs. *APRIL 1946 NATIONAL ARCHIVES*

BELOW RIGHT: Low-tech launching method of TDN in January 1943. A pilot started engines and taxied into takeoff position. Drone was then secured with rope and the pilot exited the cockpit. When all was ready, the rope was cut and the drone sent on its way. *NATIONAL ARCHIVES*

BELOW: The drone was developed and initially manufactured by the Naval Aircraft Factory as the TDN. The production version was made by Interstate Aircraft of El Segundo, California as the TDR. *NATIONAL ARCHIVES*

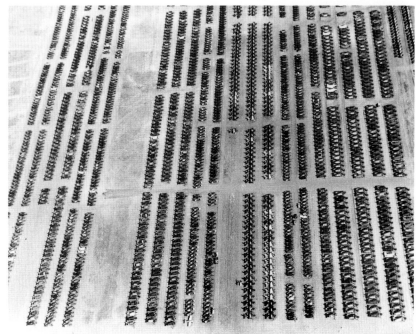

Almost 9,000 aircraft, sold for pennies on the dollar, await the smelter in April 1946. Such scenes of the aircraft disposal areas at Clinton are almost inconceivable to the present day reader. How could something so plentiful then, be so precious and sought after today? The present day historical appreciation and proliferation of aircraft museums will insure that many examples of modern aircraft will be preserved for future generations. *NATIONAL ARCHIVES*

MARCH 1945 NATIONAL ARCHIVES

NAAF Conroe, Texas

Conroe, the seat of Montgomery County, is located 40 miles north of Houston and in 1940 had a population of 4,600. In 1943, the CAA offered to build an airport if the local government provided the land. The County purchased the necessary property for $17,000 and the CAA spent $1.425 million on the construction of three 4,600 x 150-ft. asphalt runways. In the meantime, the Navy developed an interest in the site and arranged to lease the airport's 1277 acres. The Navy spent $348,000 building a hangar plus other buildings. The station commissioning on September 15, 1943, as an auxiliary of NAS Clinton, Oklahoma. Conroe's facilities were essentially identical to Clinton's other auxiliary at Durant, Oklahoma.

The Author had a difficult time discovering the extent of Naval aviation activities at the station during the war. After contacting several men who had been assigned to Conroe, the Author learned there was a good reason for this lack of information -- for all practical purposes, nothing happened at Conroe during the war! One possible explanation was the fact the auxiliary was located over 400 miles from the parent station. Clinton was home to the Training Task Force that developed drones, remotely controlled aircraft, and weapons during the war. Rumors abound at Conroe that the field was intended to serve as a gunnery training facility for the gunners of the PV Ventura drone control aircraft. Arrangements were believed to have been made for use of Army gunnery ranges over the Gulf and targets at Galveston. Another rumor suggested that the station be used for testing and development of drone aircraft and airborne electronic equipment. None of these activities ever took place and the station remained essentially in caretaker status the entire war! When the Navy took over Eagle Mt. Lake from June 1944 to March 1945, Conroe was placed under the command of that station; however, no increase in

activity took place. When the Navy transferred Eagle Mt. Lake back to the Marines, Clinton resumed command of Conroe.

At the most, the station had 100 men and three officers. The men kept themselves occupied with the locally good deer, quail, and dove hunting. The station had regular air service from Clinton that provided logistics support. Conroe also serviced lost, emergency, and low-fuel military aircraft. In May 1944, the CAA installed permanent airfield lighting. The station's main structure was the 120 x 200-ft. hangar with officer's quarters on one side and enlisted quarters on the other. The Officer in Charge of the base had an SNV that he used, "for what he saw fit." In March 1945, Conroe went onto official caretaker status with three officers and 30 men. For a time, supplies were drawn from the Army Prisoner of War camp at Huntsville. After the complement fell to 15 men, this practice ended and the men moved into town. The most lasting result of the Navy's presence at Conroe was the marriage of at least six of the base's men to local girls.

Following the war, the Navy eventually gave the airport back to the County along with the hangar, a fire truck, a grass cutting tractor, and other equipment -- everything necessary to operate an airport. Today, the Montgomery County Airport is used for general aviation and by an Army Reserve helicopter unit. On June 12, 1993, the former Navy hangar burned down, taking an aircraft collection with it.

The only aircraft ever assigned to Conroe was a lone SNV, that the O. in C. used, " for what he saw fit!" *USN*

JUNE 1944 NATIONAL ARCHIVES

NAS Corpus Christi, Texas

The National Defense Act of May 17, 1938, resulted in the forming of a Board of Officers led by RAdm. Hepburn. One of the first recommendations of the Hepburn Board was an additional Naval Air Training Center. Modeled on Pensacola, the Center was to have a main station and three auxiliaries. Of the locations considered, the Board found Corpus Christi, Texas to be the best site. Further deterioration of the world situation, spurred Congress to appropriate the necessary funds on June 11, 1940. Contracts were signed the same day and nine days later, work began on a 2050-acre site for the main station 10 miles southeast of Corpus Christi near the community of Flour Bluff. The first order of business involved the construction of a 20-mile railroad spur to the site that was completed in an incredible 35 days! The City of Corpus Christi assumed responsibility for building a military highway and 16-inch water line from town. Work progressed rapidly. In August, construction began on the three auxiliary fields that ran on a line from five miles west of the main station and continued approximately every five miles to northwest. Construction crews started on the 858-acre Rodd Field in August, the 1003-acre Cabaniss Field the next month, and the 789-acre Cuddihy in November. By Christmas, the construction at Mainside was about 50% completed. Additionally, the Navy acquired 6500 acres for 25 OLFs -- purchasing 3000 acres and leasing the remainder. In Nueces County alone, 5,571 acres of the 14,000 acres the Navy acquired were removed from cultivation. The locals were not happy since the government set a ceiling of $110 per acre for land that normally sold for as much as $200 per acre. While only 80% complete, the commissioning of Corpus Christi took place on March 12, 1941.

Although Corpus was intended for intermediate training, VN-11 commenced primary training of cadets on April 1. VN-11 was followed by VN-12,

basic training; VN-13, instruments; VN-14, fighters; VN-15, dive bombers; VN-16, torpedo bombers; VN-17, scout/observation; VN-18, multi-engine land and sea; and an instructors school. Rodd Field commenced operations on June 7, Cabaniss on July 9, and Cuddihy on September 3. Squadrons were transferred to the auxiliaries as they opened. By the end of December 1941, the original contracts had essentially been completed. The Navy's largest single base project of the war had cost over $40 million. The peak work force of 9,348 had labored over 10 million man hours completing 52 miles of railroads, 79 miles of roads, 16 miles of runways, two miles of sea walls, and 374 buildings.

After the U. S. entered the war, work got under way on an additional auxiliary at Kingsville, known as P-4. The commissioning of Kingsville took place on July 4, 1942, as VN-14's fighter syllabus transferred from Corpus Christi. Later in 1942, construction began on additional auxiliaries at Beeville and south of Mainside at Field #21305. On April 1, 1943, Field #21305 commissioned as Waldron Field and began the torpedo bomber syllabus with VN-16. Three weeks later, President Roosevelt arrived at Corpus Christi to inspect what had become the Navy's largest air training center. As additional primary stations opened, Corpus ended primary training during the spring. That same year, the station added four Celestial Navigation Trainers at a cost of $55,000 each. Future President George Bush received intermediate training at Corpus and its auxiliaries between March and May 1943. At Beeville, Chase Field commissioned on June 1 with VN-13 conducting the basic instrument course.

Corpus Christi became known as the "University of the Air." A cadet arriving at Corpus Christi for Intermediate Training in the latter half of 1943, was first sent to Cabaniss or Cuddihy for a four-week

basic training course of 34 hours. Next came instrument training. If the student was lucky or had some pull, he went through the instrument squadron at Mainside. The alternative was Chase Field at Beeville -- deemed by some to have the worst facilities in the training command. During instrument training, cadets declared their preference for the type of further training desired and could volunteer for the Marine Corps. Selection was determined by the cadet's preference, ranking based on grades, and the needs of the Navy. A full 70% of the students were sent to specialized fighter, dive bomber, or torpedo bomber squadrons. Initially, this training was separate, but problems arose producing the exact numbers required by the fleet. As a result, in late 1943, this specialized training changed to a more generalized CV syllabus. The seaplane syllabus received 15% and land-base multi-engine 8%. Land-base multi-engine was highly desired and difficult to get. The remaining 7% were sent to the scout and observation floatplane squadron -- considered a less desirable assignment by many.

By the end of 1944, the flight training load diminished. Training time was also extended. With the addition of VN-19, CV students received a three-week, 26-hour, pre-operational course in the Douglas SBD. This squadron commissioned at Cuddihy but moved shortly thereafter to Chase. At Mainside in December could be found VN-13A, an instrument squadron with 86 SNVs; VN-14B, a CV unit with 149 SNJs; VN-17, the scout/observation squadron with 27 OS2U Kingfishers and nine N3N floatplanes; and two seaplane squadrons, VN-18A and VN-18B with a total of 58 PBYs. Additional units included Operational Training Unit VPB2 #4 with 78 PBMs, seven planes assigned to the Naval Air Technical Training Center at Ward Island, and a 31- aircraft miscellaneous unit that operated nine different types of aircraft, ranging from Stearmans to a

Lockheed R5O Lodestar. The station's Assembly and Repair Department had an additional 232 aircraft in various stages of overhaul and repair. The grand total of aircraft present totaled 727.

By the end of the war, Corpus Christi and its auxiliaries had designated a total of 35,000 Naval aviators -- 7,000 more than Pensacola. These included a number of foreign students from Great Britain, France, Argentina, Brazil, Chile, Columbia, Cuba, Ecuador, Mexico, Peru, Uruguay, and Venezuela. Inevitably, the foreign students suffered their share of fatalities. The Navy purchased a section of Corpus Christi's Rose Hill Cemetery where at least 26 foreign students were buried. Interred at Rose Hill were students from Great Britain, France, Brazil, Peru, Argentina, and Mexico. All of the remains, with the exception of two, were removed to their native lands, following the war.

Corpus Christi's original 2,050 acres were increased an additional 450 acres by hydraulic-fill. The station had four 5,000 x 300 ft. asphalt runways and 17 seaplane ramps. In March 1944, complement stood at 831 officers, 2448 student aviators, 9878 enlisted men, and 1739 civilians. In September 1945, Corpus had accommodations for 23,000 officers and men. The Center's over 55 OLFs included the Corpus Christi Municipal Airport and the Aransas Co. airport at Rockport with three 4,500-ft. runways completed by the CAA in 1944.

Following the war, the Navy reorganized the Training Command and all of Corpus' auxiliaries eventually closed. On November 8, 1946, the worst accident in the Training Command's history occurred when two PBMs had a night midair collision. Only five men of the 27 men on board the planes survived. Corpus Christi became a subordinate command until 1948, when the Naval Air Advanced Training command transferred aboard from Jacksonville. In 1950, the Coast Guard established an air station at Corpus

with a search and rescue mission. The Korean War caused renewed growth and Cabaniss, Kingsville, and Chase Field were reopened. In 1949, the station also hosted the Navy's Plane Commander's School for the Douglas R5D (C-54). From 1948 to 1955, Corpus became home for the Blue Angels on two different occasions. In 1958, Cabaniss closed and its Douglas AD (A-1) Skyraider squadron moved to Corpus. The next year the Overhaul and Repair Department closed, but the void was filled in 1961 by an Army repair depot.

The Author received advanced training for a six month period beginning in August 1962. Compared to today's training, advanced training in those days was quite unique. Antisubmarine training took place at New Iberia, Louisiana, in earlier versions of the Grumman S2F (TS-2A) Tracker -- the same aircraft the students would fly in the fleet. The jet pipelines were located at Kingsville and Beeville, Texas. Jet students trained in the swept-wing Grumman F9F Cougar and received a checkout in the supersonic Grumman F11F Tiger before receiving their wings. At Corpus Christi could be found the prop-attack syllabus. After a few flights in the T-28, these students flew the early versions of the Douglas AD Skyraider -- the same aircraft in fleet use. Also at Corpus, was the multi-engine program. After about four months of training in the S2F, this program was further subdivided into the patrol (VP) and transport/early warning syllabus (VR/VW). Depending on whether they were going to seaplanes or landplanes, the patrol students received a checkout in either the Lockheed P2V Neptune or the Martin P5M Marlin -- once again, the same aircraft used in fleet squadrons. The Author, with a future airline career in mind, opted for VR/VW. This was somewhat of a risk, since this pipeline could be very good or very bad. The very good option resulted when the new pilot received orders to a transport squadron -- the most luxurious flying duty in the Navy. The bad option was the assignment to the radar barrier

Lockheed Super Constellation squadron in Argentia, Newfoundland. In order to obtain the required number of flight hours to receive their wings, VR/VW students were given a training course that confounds normal logic. Although VR/VW students were bound for landplane duty and would not normally set foot on an aircraft carrier, they were put through an S2F carrier qualification program -- yours truly included! Then, after spending 17 months and several hundred thousand dollars training the multi-engine student as a pilot, the Navy then sent the student through air navigator school! In a throwback to shipboard duty, the Navy trained its officers in all facets of ship operations, including navigation, to be future ship captains. Somehow that philosophy was carried to aviation as well. Airborne navigation training was conducted in Navy R4Ds and T-29's on loan from the Air Force.

Seaplane training ended in the mid-60's, when the Navy retired its Marlins. During the 1970s, several changes took place. First, the headquarters of the Naval Air Training Command transferred aboard from Pensacola. The Navy's Integrated Flight Training Program saw the return of primary and basic training to the station. In 1976, Beechcraft T-44A King Airs replaced the TS-2As. The next year, navigator training ended with the Air Force assuming the training for all of the Services.

In 1997, Corpus Christi is home to Training Air Wing Four and its three squadrons. VT-27 conducts primary and intermediate training in the Beech T-34C. VT-28 is the instructor training squadron. Finally, VT-31 operates T-44s in the advanced multi-engine propeller syllabus. The headquarters of the Training Command has remained as well as the Coast Guard station, the Army maintenance depot, plus an anti-drug U.S. Customs unit. During 1996, two Navy mine-clearing helicopter squadrons moved to the station. Two more of the squadrons are scheduled to arrive in late 1997 or early 1998.

Initially, VN-11 conducted primary training at Mainside beginning with the station's opening in March 1941. The predominant aircraft in use were Naval Aircraft Factory N3Ns. VN-11 was expanded into four additional squadrons: VN-11A, VN-11B, VN-11C, and VN-11D. N3N production ended in 1942 and the aircraft was eventually replaced by N2S Stearmans. All primary training at Corpus moved to Rodd Field during 1943. *NATIONAL ARCHIVES*

Flight training entailed a multifaceted program in addition to flying. Photographs on this and the next page depict a few examples of the activities given to aviation cadets at Corpus Christi during the war.

ABOVE: Cadets received small arms training that included rifle, machine gun, pistol, and shotgun. Skeet shooting, shown here, taught the principal of leading.

NATIONAL ARCHIVES

ABOVE LEFT: Everybody's favorite -- the Obstacle Course. *NATIONAL ARCHIVES*

LEFT: Group calisthenics taking place on the seaplane apron in September 1941.

NATIONAL ARCHIVES

ABOVE: Student pilots were introduced to instrument flying in the Link Trainer. After a syllabus in the Link, the pilot then received an aircraft instrument course. Training in the Link was continued for instrument proficiency throughout the pilot's career. During the war, the Navy utilized women, many with pilot licenses, as Link instructors.

NOVEMBER 1942 NATIONAL ARCHIVES

ABOVE RIGHT: Aviation cadets study map of local flying area painted on hangar floor -- what an ingenious idea!   *NOVEMBER 1942 NATIONAL ARCHIVES*

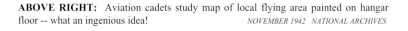

RIGHT: A ship and aircraft recognition class -- an absolute necessity for combat pilots.

MAY 1943 NATIONAL ARCHIVES

ABOVE AND ABOVE LEFT: Following primary training, students were put through a four week, 34-flying hour, basic training course by VN-12. This phase helped the student transition from the light primary trainers to the heavier and faster SNJs. Basic trainers went from OS2U Kingfishers on wheels and the Curtiss SNC Falcons; to the SNV Valiant; and at war's end, to the SNJ. VN-12's squadrons eventually moved to Cabaniss and Cuddihy. *NATIONAL ARCHIVES*

LEFT: A few N2T Tudors were used at Corpus for primary training and the instructor's school. *NOVEMBER 1942 NATIONAL ARCHIVES*

ABOVE: VN-13 conducted a four to five week instrument course following basic training. The aircraft used for most of the war was the SNV. The majority of this training took place at Chase Field; however, VN-13A remained at Mainside through 1944. During the instrument phase, students declared their preference for the type aircraft to be flown in the fleet and could volunteer for the Marine Corps. Further training received or assignment to the Marines, was determined by the students preference, grades, and the needs of the Navy. Instrument aircraft were identified by green stripes around the fuselage and wings. *NATIONAL ARCHIVES*

ABOVE RIGHT AND RIGHT: At the outset, carrier or CV training was conducted by specialized squadrons: VN-14, fighters; VN-15, dive-bombers; and VN-16, torpedo-bombers. Difficulties with providing the exact numbers required by the fleet, led to the introduction of a more generalized CV syllabus in the fall of 1943. VN-14A remained at Mainside until April 1945. Most of the squadrons were formed at Mainside and then moved to the auxiliary stations.

NATIONAL ARCHIVES

ABOVE: Mainside's VN-17 taught the scout and observation syllabus. Initially, students learning the basics of water operations in N3Ns on floats. In November 1942, VN-17 operated 21 N3Ns. Many students considered the scout and observation the least desirable pipeline.

NATIONAL ARCHIVES

ABOVE LEFT: Following the N3N, students transitioned to the Vought OS2U Kingfisher. The majority of the students would go on to fly the Kingfishers in the fleet from battleships and cruisers.

NOVEMBER 1942 NATIONAL ARCHIVES

LEFT: Kingfishers were difficult to work with in the training environment, since the beaching gear had to be manually attached and removed. Once launched in the morning, the aircraft remained on the water until the final training flight of the day. Crew changes and servicing was accomplished afloat.

JUNE 1942 NATIONAL ARCHIVES

ABOVE: VN-17 operations are secured in November 1942 due to high winds.
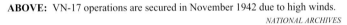
NATIONAL ARCHIVES

ABOVE RIGHT: Judging by the smiles, instructor and student exchange pleasantries after a satisfactory training hop in November 1942. VN-17 did not received the new Curtiss SCs before the end of the war, as its sister squadron, VN-7, did in Pensacola. *NATIONAL ARCHIVES*

RIGHT: VN-18 taught the multi-engine syllabus with PBYs. In February 1943, VN-18C, a landplane multi-engine squadron, formed and moved shortly thereafter to Rodd with SNBs. VN-18C decommissioned before the end of the war and Mainside's VN-18A assumed the landplane syllabus. Initially, VN-18 operated early non-amphibian versions of the PBY, shown here. Training operations were difficult since beaching gear had to be installed and removed manually. The situation improved greatly with the arrival of the amphibian PBY-5A, beginning in 1943. *NOVEMBER 1942 NATIONAL ARCHIVES*

ABOVE: Every one of the Corpus Christi area's 55 plus OLFs had to have a crash truck in attendance during flight operations. Road signs were erected to help the crash crews find their assigned field. In Nueces County alone, landowners were outraged when the Navy summarily removed 2,376 acres from cultivation for OLFs. The locals were further incensed when the Navy set a ceiling of $110 per acre for land that brought up to $200 per acre. *NATIONAL ARCHIVES*

ABOVE LEFT: When Intermediate Flight Training diminished, the Navy added a PBM Operational Training Unit at Corpus Christi in late 1944. *NATIONAL ARCHIVES*

LEFT: A well composed photograph of an SNB in a Corpus hangar.

NOVEMBER 1942 NATIONAL ARCHIVES

ABOVE: One of the proudest and happiest days in a young man's life -- one and a half years of hard work finally pays off! The Author receives his wings from Capt. F. Upham, C.O. of NAS Corpus Christi, on February 21, 1963.

RIGHT AND ABOVE RIGHT: WW II burial plot for foreign students at Corpus Christi's Rose Hill Cemetery in 1996. All the remains, except two, were returned to their native lands following the war. In a rather sad state of present affairs, when former Navy Flight Surgeon, Dr. James Morrow, inquired about the plot on behalf of the Author, the caretaker remarked that this was the first inquiry in 25 years!

JAMES MORROW

JUNE 1945 NATIONAL ARCHIVES

NAAS Corvallis, Oregon

In 1940, the City of Corvallis purchased 491 acres four miles south of town for a municipal airport. The CAA then allocated $400,000 for two runways and a hangar; however, very little work had been done on the project prior to December 7, 1941. After that date, the Army took over the project and started construction in February 1942. The Army enlarged the airport by purchasing a total of 1597 acres and building three 5,100-ft. runways, taxiways, hardstands, and a 160 x 200-ft. hangar. A total of 130 temporary buildings were constructed that included barracks for 140 officers and 900 enlisted men. Meanwhile, the Army established Camp Adair -- a 50,000-acre infantry training center north of Corvallis. Presumably to support the training at Camp Adair, two tactical reconnaissance, one photo reconnaissance, and one liaison squadron passed through the base during 1943. Very little flying activity occurred at the base after October 1943. The Army inactivated the field in April 1944.

On April 20, 1944, Marine Air Group 35 departed Cherry Point, North Carolina for Camp Kearny, California. Four days later, the Army transferred Corvallis to the Navy on a temporary basis. MAG 35's orders were changed en route and the group arrived at Corvallis on April 27. Corvallis was redesignated a Marine Corps Air Facility with the mission of training crews and furnishing aircraft for transport operations. Meanwhile, the last division had departed Camp Adair and the Army turned over the camp's hospital to the Navy as well. The Army utilized the remainder of Camp Adair as a POW camp for Germans and Italians. On May 2, VMJ-953 arrived from Camp Kearny. The Marines carried out training on the Douglas R4D and the Curtiss R5C Commando (C-46). The Marines redesignated VMJ-953 as VMR-953 in July and the next month the squadron departed for the South Pacific. In September, the Marines aircraft at Corvallis totaled

59 including 31 R5Cs and 20 R4Ds. During October, prevailing poor flying weather set in and MAG 35 moved to El Centro, California. A Marine Headquarters Squadron retained possession of the base, although no units were stationed there.

On June 1, 1945, the Navy took over the base redesignating it an NAAS. CASU 10 formed the same day with five officers and 20 enlisted men. During the next two months, base and CASU personnel had their hands full making the base both workable and livable -- former Army accommodations were considered to be "primitive." CASU 10 soon received 58 aircraft to be transferred to CAG 151 -- the leading elements of which started arriving on July 26

from Oceana. During August, operations reached full swing. The Navy completed the erection of 23 prefabricated buildings that measured 20 x 100 ft. and the installation of runway lighting. The air group's 100-plus aircraft, including VBF-151's new F4U-4s, logged an average of 400 hours a day. In September, CAG 151 transferred to Santa Rosa where it decommissioned the next month. CASU 10 departed shortly thereafter for Port Hueneme and decommissioning. Although all flying operations had ceased, the Navy retained Corvallis through the end of 1945. The Navy eventually returned the base to the Army who, in time, deeded the property to the City. In 1995, the original Army hangar had survived among other structures.

Avengers taxi into chocks after training mission.

NAAS Crows Landing, California

In late 1942, the Navy chose a site in the San Joaquin Valley, 71 miles southeast of Alameda, for an auxiliary air station. An 804-acre parcel of land was purchased for $86,708 and ground broken on December 1, 1942. The site was located near the agricultural community of Crows Landing, 1940 population of 363, that consisted of a gas station, country store, and a freight train stop. During construction, the project was known as NAAF Patterson for the nearest post office, six miles to the north. After the Navy decided to include a post office on the station, the base commissioned on May 25, 1943, as NAAF Crows Landing.

On June 18, 1943, VC-36 became the first unit assigned. A detachment of Alameda's CASU 6 also arrived in support. For the next nine months, Crows Landing hosted various carrier units. These units included VC-65, and elements of CAG 28, CAG 18, and CAG 11. In the meantime, a detachment of CASU 37 replaced CASU 6 and Crows Landing was upgraded to an NAAS. Up to the spring of 1944, multi-engine patrol aircraft were based at NAAS Vernalis, 18 miles to the northwest. The Navy realized that Crows Landing's 7,000-ft. concrete runways would be better suited for the heavier weight multi-engine aircraft than Vernalis's asphalt runways; thereafter, Vernalis was designated for carrier units and Crows Landing for multi-engine types.

In March 1944, the first multi-engine squadron, VPB-137 arrived from Alameda with PVs. From June to November, the station embarked on an expansion project that added housing, a hangar, and other improvements. The runways were widened from 150 to 200 ft. The station's ramp that initially was 200 x 400 ft. was enlarged by a 1200 x 200-ft. and a 1890 x 260-ft. section. In August 1944, the first PB4Y-2 Privateer squadron, VPB-118, arrived from Camp Kearny. In January 1945, Crows

Landing added six enlisted barracks, a warehouse, and a 100-man ground training building. From February 2, to March 27, 1945, a VRE-1 Detachment with 12 R4Ds was based at the station. VRE-1 was one of the Navy's three evacuation squadrons that transported wounded men from combat areas in the South Pacific to the various Naval Hospitals in the U.S. In addition, Oakland's VR-4 and VR-11 used Crows Landing for training throughout the station's existence.

Crows Landing's isolated location prompted the Navy to run 10 liberty buses a day to Modesto and Patterson. Navy men were allowed to use the swimming pool at Patterson High School. In June 1945, the station's complement stood at 27 officers and 185 men -- squadron personnel added an additional 245 officers and 1220 enlisted men. Available

billeting accommodated 268 officers and 2116 men. Patrol squadrons that passed thought the station during the war included VPB-115, 122, 101, 103, 107, 133, 140, 118, and 108. The PV operational training squadron, VPB-198, also spent time aboard. Patrol squadrons were supported by PATSUs 8-2, 8-4, 8-5, and 8-7. Other units that operated and trained at Crows Landing were VJ-12 and ABATU 105. By war's end, the station was valued at $4 million.

Crows Landing decommissioned on July 6, 1946, becoming an OLF to Alameda and later Moffett Field. In recent years, the Navy maintained a permanent detachment at the field that supplied crash equipment and refueling services for Naval aircraft from the stations in the area. With the closing of Moffett, the Navy turned Crows Landing over to NASA's Ames Research Center in 1993.

PB4Y-1 has come to grief on takeoff or landing -- details are lacking.   *CURTISS SILVERNAIL*

JANUARY 1944 NATIONAL ARCHIVES

NAAS Cuddihy Field, Texas

Work on P-3, the third auxiliary of the initial Corpus Christi Air Training Center plan, started in November 1940. Located 22 miles WNW of NAS Corpus Christi, the site consisted of 899 acres of farmland and pasture. Construction costs totaled $2.7 million plus a railroad spur of the Texas-Mexican Railroad and an all-weather road to Cabaniss and Rodd fields. The Navy named the station in honor of Lt. George T. Cuddihy when the base opened on November 3, 1941. Lt. Cuddihy was killed in a flight test at Anacostia in 1929.

Cuddihy was home to the basic training squadrons VN-12A and VN-12B. Initially, basic squadrons used the land version of the OS2U Kingfisher and the SNV Valiant. VN-12C, an additional squadron, commissioned at the station on June 1, 1942, but transferred to Cabaniss two and a half months later.

The four-week basic training course consisted of 15 hours of familiarization, 15 hours of formation, and four hours of night flying. The purpose of the course was to provide a transition from light primary trainers to heavier and faster intermediate trainers. Cadets referred to Cuddihy as the "Country Club." Well landscaped and compact, the station was purported to be lenient on military discipline and have an easy ground school. In September 1942, the Navy conducted an enlisted boot camp for 250 men at Cuddihy. An additional 250-man boot camp was held in March 1943.

During the war, the predominant basic trainer in use was the Vultee SNV Valiant. Nicknamed the "V" or "Vibrator", the SNV had an irritating vibration with the propeller in high pitch and was restricted from acrobatics and violent maneuvers. The instructor demonstrated stalls and spins, but the students were not allowed to practice those maneuvers on solo flights. The Navy purchased a total of 2,000 SNVs

during the early part of the war and used the aircraft for intermediate instrument training in addition to basic training. With fixed-landing gear and 100 less horsepower than the equal weight SNJ, the "V" was under-powered and slow. No one that the Author has ever heard of liked the SNV.

Beginning in 1944, SNJs began to replace the SNVs. During the second half of the year, Cuddihy went through a series of squadron changes. On August 17, VN-19, a pre-operational squadron with SBDs, commissioned at the station while the basic training squadrons decommissioned. VN-19 syllabus consisted of a three-week course and 21 hours of flight training. In December, VN-19 transferred to Chase Field and Chase's VN-13C, an instrument training squadron, moved to Cuddihy.

The next month, basic training returned to Cuddihy when VN-12D moved aboard from Cabaniss. In April 1945, VN-12D decommissioned and at the end of the war, only VN-13C remained. In March 1944, Cuddihy's complement numbered 223 officers, 400 cadets, and 1014 enlisted men. Barracks existed for 150 officers, 448 cadets, and 1300 enlisted men.

Cuddihy had four 5000 x 300-ft. asphalt runways and seven OLFs. Although the station was designed to accommodate 200 aircraft, in March 1945, 288 were on board -- including 38 SNVs in a storage pool. On December 15, 1945, in a reorganization of the training command, VN-13C changed to VN-2A.

In January 1947, VN-2A transferred to Cabaniss and Cuddihy Field closed. The former base became a general aviation airport for many years. In 1997, the airport has been abandoned, but several WW II buildings remain.

OLF #30   *NATIONAL ARCHIVES*

NAS Dallas, Texas

In the late 1920's, the City of Dallas purchased 310 acres 10 miles west of town for an airfield on the northern shore of Mountain Creek Lake. The City leased the property to the Army for the nominal sum of $1 per year. On August 16, 1929, the Army dedicated the reserve air base in honor of Major William N. Hensley who had passed away earlier that year. Hensley had been an observer on the British airship R-34's transatlantic crossing in 1919 and a flight instructor in the Dallas area.

In November 1940, construction began at a 30-acre site for a Naval Reserve Aviation Base on the southeast side of the airfield. On May 15, 1941, Lt. Harry Sartoris commissioned NRAB Dallas with 15 officers, 109 enlisted men, 35 students, and six Spartan NP biplane trainers. Also in 1941, North American Aviation completed construction of a plant on the west side of the airport and transferred production of the Army T-6 and Navy SNJ there from Ingelwood, California. Although the main mission of the NRAB was the conduction of primary training, an additional duty was accepting and testing SNJs built by the North American plant. On December 23, 1941, the Army installed the Midwest Headquarters of the Ferry Command at Hensley.

After the U.S. entered the war, the Navy expanded Dallas rapidly including an additional 71 acres. Both the Army and the Navy took a quite different approach to primary training during WW II. While the Army farmed this training out to private contractors in remote locations, the Navy conducted the

training in-house at busy airports such as St. Louis, Minneapolis, and Dallas. With air operations at Hensley by North American, the Army, and the Navy, the Army took a dim view (perhaps justifiably) of solo flights by the Navy's primary training cadets. Since the Army owned the airfield and the Navy's status was that of tenant, the Army forbad the student solo flights. As a result, the Navy entered negotiations to purchase the Lou Foote Airport, located a couple of miles to the west at Grand Prairie. Mr. Foote, who operated a Wartime Training School at the field, paid $55,000 for the land two years earlier. Although the airport had been appraised for $170,000, Mr. Foote asked a price of $250,000. After the Navy and Mr. Foote failed to reach an agreement, on June 5, 1942, the government condemned the property. Mr. Foote relocated his operation south of Dallas. The Navy built two 1500 ft. hexagon landing mats, two enlisted barracks, a hangar, and other buildings. Grand Prairie was known as Squadron Two and all primary training gradually moved there. In October 1942, the Army's Ferry Command moved to Dallas' Love Field and the situation improved at Hensley. The Army's resolve remained and the restriction on solo fights continued. During the entire year of 1942, the station incurred only one flight fatality.

In January 1943, the Navy changed Dallas' designation to a Naval Air Station. Although authorized for 230 primary trainers at that time, the station only operated 145 Stearmans and 13 Spartan NPs. On March 8, 1943, all primary training at Dallas moved to Grand Prairie. Also during 1943, a contingent of Free French students began flight training. In the first class of 18 students, 13 received the *Croix de Guerre* for heroism at Dunkirk. Training continued to expand and by the end of the year, 280 Stearmans were on board. The station suffered six fatalities in the last 12 months.

The primary function of Mainside became aircraft overhaul and SNJ acceptance. The Navy encountered a considerable number of problems with the SNJ acceptance. Wrenches, hammers, pieces of hose, and rags left by production workers were found in the aircraft by Navy inspectors. When the Navy complained, a North American test pilot replied: "What do you expect when you have women, children, and old men building them." A more serious problem involved the wings. On May 17, 1944, the Navy claimed that a wing on a particular airplane was faulty. When North American begged to differ, a Navy test pilot took the aircraft on an acceptance flight. When the test pilot pulled out of a 200-kt. dive, a required maneuver, both the wing and tail failed. The test pilot bailed out and the aircraft hit the corner of the station's drill hall. Incredibly, no one was injured or killed.

In 1944, SNJ and T-6 production lessened and North American retooled to produce the B-24. Hensley's airfield, which up until then consisted of a single 3000 x 200-ft. hard-surfaced strip, had to be enlarged. On July 1, three concrete runways, the longest 5200 ft., reached completion. Additional land was gained by filling in portions of Mountain Creek Lake and relocating a creek. In August, Grand Prairie was also used as a temporary storage site for SNVs, early model Stearmans, and N2Ts. North American's B-24 production got under way in November. With the slowdown in primary training in the second half of the year, Dallas' trainers had been reduced to 86 Stearmans.

With termination of primary training at other bases, Dallas' training load increased with 282 Stearmans on hand in March 1945. Grand Prairie had almost 300 SNVs awaiting disposal. As the Navy's blimp program wound down, 150 blimp pilots began primary training in July 1945. By the end of the war,

Dallas' Aircraft Delivery Unit had accepted 4,421 SNJs from North American. The Dallas plant also produced a further 8129 AT-6s, 4552 P-51s, and 969 B-24s for the Army.

Dallas operated a total of 15 OLFs -- five were owned, the remainder leased. At the owned OLFs, the Navy built hard-surfaced runways -- usually the eight-point stars or variations thereof. Dallas supported one auxiliary at Fort Worth's Meacham Field. Prior to the opening of Meacham, the Naval Ferry Command used Hensley. Primary trainers also utilized Meacham during wet weather. In March 1944, station personnel stood at 363 officers, 1000 cadets, 2329 enlisted men, and 143 civilians. Barracks were available for 194 officers, 1077 cadets, and 2210 enlisted men. Station aircraft numbered nine miscellaneous types. The total number of aircraft present reached almost 900 in April 1945.

Following the war, Dallas became a Reserve base and Chance Vought took over the North American factory. Chance Vought and its successor Ling Temco Vought went on to produce the last versions of the F4U Corsair, the F6U Pirate, the F7U Cutlass, the F-8 Crusader and the A-7 Corsair II for the Navy. On May 1, 1949, the Air Force turned control of Hensley Field over to the Navy, although the Air Force Reserve and Air National Guard remained as Navy tenants. In the early 1950s, the north-south runway was extended to 8,000 ft. by once again filling in a portion of Mountain Creek Lake as Dallas' first jets, FH-1 Phantoms arrived. In 1987, Dallas' VF-201 received the F-14 Tomcat.

In 1997, NAS Dallas is in the process of moving to the former Carswell AFB in Fort Worth. NAS Dallas reserve units, Air Force and Navy, as well as Navy and Marine units from Memphis and Glenview will relocate to Fort Worth. The new base will be named NAS Fort Worth, Joint Reserve Base.

Instructor gives last minute briefing to student on solo flight. *JUNE 1942 NATIONAL ARCHIVES*

RIGHT: Dallas's flight line in July 1942.   *NATIONAL ARCHIVES*

LEFT: The secondary mission of NAS Dallas was the acceptance point for SNJs manufactured by North American at Hensley. During 1941, an anticipated shortage of aluminum alloy prompted North American to develop the SNJ-4. Spot-welded low-alloy steel was used for the wing, center section, vertical stabilizer, rudder, elevators, ailerons, and flaps. Portions of the fuselage, cockpit floor, and other parts were made of plywood. A savings of 1,246 lbs. of aluminum alloy was realized. The shortage never materialized and future models reverted to traditional materials. All the Navy's 2400 SNJ-4s were produced at Dallas. A group of SNJ-4s, pictured here, await the delivery process -- probably during early 1942.   *NATIONAL ARCHIVES*

ABOVE: Mansfield OLF had a common layout repeated many times throughout the Navy's Training Command bases. Dallas's Polo OLF had an identical scheme.

FEBRUARY 1943 NATIONAL ARCHIVES

ABOVE LEFT: Five-Point OLF. The white circles are targets the student must land in. This was known as spot-landing practice. *FEBRUARY 1943 NATIONAL ARCHIVES*

LEFT: Arlington OLF was a large area with combination of a hard-surfaced octagon and a grass landing area. Adjacent to the octagon is a parking area. Possibly, this could be a solo check field, where the instructor exited the aircraft and observed the student take a few solo circuits in the landing pattern. *FEBRUARY 1943 NATIONAL ARCHIVES*

OLF Grand Prairie: For all practical purposes, the story of primary training at Dallas is the story of Grand Prairie, located three miles west of Hensley. The field had two 1500-ft. hexagon landing mats, a hangar, and enlisted barracks. Initially known as Squadron Two, the field was first used for cadet solo hops. By March 1943, all of Dallas' primary training moved here. *1943 NATIONAL ARCHIVES*

SEPTEMBER 1943 NATIONAL ARCHIVES

NAAF Del Mar, California

Del Mar is a seaside resort community located 20 miles north of San Diego's North Island. The town is the location of the San Diego County Fairgrounds, the Del Mar Race Track, and the luxurious Del Mar Hotel. An unpaved military outlying field, known as San Dieguito Valley or Del Mar, existed one mile east of town as far back as the 1920's and possibly earlier. In June 1941, the Navy, previously leasing the airfield's 80 acres, purchased the property with the intention of building two hard-surfaced runways. When the cost of building a dike to prevent possible flooding by the San Dieguito River proved prohibitive at that time, the proposal was cancelled and the airfield remained unimproved.

Wartime needs for a blimp facility to patrol the sea around San Diego, prompted the Navy's return to the site in 1943 to construct a small blimp base. Although Lt. Hugh Talford landed the first blimp there on July 1, 1943, the facility was not commissioned until August 8 as an auxiliary of NAS Santa Ana. The station was essentially identical in make-up to Santa Ana's other auxiliary at Lompoc, California consisting of a 500 by 1000-ft. asphalt mat with two mooring circles and barracks for 26 officers and 112 enlisted men.

Normally, Santa Ana's ZP-31 or Blimp Headquarters Squadron Three maintained a detachment of one to two K-ships at Del Mar. During the summer of 1944, MGM studios used the station to film segments of the motion picture, *This Man's Navy*. The typical implausible action feature of the day, the film ended in Burma -- Del Mar was the location for this segment. The film starred the late Wallace Beery, who had been made an honorary LCdr. and Naval Aviator in the 1930s in appreciation of his promotional contributions to the Naval Aviation Reserve at NRAB Long Beach.

On October 17, 1944, K-111 of Blimp Headquarters Squadron Three from Tillamook, Oregon crashed on Santa Catalina Island. Temporarily deployed to Del Mar, the fully armed blimp was conducting a night navigation training flight when it hit high terrain on the island. The blimp's depth charges and gasoline tanks exploded, killing five of its nine-man crew. In spite of this tragedy, duty at Del Mar must have been quite pleasant. One former blimp pilot recalled: "We'd get our orders for the next day's patrol from the end of the bar at the Hotel Del Mar."

The Navy closed Del Mar in September 1945 and eventually sold the property to San Diego County for $1. The County then leased the property for an airport. The fixed-base operators had both been stationed at Del Mar during the war -- one of which was former Lt. Hugh Talford, who landed the first blimp at the station. The runway was ultimately extended to 3,500 ft. The airport, frequented by visitors to the Del Mar Hotel and race track, remained open until October 8, 1959, when Interstate 5 was constructed through the middle of the property.

During the summer of 1944, MGM filmed a segment of *This Man's Navy* at Del Mar. Pictured here is the motion picture's star, Wallace Beery, an honorary LCdr. and Naval aviator for his role in promoting Naval Aviation in the 1930's.   *NMNA*

MARCH 1945   NATIONAL ARCHIVES

NAAF Durant, Oklahoma

Durant is located in southern Oklahoma, approximately 100 miles NNE of Dallas, Texas. In the early 1940s, the CAA offered to build a municipal airport if the City purchased the property. A small airport existed north of town, but that site was deemed unsuitable for the airport proposed by the CAA. The City purchased a tract of farmland three miles SSW of town for $75,000 on which three 4,000-ft. runways were built. During the construction of NAS Clinton, Oklahoma, 190 miles to the northwest, the Navy took an interest in the airport and reached an agreement with the City to lease the property. Work on a hangar, aircraft parking apron, garage, and fence began in September 1943. The runways were also extended an additional 1000 ft. for Navy use. During construction the Navy used the National Guard Armory in Durant as quarters. At a cost of $346,000, the station opened on October 1, 1943, as an auxiliary of Clinton. An additional auxiliary at Conroe, Texas was also established by Clinton with facilities almost identical to Durant's.

The mission of the station was to support the operational phase of the Special Task Air Group. Specifically, the base operated a training school for Target Drone Units. The course covered drone rigging, pre-flight, launch, flight, and recovery. The drones used were TDDs originally developed by the Army as the OQ-2 series and manufactured by Radioplane Corporation. The TDD-1, powered by a six-HP engine, had a 146" wing span and weighed 108 lbs. The TDD-2 had similar dimensions but weighed 97 lbs. with an eight-HP engine. The drones were radio controlled, launched by a bungee catapult, and parachute recovered. The training school's staff consisted of three officers and 30 enlisted men that instructed classes of 30 officers and 100 enlisted men at a time.

Durant had three 5,000 x 150-ft. asphalt runways on 850 acres. The Navy allowed Army basic trainers from Perrin AAF, 30 miles south at Sherman, Texas, to use the airfield as a bounce field. The Navy operated three transport flights a week to the main station at Clinton. The CAA installed lighting on the airfield in April 1944. The station operated one aircraft, an SNV.

In 1947, the Navy returned the airport, currently known as Eaker Field, to the City. In 1997, the hangar built by the Navy survives.

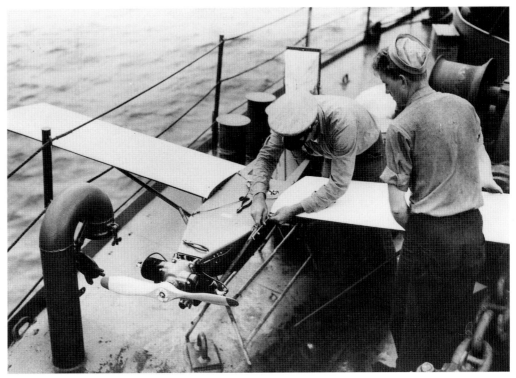

RIGHT: A TDD-2 target drone is prepared for shipboard use. About the size of today's large radio-controlled models, the drone did not have wheels. Normally bungee launched and parachute recovered, the drone was probably not retrieved aboard ship. *NATIONAL ARCHIVES*

NAS Dutch Harbor, Alaska

The Naval Air Station and submarine base at Dutch Harbor was the third Alaskan station constructed by the Navy in the buildup prior to WW II. The Navy first acquired the land in the early 1900s and later established a coaling station and radio facility. The air station commissioned on September 1, 1941. After the beginning of the war, a detachment of three floatplanes operated from the base.

In June 1942, the Japanese mounted a diversionary raid on Dutch Harbor as part of the Midway Islands attack plan. On June 3, two Japanese aircraft carriers launched a 35-plane attack force against Dutch Harbor. The Americans, having broken the Japanese code, knew a raid was imminent. En route to Dutch Harbor, the attacking force shot down an American patrol plane. The weather was not particularly good and only 17 aircraft found their way to Dutch Harbor. Attacking aircraft bombed and strafed the base, killing approximately 25 American soldiers and sailors. Dutch Harbor's antiaircraft guns shot down two of the attackers and damaged two others. The next day, the Japanese attacked again killing an additional 18 defenders. The raiders' withdrawal to their carriers produced one of the great American windfalls of the war. A Zero, hit by antiaircraft fire at Dutch Harbor, developed engine trouble and crash landed on an island. The ground was very soft and the aircraft nosed over, breaking the pilot's neck. Five weeks later, American forces discovered the wreck and recovered the aircraft. The Zero was brought to the U.S., repaired, and returned to flying status. American intelligence had recovered wrecks of Zeros shot down at Pearl Harbor and knew a great deal about the aircraft's construction -- now they learned everything else. The aircraft was thoroughly flight tested and flown in mock combat against all American fighters. The Zero's strengths and weaknesses as well as recommended tactics against it were passed on to operational units. In retrospect, the raid on Dutch Harbor may well have cost the Japanese the Battle of Midway. If the two Japanese aircraft carriers had been at Midway, the outcome of that battle may have been quite different.

After the opening of Adak, the importance of Dutch Harbor diminished with the base becoming a support and staging facility. In 1945, the submarine base closed as the air station was reduced to a Naval Air Facility. The Navy finally closed the base in 1947. Dutch Harbor's 2095 acres had a 4300-ft. runway, one seaplane ramp, and two landplane hangers. The base could support 18 carrier aircraft and 12 observation floatplanes. The seaplane operating area was not very large, handling PBY aircraft only on an emergency basis. Barracks existed for 295 officers and 3790 enlisted men. By the end of the war, the base's complement had been reduced to 42 officers and 472 enlisted men. Today, the former facility is Dutch Harbor's municipal airport.

Dutch Harbor's barracks area shortly after the Japanese attack on June 3, 1942.   *NATIONAL ARCHIVES*

Dutch Harbor's seaplane and barracks area in March 1943.   *NATIONAL ARCHIVES*

APRIL 1943 NATIONAL ARCHIVES

NAS Eagle Mt. Lake, Texas

Impressed by German glider assaults in Belgium and on Crete, Secretary of the Navy, Frank Knox, ordered the Marines to develop a glider program. Three locations were selected for glider training bases: Edenton, North Carolina; Shawnee, Oklahoma; and Eagle Mt. Lake, Texas. The Navy selected a 2,931-acre site on the eastern shore of Eagle Mt. Lake, 25 miles northwest of Fort Worth. Construction began on July 24, 1942, with the base commissioning on December 1, 1942, at a cost of $4.35 million. An auxiliary, NAAF Rhome Field, was also built seven miles to the north.

Marine Glider Group 71 (MLG 71) commissioned at Parris Island, South Carolina on January 10, 1942. On May 1, 1942, Marine Glider Squadron 711 (VML-711) formed as a subordinate unit of MLG 71. During November, MLG 71 and VML-711 transferred to Eagle Mt. Lake. Soon Naval strategists realized that glider assaults would be impractical in the island hopping campaign planned for the Pacific; however, the Navy developed seaplane gliders in the meantime. Two prototypes were built by Allied Aviation Corporation as the XLRA-1 and two by Bristol Aeronautical Corporation as the XLRQ-1. The Marines cancelled the glider program in May 1943. The base closed and the program's 36 officers and 246 enlisted men transferred to other duties. Following the war, the Germans revealed Hitler had forbidden further glider assaults because of the unacceptable losses suffered on Crete.

The Training Task Force (TTF) Command at NAS Clinton, Oklahoma, took over the base commissioning an NAS there on June 1, 1943. The station also assumed command of the NAAFs at Rhome and Conroe, Texas. When the Marines departed, they apparently left their gliders behind. On June 30, gliders on board consisted of 34 Pratt-Read LNE wood trainers, 10 LRW transports (Army Waco

CG-4A) and six Schweizer LNS trainers. Aircraft present included one R4D, four NE Piper Cubs, three N3Ns, 17 Timm N2T Tudors, and one Curtiss SNC. The TTF experimented with remote controlled bomb carrying gliders, but the main development effort was with drones. The TTF transferred the Special Task Training Group (STAG) 2 and its PV squadrons, VK-11 and VK-12, to the new station. The STAGs also conducted experiments with

remote controlled landing craft and torpedo boats -- it is possible that this work was conducted on Eagle Mt. Lake. The concept involved the launching of remote controlled high explosive laden boats against beach obstacles. The Navy remained at Eagle Mt. Lake for less than a year, and transferred STAG 2 with VK-11 and VK-12 to Traverse City, Michigan. When the Navy departed, the command of Conroe returned to NAS Clinton.

Rhome Field, located seven miles north of Eagle Mt. Lake, was used by the Marines for glider operations. Under the Navy, Rhome was deemed "not usable." The Marines installed a GCI radar site at Rhome when they resumed command. *NATIONAL ARCHIVES*

The Marines returned recommissioning an MCAS on April 1, 1944. Marine Air Group 33 arrived nine days later for training. The next month, three VMSB squadrons of SBDs also arrived. In August 1944, MAG 33 departed for San Diego and deployment to the South Pacific. The SBD squadrons remained until November, when they moved to Oak Grove, North Carolina. MAG 53, a night-fighter training group, then arrived and trained seven squadrons until the end of the war.

Eagle Mt. Lake had three 6,000-ft. asphalt runways. Station complement during the Navy's stay at the base numbered 144 officers, 969 enlisted men, and 253 civilians while barracks could accommodate 188 officers and 1200 enlisted men. Rhome Field had a sod landing field, barracks for 464 enlisted men, a BOQ for 60, and a nose hangar. The Navy deemed Rhome Field "not usable" for aircraft use, but after the Marines returned, MAG 33 installed a radar Ground Control Intercept (GCI) there for night fighter training. The Marines also used the airport at Beaumont, Texas as an OLF and sent its fighter squadrons there for gunnery training.

Eagle Mt. Lake had a seaplane ramp that serviced 457 transient seaplanes during the base's existence. This service was provided by HEDRON 52 and then by Ferry Service Unit 10. Duties of the ferry service unit were finally assumed by a detachment of VRS-1 -- the ferry service squadron headquartered at NAS New York. The station also supported an additional seaplane transient facility at Bridgeport Lake, 28 miles to the northwest. At Bridgeport Lake, the Navy had a seaplane ramp, administration building, boathouse, and seaplane parking area.

Eagle Mt. Lake was deactivated on July 1, 1946. For a time, NAS Dallas utilized the airfield as an OLF. The government eventually disposed of the the property. Today, the airfield is a private airport.

ABOVE AND ABOVE RIGHT: The TDN, the world's first guided missile, was flown by a remote control operator with the help of a TV camera in the drone's nose. The TDN could carry 2000 lbs. of bombs 300 miles. Developed by the Naval Aircraft Factory, the production model was manufactured by Interstate as the TDR. In the fall of 1944, a month long demonstration of the TDR took place in the Pacific with the launching of 42 drones. STAG Two and its two squadrons, VK-11 and VK-12, operated TDN drones with PV-1 control aircraft at Eagle Mt. Lake.   *NATIONAL ARCHIVES*

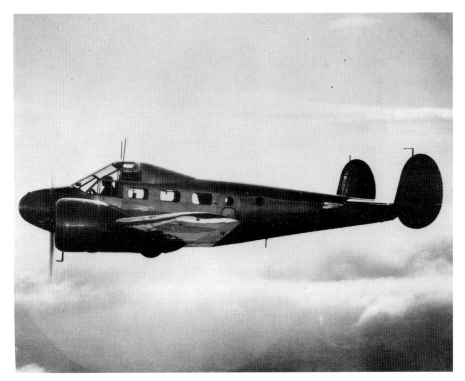

RIGHT: Beech JRB-1 equipped with a cupola for drone control.   *USN*

OPPOSITE PAGE: Whether the Marines or the Navy were at Eagle Mt. Lake, the station served as the main refueling stop on the transcontinental seaplane route and serviced 457 seaplanes during the facility's existence. Seaplanes from Corpus Christi also used the lake during hurricane evacuations. Servicing was first provided by HEDRON 52, then Ferry Service Unit 10, and finally by a detachment of VRS-1.   *AUGUST 1945 NATIONAL ARCHIVES*

SEPTEMBER 1945 NATIONAL ARCHIVES

NAAF Eureka, California

Eureka is located 280 miles north of San Francisco. The local North Peninsula is ten miles long and one mile wide between the Pacific Ocean and Humboldt Bay. The community of Samoa is located on the peninsula and in 1878, a U.S. Life Saving Station was built nearby. The U.S. Coast Guard took over the station in 1915. Eugene Ely conducted the first landing on a warship, the USS *Pennsylvania*, in San Francisco Bay on January 18, 1911. In May, Ely and his aircraft arrived in Humboldt Bay on a steam boat and held a flying exhibition with a Curtiss pusher aircraft on the peninsula.

Two weeks after Pearl Harbor, a Japanese submarine torpedoed the tanker *Emidio* just south of the Bay. This act abruptly brought the distant war to the area. In a few weeks, an activated Mississippi National Guard cavalry unit arrived with caissons and horse-drawn equipment. The Guard set up camp in the buildings of an old lumber mill and later received motorized equipment. Before the Guard departed, it had been joined on the peninsula by an increased Coast Guard complement of 80 men that patrolled the beaches. The Humboldt Bay area became a strategically important area with the only harbor and airfield along the mountainous coast of Northern California. The Army began operating antisubmarine patrols out of Murray Field, a grass field northeast of Eureka. The Navy built a section base near the Coast Guard station and a small seaplane facility at the Samoa boat basin with a wooden seaplane ramp. Fleet Air Wing 8 Headquarters Squadron 3 operated three Vought OS2U Kingfishers from here during the winter of 1942-1943. The seaplane facility never commissioned. The Navy then built a blimp base nearby commissioning NAAF Eureka on August 6, 1943, as an auxiliary of Moffett Field.

Moffett's ZP-32 then maintained a detachment of one to two K-ships at the facility except in the dead of winter. Operations were further complicated by the fact that Humboldt Bay had some of the foggiest weather in the U.S. Meanwhile, NAAS Arcata, a heavier-than-air station, was built 10 miles north of Eureka and commissioned in July 1943. In March 1944, Eureka had a complement of 19 officers and 72 enlisted men with barracks for 50 officers and 441 men. The base's 429 acres had a 700 x 1400-ft. paved blimp operating mat with two mooring circles and a 2400 x 200-ft. asphalt runway over the mat. Kingfisher scouting aircraft continued to operate from the seaplane base throughout the war and a taxiway was eventually built to the airfield for use by amphibian aircraft.

The Navy closed the facility on October 15, 1945. Following the war, the airfield became the Eureka Municipal Airport and remains so to this day. In 1995, the former BOQ had been converted to a bed and breakfast establishment.

The Eureka Naval Section base with the seaplane facility in the lower right of the photograph. The blimp facility is located a short distance to the right. A taxiway was eventually built to the blimp base for use by amphibians. *JUNE 1943 NATIONAL ARCHIVES*

MARCH 1944 NATIONAL ARCHIVES

NAAS Fallon, Nevada

Located 55 miles east of Reno, Fallon's population only amounted to 2000 souls in 1940. The CAA selected a site for an airport here as early as March 1939, although no work would be done for three more years. Once the U.S. entered the war, the Army developed a plan to build several airfields east of the Sierras from where the West Coast could be defended in the event of a Japanese invasion. In Nevada, the places selected included Minden, Winnemucca, Lovelock, and Fallon. In December 1942, the Army Corps of Engineers completed two 5200-ft. runways on land leased by the CAA from the County -- the Army never used the airfield.

The Navy, attracted by the excellent flying weather, isolated location, and existing runways, took over the airport in August 1943. Construction of the base began one month later and included the CAA's contribution of an additional runway plus the extension of an existing runway. In December, the Navy opened a torpedo, gunnery, and rocket range at Pyramid Lake. The commissioning of Fallon occurred on June 10, 1944, with the intention of basing one CAG at the station. Meanwhile, CASU 54 set up in preparation for the first unit, CAG 5, that arrived in July. Some time later, the Navy enlarged the base to accommodate two CAGs. The squadrons based at Fallon during the war besides CAG 5's, included the units of CAG 1, CAG 11, CAG 13, CAG 17, and CAG 60. PV Venturas and Harpoons also used the base for rocket training. On June 1, 1946, the Navy placed Fallon on caretaker status.

Fallon had three asphalt runways, the longest 7,000 ft. on 2500 leased acres. The base's complement totaled 2500 with a BOQ capacity of 405 and enlisted barracks for 2088 men. The station's OLFs were located at Austin, Lovelock, Winnemucca, and the Churchill Strip at Lahontan Dam -- used for FCLPs. Total number of aircraft on the station reached a high of over 160. In the month of June 1945, a total of 21,393 takeoff/landings and 12,645 flying hours were logged.

Following the closing of Fallon, the Navy turned the base over to Churchill County and the Bureau of Indian Affairs. Many of the station's buildings and equipment disappeared during this time and the base's swimming pool was used as a pig sty. In June 1948, the station became an OLF to Alameda. During the Korean War, Navy personnel returned to the base to operate the gunnery ranges in the area and the station became an ALF.

On October 1, 1953, Fallon was recommissioned as an NAAS with the primary mission of providing support for gunnery, rocket, and bombing training. The Navy completed a 10,000-ft. runway the next month. On November 1, 1959, the Navy dedicated the airfield in honor of LCdr. Bruce Van Voorhis, WW II Medal of Honor posthumous recipient who grew up in Fallon. In 1972, the Navy upgraded Fallon to an NAS. In 1997, Fallon is home to the Naval Strike Warfare Center -- commonly called "Strike University." The only squadron permanently attached to the base is VFA-127, an adversary unit that flies the FA-18 Hornet and F-5. Entire carrier air wings of Navy aircraft routinely rotate to Fallon for three weeks of training. The station will be the new home of the Navy's Top Gun school with the transfer of NAS Miramar to the Marines. Fallon now has a 14,000-ft. runway.

An SNJ with an aerograph, a weather instrument, mounted on the wing.   *NATIONAL ARCHIVES*

NAS Hilo, Hawaii

In 1925, the Territorial government appropriated $10,000 to establish a prison camp on the island of Hawaii for the purpose of using prisoner labor to construct an airport. Initially situated on 100 acres, 800 ft. of the planned 3,000-ft. runway was available by September 1927 for emergency landings. When Inter-Island Airways inaugurated service in November 1929, Hilo was regarded as the finest airport in Hawaii. Improvements continued to take place throughout the 1930s.

In March 1941, the Army began developing the airport for national defense and on December 25, 1941, took over the property. Although the airport was spared on the December 7 attack, at midnight December 30, a surfaced Japanese submarine shelled Hilo and the base, causing very little damage. During 1942, the Army embarked on the construction of a major base, while observation and fighter aircraft used the airfield. The Army officially established Hilo Army Air Base on April 1, 1943, with three hard-surfaced runways, 24 revetments, and accommodations for 70 officers and 1200 men. That month the airport was named General Lyman Field. BGen. Albert K. B. Lyman, who had passed away the year before, was the first person of Hawaiian ancestry to reach the rank of General.

Meanwhile, the U.S. Navy entered the picture. Adm. Chester Nimitz, CinCPac, directed a joint Army and Navy board to find an airfield in Hawaii to support two carrier air groups of 180 aircraft. The board determined that Hilo could be expanded to meet this need. In March 1943, the 59th Seabees arrived with 27 officers and 1,036 men to construct buildings. Although only 20% complete, NAS Hilo was commissioned on August 1, 1943. CASU 31 formed at Hilo 12 days later. The station's first tenant, CAG 1, arrived on August 24. The officers' club and mess opened in September, followed the

next month by the completion of an additional 24 buildings. In December, with another BOQ and nose hangar ready for use, a second air group, CAG 5, came aboard. In March, the Seabees finished the widening of the runways from 200 to 400 ft. With the major part of the construction completed, the 59th Seabees were relieved by Seabee Maintenance Unit 562 on April 21, 1944.

As the threat of a Japanese air attack diminished, Army fighter aircraft were withdrawn from Hilo by the end of 1943. The Army planned to use the base for heavy bombers in the middle of 1944, but concentrated its forces on Oahu. An Army Air Transport Command Service Unit remained, but Hilo became an almost exclusive Navy operation. Navy carrier units spent an average of two months at the station, conducting final training before departing for the South Pacific. CAGs 2, 18, 11, 3, 4, 46, 17, 6, 88, and 31 were aboard during 1944 and 1945.

The Hilo complex encompassed a total of 1976 acres leased by the Army. In turn, the Army subleased the land occupied by the NAS to the Navy. By the end of the war, the station had accommodations for 464 officers and 3521 men, as well as a hospital and two swimming pools. Two OLFs existed on the island: Suiter Field at Upolu Pt. and Morse Field at South Pt. Suiter Field was used for FCLPs with messing and housing available, while Morse Field was an emergency strip.

After the war, operations at Hilo slowly diminished. Following a tsunami on April 1, 1946, that demolished many homes, former barracks were turned into low-cost housing. The Navy gave the hospital to the Territory and the facility became a tuberculosis asylum. The station was finally disestablished on July 15, 1947. A portion of the former air station was used by the National Guard. Today, General Lyman remains as Hilo's municipal airport.

The men of Hilo's CASU 31 celebrate VJ-Day.   *NATIONAL ARCHIVES*

NAS Hitchcock, Texas

Hitchcock, located 10 miles north of Galveston, is a classic example of a base built during the war to counter a threat; however, after the completion of the base, the threat no longer existed. Following Pearl Harbor, the Navy's master blimp base plan, started in 1940, proceeded full speed ahead. Part of this plan included two blimp facilities in the Gulf states to protect the United States' major petroleum supply shipping lanes -- the passes of the Mississippi and the Houston ship channel.

In April 1942, the Navy condemned 3000 acres at Hitchcock, paying the 95 owners $142,921. Construction began shortly thereafter on a railroad spur to the station, a 1000-ft. wooden blimp hangar, and a 2000-ft. asphalt landing mat, among other facilities. During 1942, the Germans sunk a staggering total of 1664 Allied ships with the loss of 87 U-Boats -- the German's "Happy Time." By the spring of 1943, the Allies attained the upper hand and the U-Boats had been driven out of the Gulf of Mexico. Nevertheless, the Navy commissioned Hitchcock on May 22, 1943, at a cost of $8.5 million. ZP-23, commissioned at Lakehurst on June 1, arrived at Hitchcock with K-62 three weeks later and commenced antisubmarine patrols. In September, Blimp Headquarters Squadron Two was commissioned to provide support for ZP-23. In December, blimps, previously moored in the open, used the hangar for the first time. By the end of 1943, Allied ship losses had been reduced to 597 with 237 U-Boats being sunk. The Navy cancelled a second blimp hangar planned for Hitchcock.

Hitchcock's blimps patrolled the Texas coast south to Brownsville, and maintained a portable mooring mast at San Benito, Texas. In February 1944, the station reached its high-water mark with five blimps on board. At that time, personnel numbered 98 officers, 587 enlisted men, and 122 civilians. Available

berthing accommodated 154 officers and 616 enlisted men. Station aircraft consisted of one SBC, one SNJ, and a GB Staggerwing Beech. ZP-23 moved on to Vernam Field, Jamaica and was replaced by ZP-24 which commissioned on February 9, 1944. On May 31, 1944, ZP-24 transferred to NAS Weeksville, N. C. Houma's ZP-22 then deployed a detachment to Hitchcock. When ZP-22 decommissioned in September, lighter-than-air operations ended. On October 18, 1944, the Navy redesignated Hitchcock as a Naval Air Facility and made the station available for heavier-than-air operations. On January 1, 1945, the mission changed to provide housekeeping for personnel from the Naval receiving station at Galveston and as a storage facility for aeronautical materials, equipment, and helium -- no further flight operations were conducted.

The station closed on September 15, 1947. For a time after that, the hangar was used to store rice -- if need be, the hangar could hold the entire rice crop of Texas! In 1949, the government disposed of the property, giving the former owners first option -- 51 of the 95 original owners took advantage of this offer. In the early 1950's, the hangar was used to remanufacture Army tanks and half-tracks. In 1961, the hangar suffered damage from a hurricane and was demolished by dynamite the next year. Today, several of the base's buildings have survived, including the former administration building.

The cockpit of a blimp. Blimps of this time required two pilots -- one pilot operated the elevators and the other pilot the rudder.   *NATIONAL ARCHIVES*

NAAS Hollister, California

Hollister is located 80 miles southeast of San Francisco. On April 14, 1912, the first local flight took place from a pasture three miles north of town that would later become an NAAS. The field was used for various flying activities during the ensuing years. In the mid-1920s, Everett Turner, a local crop duster, purchased the property naming the airport Turner Field. In February 1942, the Army from Moffett Field inspected the airport with the intention of forming a primary training Contract Pilot School. At that time, the CAA was conducting flight training at the airport -- still a grass strip. The Navy visited the airport the following November and evaluated it for an auxiliary station. After the beginning of the war, the Navy condemned the property purchasing it for $18,500. Construction proceeded slowly with only two 2700-ft. gravel runways completed by October 1942; however, work began in earnest during December to add lengthened hard-surfaced runways and buildings. Initial expenditures at Hollister totaled $725,000, when it commissioned on June 26, 1943, as an auxiliary of Alameda.

Hollister served as an operational training base for torpedo and fighter squadrons that formed or reformed at Alameda. Since the torpedo range at Monterey Bay was only 20 miles to the west, Hollister was ideal for torpedo squadrons and composite squadrons of torpedo and fighter aircraft. VC-39 was the first squadron to report, shortly after the opening of the base. During the remainder of 1943, VC-42, and VC-68 passed through the station. Meanwhile, an $890,000 program enlarged the base to accommodate two light carrier air groups of four squadrons. Additions included two hangars and a ground training building. Light carrier air groups consisted of one fighter and one torpedo squadron of Hellcats and Avengers. In early 1944, VT-18 and CAG 27 trained at Hollister for several months. CASU 37 serviced and supported the carrier aircraft

at Hollister as well as Monterey. VF-17, CAG 33, and VC-41 were on board during the rest of the year. A tragic accident occurred on June 8, when a VF-33 pilot lost his life in the crash of an F6F -- five days after his wedding.

During early 1945, CAG 31 trained at the station. VF-31 suffered an unfortunate accident during its stay, when its LCdr. commanding officer was killed in an F6F crash at Monterey Bay. CAG 32 arrived at the station following CAG 31's departure. In June, Hollister reached operational peak with CAG 22 and 37 and a total of 88 aircraft on board. On June 26, two F6Fs of VF-22 had a midair collision that claimed the life of one pilot. Another fatal accident happened less than two months later on August

17, when a TBM of VT-37 was lost with its crew of three. The Navy placed the station on caretaker status, October 15, 1945.

Hollister's 210 Navy-owned acres had two 200-ft. wide tarmac runways of 4300 and 4000-ft. lengths. In August 1945, complement stood at 146 officers and 927 men. The base had billeting for 167 officers and 928 enlisted men. Station aircraft usually consisted of a GH Howard ambulance aircraft and a GB Beech for light transport.

In 1947, the U.S. Government deeded the airport to the City. In 1995, several Navy buildings survived. The airport is used for general aviation and in the summer by California forest fire fighting aircraft.

Hollister's ramp in May 1944.

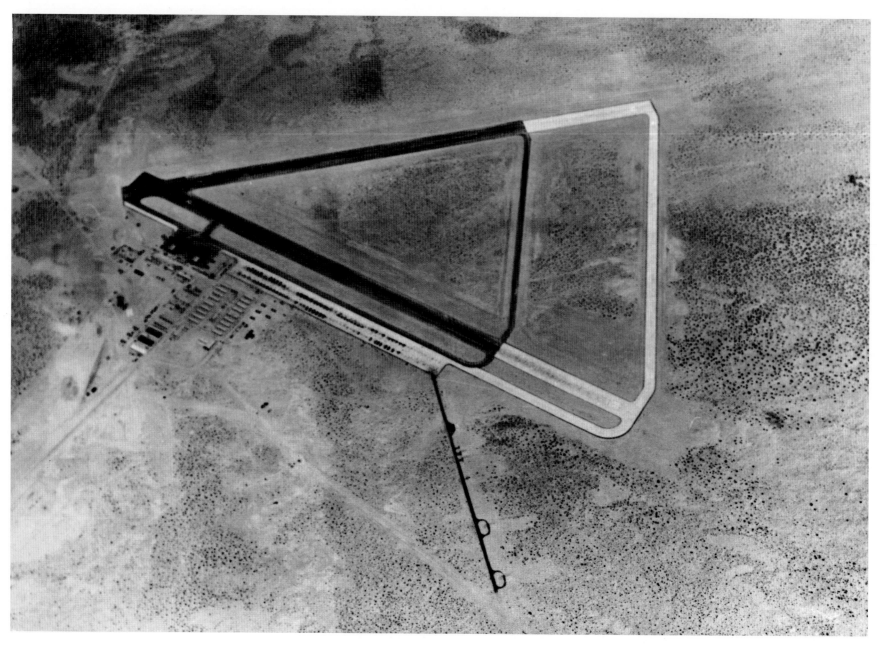

MARCH 1944 NATIONAL ARCHIVES

NAAS Holtville, California

Holtville is located in California's Imperial Valley, 115 miles east of San Diego on the Mexican border. In 1942, the Navy purchased 1397 acres in the desert, eight miles east of town, for an auxiliary air station. Construction began in January 1943 and the flag was run up the flagpole on July 4, officially commissioning the station under the command of Naval Air Center San Diego.

The first squadrons arrived thirteen days later supported by a detachment of San Diego's CASU 5. The flying weather at Holtville was outstanding with VFR conditions 360 days a year. The nearby desolate mountains and desert provided ample gunnery and bombing ranges. The Salton Sea also provided skip-bombing ranges. Despite the remote location, the base was considered to be well appointed and comfortable. On the downside, summer temperatures averaging over 100 degrees F. made daytime flying operations very difficult -- for aircrews, as well as ground crews servicing the aircraft. During 1943, the station suffered nine fatalities.

Many changes occurred at Holtville during 1944. In February, two ground training buildings were completed that housed Link trainers and a Gunairstructor. Initially, the base hosted VC squadrons and up to late 1944 a total of 45 such squadrons had spent several months at the base for operational training. In May 1944, an expansion project increased the station's capacity from three to six squadrons. The only blimp to pay Holtville a visit, K-29, passed through on July 2. CASU 53 commissioned out of CASU 5 in August as the station became primarily a rocket training base. CAG 98, the replacement training air group, also had a contingent at Holtville. During all of 1944, 11 lives were lost in flight accidents.

In March 1945, an adjustment was made by all personnel as the first group of Waves arrived. During the year, 53 aviation units were hosted for an average of a one month stay with five fatalities. Beginning in December 1945, Holtville served as the short-time storage site for 111 PV-2 Privateers. The last of the PV-2s departed in April 1946 and the station went into caretaker status.

Initially, Holtville had two 4,500 x 200-ft. concrete runways that were later extended to 6,000 ft. Eight miles east of the station in the desert was the Sand Hill OLF with a catapult and arresting system, also used by the Marines from El Centro. In March 1944, complement stood at 330 officers and 2650 enlisted men with barracks for 175 officers and 1020 men. Station aircraft consisted of a Staggerwing Beech light transport, an AE Piper ambulance plane, and a Stearman. Holtville also provided supply and personnel support for the small NAAS on Salton Sea, 40 miles away.

Following the war, the Navy eventually gave the airport to the local community. For a time, the former base was used as a tuberculosis sanitarium. The airport has remained open, but sees very little activity. The Navy from El Centro occasionally uses the airfield for touch and go landings. The British Army parachute team has practiced here as well. No Navy built structures have survived.

Holtville's ramp in March 1944 with possibly VC-11 and VC-20 present.   *NATIONAL ARCHIVES*

JANUARY 1945   NATIONAL ARCHIVES

NAS Honolulu, Hawaii

In 1927, the Territory of Hawaii purchased 885 acres, 119 on land and 766 under water, on Keehi Lagoon and developed a municipal airport for Honolulu. The airport was named John Rodgers in honor of the Navy Cdr. who attempted the first mainland to Hawaii flight in 1925. Rodgers, Naval Aviator #2, lost his life in a crash near the Naval Aircraft Factory at Philadelphia in 1926. The airfield was used for private flying until 1935, when Hawaiian Airlines began inter-island service.

In October 1941, the Army Corps of Engineers began a project to dredge seaplane runways in the lagoon and use the fill obtained to create additional land at the airport. By December 7, only 5% of the work had been completed. The Army continued on the project and agreed to turn the facility over to the Navy, provided the Army could use the airfield as well. Initially, the Navy planned the facility for two carrier air groups and five VP squadrons. Later, the situation changed with a decision to use the airfield for a NATS terminal. Pearl Harbor had become too busy for seaplane operations and the runway at Ford Island was too short for fully loaded R5Ds (C-54). The Army completed the initial work at Rodgers at a cost of $16 million. In September 1943, the 1400 men of the 5th Seabees arrived and started construction of the Navy's buildings and hangar. In anticipation of the station's opening, VR-11, commissioned at Oakland in September, moved its headquarters to Honolulu on December 15, 1943. The station officially opened on January 1, 1944, although work continued on additional dredging, filling, and runway construction.

On April 1, 1944, the station received its first permanent C.O., Cdr. David Ingalls, Naval Aviator #85. Ingalls was the first Navy ace and the only Navy ace of WW I, achieving five aerial victories while attached to the 213 Squadron of the British Royal Air Force. Following the war, he finished his education at Yale and went on to Harvard earning a law degree. From March 1929 to June 1932, Ingalls served as the Assistant Secretary of the Navy for Air. After leaving government service, he held an executive position with Pan American. A more fitting man for the C.O. of the Navy's largest transport base could not be found. At the end of the war, Ingalls was promoted to Commodore, although he was undoubtedly a civilian at heart and sympathetic to his pilots. This was demonstrated when an inspecting Admiral took objections to the inevitable personal relationships between the Navy nurses and the male officers on the station. The Admiral ordered Ingalls to build a fence around the nurses' barracks. After the Admiral's departure, Ingalls followed his orders and had a one foot high fence installed around the barracks!

Following the station's commissioning, the Commander of NATS Pacific moved his headquarters aboard. On January 23, 1944, the Martin PB2M-1R Mars landed at the new facility on a proving run. Two months later, the Mars was assigned to Alameda's VR-2. In May, an additional support squadron, VR-12, commissioned as a Headquarters Squadron to support transport operations. VR-10, strictly a maintenance squadron, supported the Navy transport squadrons and Pan Am. The next month, VRJ-1, a utility transport squadron moved aboard from Pearl Harbor. VRJ-1 provided VIP transport service between the Navy's stations in the area, flying seven flights a day with four PB2Ys, eight R5Ds, and one JRB. VRJ-1 eventually became VR-21 after the war. On November 17, the first R5D with special refrigeration equipment passed through the station with 160 pints of whole blood. By the first of 1945, whole blood shipments had risen to 14,500 pints per month and by the time of the Iwo Jima invasion, 1000 pints daily.

In March 1945, the Navy formed VRE-1, a wounded evacuation squadron, out of VR-11 and moved the squadron to Guam. That same month, the NATS terminal processed 17,836 passengers. VR-11, operated along the lines of an airline, became the largest squadron in the Navy. The squadron relied heavily on personnel with airline experience and at one time had 47 officers and 10 enlisted men that previously worked for 15 different airlines. In August 1945, the squadron had 700 pilots, 89 R5Ds, 10 R4Ds, and three miscellaneous aircraft. A VR-11 flight passed through Honolulu every hour, 24 hours a day, seven days a week!

The total area of NAS Honolulu encompassed 56 acres owned by the Navy and an additional 4107 leased acres. Eventually, Honolulu had three seaplane runways -- the longest three miles and four landplane runways -- the longest 7,700 ft. There were four miles of taxiways including one that ran to Hickam Field. The station had 700 vehicles and its galley turned out 7,000 meals a day. Barracks were available for 1447 officers and 9785 enlisted men. Transient VR pilots were housed at a wing of the Royal Hawaiian Hotel -- the submariners occupied the other wing. In addition, the Army had a troop carrier squadron, an Air Transport Command terminal, service squadrons, and barracks for 2160 men on the airfield. Total government investment in the station reached $50 million.

In March 1946, the Navy reduced Honolulu to an NAF and returned control of the airport to the Territory in October of that year. The station finally closed on June 30, 1949, becoming an OLF to Barbers Pt. for seaplane operations only. After the government of Hawaii resumed control of the airport, the name was changed from John Rodgers to Honolulu International. Hickam AFB now uses the runways at Honolulu.

ABOVE: NAS Honolulu probably had one of the world's largest nose-hangars. In July 1944, a minimum of six PBMs and one PB2Y are present. *NATIONAL ARCHIVES*

ABOVE LEFT: At least 17 R5Ds can be counted in June 1944. The station had eight seaplane docking piers for Navy and Pan Am transports. *NATIONAL ARCHIVES*

LEFT: NAS Honolulu's operations area in June 1944. The Army's area at the station was located on the far side of the airfield. *NATIONAL ARCHIVES*

ABOVE: Honolulu's ramp in February 1945.   *NATIONAL ARCHIVES*

ABOVE RIGHT: A Douglas R5D wings its way over Hawaii. This aircraft revolutionized transoceanic travel, previously the domain of the flying boat. Following the war, the airlines quickly discarded their flying boats in favor of four-engine landplanes. The Navy acquired almost 200 R5Ds during the war from Army production lines.   *NATIONAL ARCHIVES*

RIGHT: Three Pan Am B-314s at Honolulu shortly after the war. The Navy placed Pan Am under contract during the war and the airline operated Navy transports as well as their own.   *NATIONAL ARCHIVES*

NAS Houma, Louisiana

To protect the passes of the Mississippi, the Navy built a blimp base at Houma, Louisiana, 55 miles southwest of New Orleans. By the time the base commissioned, the German submarine threat had been, for all intensive purposes, eliminated in the Gulf of Mexico. The Navy chose the 613 acre Houma Municipal Airport for the station. Established in the 1930's, the airport was operated by Texaco Oil Co. Although Navy construction began in August 1942, the Coast Guard had already been conducting antisubmarine flights from the airport. On August 1, a Coast Guard Grumman J4F Widgeon, aircraft number V212, depth-charged a U-boat, 100 miles south of Houma. An oil slick was spotted and the pilot given credit for the kill -- the only submarine sunk by a Coast Guard aircraft during the war. Following the war, the Germans acknowledged the loss of U-166 in the area. Today, the Widgeon, V212, is on display at the National Museum of Naval Aviation in Pensacola.

The Navy purchased additional land, bringing the total acreage to 1743. In a situation unique to Houma, the Navy improved the existing airport with two hard-surfaced runways and built a blimp facility adjacent to the airfield. Construction included a standard timber 1000 by 200-ft. blimp hangar. The hangar at Houma was unique in that it had half-dome, rather than the usual vertical flat leaf sliding doors. These doors turned out to be a constant source of trouble. The $10 million station commissioned on May 1, 1943. ZP-22, formed at Lakehurst, arrived fifteen days later beginning antisubmarine patrols. By this time, the U-boat offensive had collapsed in the Gulf, so the second blimp hangar planned for Houma was cancelled.

For a small station, Houma had an extraordinary number of accidents. On April 19, 1944, K-133 was caught in a thunderstorm while patrolling in the Gulf of Mexico. The ship went down losing twelve of its thirteen-man crew. A single crewman was recovered after spending 21 hours in the water. Two days later, the southeast door of the hangar was inoperative and chained open. A gust of wind sent K-56, K-57, and K-62 out into the night to their destruction. K-57 exploded and burned four miles from the station. K-62 came to rest against high tension electrical lines a quarter of a mile away and caught fire. K-56 travelled 4.5 miles and crashed into trees. K-56 was salvaged, rebuilt by Goodyear in Akron, and returned to service. Another incident occurred when a blimp accidentally dropped a depth charge on the Houma Golf Course. The depth charge did not explode. Thereafter, blimps were prohibited from flying over populated areas. On September 21, 1944, ZP-22 decommissioned with a detachment from Richmond's ZP-21 replacing it.

By the beginning of 1945, blimp operations ended at Houma and the station redesignated an NAF. The Coast Guard returned to the field flying air/sea rescue operations. VB-143 from Clinton trained at the station with PVs for a time. Marine PBJ squadron VMB-614 from Newport, Arkansas also used the station for six weeks. The blimp hangar became a storage site after the war with the inventory reaching 330 SNJs, 25 PBYs, 29 SB2Cs, and 64 F6Fs.

Houma had two 5,000 x 200-ft. runways, a 2,000-ft. blimp circular mat, and four mooring circles. In March 1944, complement stood at 99 officers, 607 enlisted men, and 202 civilians. Barracks existed for 196 officers and 898 enlisted men. The station operated a single GB Staggerwing Beech. The base remained active as an aircraft storage facility until October 1947, when the Navy donated it to the City of Houma. In 1948, maintenance cost of the blimp hangar became prohibitive and it was demolished. In the 1950's, the Air Force placed a radar station at the airport. Today, the former Navy base is occupied by light industry, a high school, and a park among other activities. The airport is now known as Houma-Terrebonne.

This close-up of Houma's hangar gives a good view of the unique half-dome doors and the tracks they moved on. The spherical object to the left is the station's helium storage tank. *NATIONAL ARCHIVES*

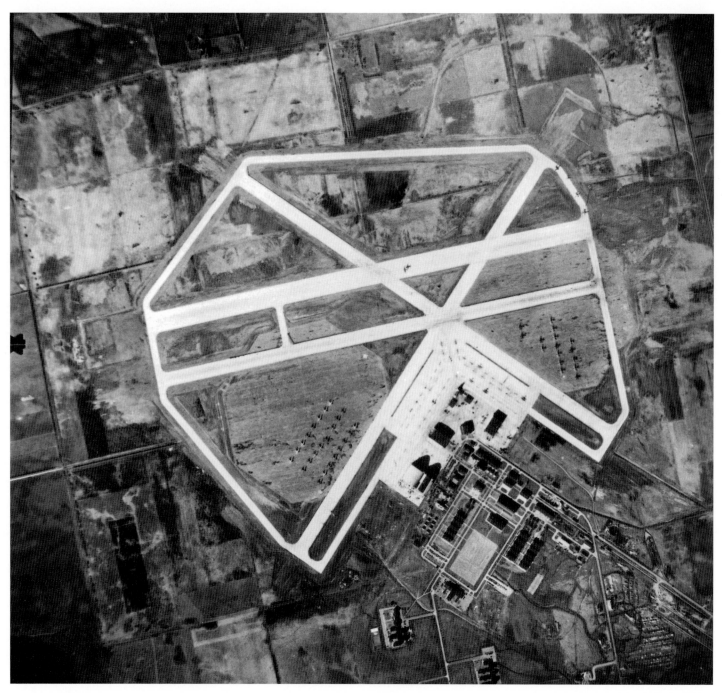

1945 NATIONAL ARCHIVES

NAS Hutchinson, Kansas

Beginning in March 1941, Hutchinson officials lobbied the Navy to build a base at their community. Following the start of the war, the Navy chose a 2565-acre tract 13 miles south of the town for a primary training base and broke ground in July 1942. The land had been previously owned by Amish farmers. The Amish reportedly gave up their property "willingly with no bitterness." Undoubtedly, the fact that the Navy paid $115 per acre for land that usually brought $75 to $100 per acre helped ease the Amish's pain. After estimating an average cost of $1400 per building to clear the existing structures, the Navy reached a mutual beneficial arrangement to allow the previous owners to remove their buildings. The resourceful and frugal Amish, with the help of their neighbors, dismantled and moved their buildings ahead of the bulldozers, saving the Navy an estimated $20,000.

A 17-day deluge of rain hit the construction project in October. Since the roads and railroad spur had been completed, the delay did not extend beyond the downpour. In spite of this, the commissioning of Naval Reserve Aviation Base Hutchinson took place on October 27 -- the base only partially completed. The first cadets arrived during the next month and ground and flight training commenced three months ahead of schedule. This was made possible with the cooperation of the Hutchinson community that leased the Navy the local fairgrounds, other buildings, and the municipal airport. On January 1, 1943, the Navy redesignated Hutchinson as a Naval Air Station; however, only 55 N2S Stearman's were on board at that time.

In the spring, a crisis over a seemingly mundane matter arose. For some reason lost in time, the base's laundry had not been completed and Navy personnel relied on the commercial laundries in Hutchinson. These laundries soon became swamped

with service taking as long as three to five weeks. Some Navy men resorted to sending their laundry home to receive faster service. As the numbers on the base increased, the situation was proclaimed "desperate" by June. All attempts to persuade the laundries to give the Navy priority failed. The Navy contemplated appropriating one of the laundries, but did not want to alienate the locals. Finally, the directors of the Hutchinson Chamber of Commerce and the Mayor acted as a mediator between the laundries' owners and the Navy. The laundries' owners revealed that the bottleneck occurred in the ironing process. Shortly thereafter, both the military and the civilian side embarked on a campaign to encourage wives to iron their husbands' shirts and adopt other laundry conservation practices. The civilian effort was led by Mayor H. H. Heaps who appeared in a photograph on the front page of the local paper watching his wife iron his shirt while dressed in an undershirt. The completion of a $105,000 laundry facility at the base finally ended the problem.

The second problem involved the contraction of venereal disease by base personnel. This situation was never overcome in spite of a vigorous campaign by military and civilian authorities. The Navy went so far as to place a prophylactic dispensing station in downtown Hutchinson staffed by pharmacist's mates 24 hours a day.

In June 1943, 185 Stearmans were on board. By the end of the year, primary training reached its zenith with 303 Stearmans. Shortly thereafter, the Navy selected the station as one of the bases to terminate primary training. In a year and a half, a total of 3,396 cadets passed through Hutchinson with 2,444 graduates and 952 failures, dropouts or fatalities -- a 72% success rate.

A large number of British cadets passed through

Hutchinson. At the risk of offending my British readers, the experience of a former instructor and now retired Delta Air Lines captain, as related to the Author, follows: "Most American young men of those days grew up operating a farm tractor or an automobile; however, the most complicated mechanical device operated by the British lads was a bicycle. Initial primary training could be a nightmare. The Brits were wonderful lads, great and polite gentlemen, and trying hard as hell; nevertheless, the problems were frequent and recurring. On one occasion, while taxiing out, I alerted the student to another taxiing aircraft. The student jammed on the brakes, standing the aircraft on its nose. The major concern was night flying. On many occasions, I felt like I was signing the student's death warrant when approving him for night flight. The next morning, I would sheepishly approach the duty officer and offhandedly ask if anything had happened the night before -- usually nothing had. I did not like this do or die situation, but there was a war on and quotas to fill. My three instructor roommates had similar experiences." The Army encountered the very same problems during primary and initially taught British cadets to ride a motorcycle, acquainting them with the operation of a machine. In the final analysis, the British learned and learned well. Once reaching operational training, British accident rates were better than their American counterparts!

Beginning in March 1944, the base transitioned to operational training with the establishment of Operation Training Unit VB4 #1 with PB4Y-1 Liberators. In conjunction with the Liberators, celestial navigation training towers were completed in October. By the first of 1945, the OTU operated 62 PB4Y-1s with an additional 20 PB4Y-1s in a pool. In March, the first of the Navy's new PB4Y-2 Privateers arrived. By the summer, the OTU's numbers stood at 45 PB4Y-1s and 19 PB4Y-2s with an additional pool of 32 PB4Y-1s and six PB4Y-2s. The station inactivated in October 1946.

Hutchinson had three 5,000-ft. concrete runways with two large asphalt landing mats amongst the runways. Primary training utilized a total of 20 leased OLFs. At the peak, a total of 5,000 personnel were present, including 146 civilian workers. Barracks existed for 166 officers, 1000 cadets, and 2348 enlisted men. In 1945, all runways were extended to 7,000 ft. and an additional 7,000-ft. runway added for the PB4Ys. At a field elevation of 1565 ft., the PB4Ys required longer runways. The OTU's PB4Ys used OLFs at the Hutchinson Municipal Airport, a 7000 x 300-ft. strip at Newton, Kansas, and the airfield at Stillwater, Oklahoma. The station aircraft consisted of a GH and an SNB.

In the years following the war, the station fell into general disrepair. Local farmers used the hangars for grain storage and a civilian leased the former recreation building for a roller skating rink. The Korean War necessitated reopening the base to relieve the congestion at Corpus Christi. On April 25, 1952, a Navy contingent of 1200 men arrived to reactivate the base. During September, advance multi-engine training commenced with PB4Y-2s and SNBs. Ultimately, the Advance Training Units 604 and 614 operated over 100 S2F Grumman Trackers and Lockheed P2V Neptunes with a total station personnel of 2,200. Hutchinson fell victim to the cuts of Naval Aviation in 1958 and the station closed for the final time on June 30.

Following the Navy's departure, the National Guard used the base for a time. With a substantial municipal airport north of town, little need existed for the airfield. In 1997, the former base is occupied by several industries and a law enforcement training center. The airfield, now known as the Sunflower Aerodrome, has kept the north/south runway open, using it for gliding and parachuting activity.

ABOVE: Hutchinson's ramp in 1943.   *NATIONAL ARCHIVES*

BELOW: The Russian Front? Hutchinson's instructors in the winter of 1943-44. Training went on until the temperature dropped below 10F(-12C). This limit was for the aircraft -- not the pilots! Note Christmas tree on top of building.   *KEN ALLERUP*

Three Stearmans fly over Hutchinson control tower. The station's ambulance plane's red cross marking is very unusual.
NOVEMBER 1943 NATIONAL ARCHIVES

Typical Navy mechanic at work in the Assembly and Repair Department. "War is Hell!"
NOVEMBER 1943 NATIONAL ARCHIVES

DECEMBER 1944 NATIONAL ARCHIVES

NAF Inyokern, California

In the mid-1930s, Trans-Sierra Airlines applied for a route between Fresno, California and Phoenix, Arizona. The CAA granted the request with the provision that an emergency landing field be built in the Mojave Desert. This resulted in Kern County purchasing land and the CAA/WPA building a paved runway one mile northwest of the small town of Inyokern (1940 population 55). The airport was inaugurated in 1935 with General Hap Arnold in attendance. In September 1942, the airfield was taken over by the Army's Fourth Air Force and assigned to the Muroc Bombing Range Air Base (now Edwards AFB), 50 miles to the south. Although the Army intended to use the airfield for dispersal and glider training, this plan was never augmented; however, Army primary training Stearmans from Lancaster regularly used the airfield for cross country flights.

Prior to the beginning of WW II, the Office of Scientific Research and Development (OSRD) was created to oversee the development of weapons by America's academic scientists. In August 1940, OSRD placed the California Institute of Technology at Pasadena under contract to develop rockets and other weapons. On July 14, 1943, a TBF fired a British 3.5" rocket and five weeks later, the first Cal Tech produced rocket was launched. The program needed a test facility near Pasadena, so the Army released Inyokern to the Navy when requested in October 1943. The Navy built a hangar plus other support facilities at the airfield. Ten miles east of Inyokern, the main base was constructed and consisted of work shops, laboratories, and barracks for 60 officers and 600 men. The Naval Ordnance Test Station commissioned on December 12, 1943, including a 900-sq.-mi. test range. Meanwhile, the Vice-Chief of Naval Operations ordered 6000 aircraft equipped for rockets by June 1, 1944. On January 15, 1944, CASU 53 formed at Inyokern with 31 officers and 617 men to support rocket training for fleet squadrons that arrived shortly thereafter. Development continued with the British designed 3.5" rocket which was forward firing and high velocity with interchangeable high explosive or incendiary warheads. Combat experience had shown that larger and more powerful rockets were needed. A modified 5" artillery warhead was mounted on a 3.5" rocket motor becoming the 5" Aircraft Rocket (AR). When the new warhead reduced the 5" AR's velocity to 710 fps (feet-per-second) from the 3.5" rocket's 1175 fps, a new motor was developed. This resulted in the 5" High Velocity Aircraft Rocket (HVAR) or "Holy Moses." The first test firing of the Holy Moses took place on March 29, 1944, from a TBF. The rocket's nickname was allegedly coined by Conway Snyder of the rocket's design group after observing a test firing. The first operational use of the rocket occurred in France by the Army. Both Army and Navy units quickly disdained the 3.5" and 5" AR for the more powerful Holy Moses. A full salvo of the Holy Moses gave an aircraft the firepower greater than a broadside from a destroyer. Demand was such that the Joint Chiefs of Staff had to ration the weapon through March 1945. At war's end, however, over one million had been stockpiled.

The popularity and effectiveness of aircraft rockets led the Navy to begin a project to develop a "really big rocket" in early 1944. The project culminated with the 11.75" or "Tiny Tim." With a total weight of 1290 lbs., the Tiny Tim, basically a rocket propelled 500-lb. bomb, was accurate at ranges to 4,000 yds., had a velocity of 820 fps, and could penetrate up to 4 ft. of reinforced concrete. The first firing took place on June 6, 1944. Several developmental problems were encountered including the launching method. A lanyard system was finally selected that fired the motor after the rocket dropped approximately three feet below the aircraft. After the German V-1s began their assault on England, the Joint Chiefs of Staff ordered *Project Crossbow*. The project provided for Marine Air Group (MAG) 60's F4Us to attack the V-1 launch sites with the Tiny Tim. MAG 60's aircraft came to Inyokern for training in July. Delays in the rocket's development and the overrunning of the V-1 launch sites by Army ground units caused the project to be cancelled. With all the problems finally overcome, production of the Tiny Tim began early in 1945. The rocket's effectiveness during the war was minimal and very few were fired in combat. One of the two Tiny Tim squadrons was destroyed when the USS *Franklin* was put out of action by the Kamikaze attack on March 18, 1945.

The airfield at Inyokern was dedicated as Harvey Field on May 10, 1944, in honor of LCdr. Warren Harvey for his contribution to the development of aviation ordnance and fighter tactics. The next month, CASU 53 moved to Holtville as rocket training began at other bases. Meanwhile, the facilities at Harvey Field became inadequate and a larger airfield was needed. In June 1944, work began on a new air station east of Inyokern near the main base

During the summer of 1944, a series of tragic accidents left the station in a state of shock. On June 20, Lt. Donald Innes was killed over the Salton Sea when a rocket under his wing prematurely exploded. Twenty days later, a similar accident claimed the life of Lt. Douglas Walhall and his crewman, Wilson Keller. On August 21, Lt. John Armitage flew into the ground from 1500 ft. in an SB2C and was killed after the launching of a Tiny Tim. Accident investigators discovered that the shock wave from the rocket's blast caused a jam in the SB2C's flight controls. The carnage continued just eight days later, when a rocket ricocheted off the ground tearing the wing off Lt. Robert Dibbs aircraft, who was killed in the subsequent crash. In spite of these grievous losses, work continued unabated.

Beginning in early 1945, Inyokern supported three Army B-29s of the atomic bomb development unit. On June 1, 1945, the Navy opened the new airfield dedicating it as Armitage Field. Harvey Field remained in use by drone utility and fleet units. At that time station complement numbered 60 officers and 732 men with 73 aircraft of 27 types. During the war, the station flew 12,000 flights and accumulated 11,000 flight hours. Rocket firings totaled 1300 Tiny Tims, 5,000 5" Holy Moses, plus 6,500 5" and 3.5" rockets. Rockets were adapted to and test fired from the TBF, PBY, PV, SBD, OS2U, FM, F6F, F4U, SB2C, and PBJ, as well as the Army's P-38, P-47, P-51, A-20, and A-26.

Following the war, Inyokern continued in the development and production of missiles. The Navy closed Harvey Field in April 1946, returning it to the County a year later. In May 1948, the Michelson Laboratory reached completion. The most famous product of the laboratory was the heat-seeking Sidewinder, named for the desert horned rattlesnake. In 1967, the complex became the Naval Weapons Center, China Lake. During the Vietnam War, 75% of the air-to-air and air-to-ground missiles in use were developed by the Navy at the Center. In 1979, the joint service National Parachute Test Range moved to China Lake from El Centro, California. Today, the Center encompasses over 1,000-sq.-mi.

ABOVE RIGHT: The wartime insignia of the United States Naval Ordnance Test Station.   *NATIONAL ARCHIVES*

RIGHT: A Corsair with eight 5" Holy Moses rockets gave the aircraft greater firepower than a broadside from a destroyer.
JUNE 1945 NATIONAL ARCHIVES

ABOVE: Ordnance men learn the details of the 5" Aircraft Rocket, a modified 5" shell warhead fitted to a 3.5" rocket motor. The low velocity of this combination led to the development of the 5" High Velocity Aircraft Rocket or Holy Moses. *NATIONAL ARCHIVES*

ABOVE RIGHT: This F6F-5N Hellcat at Armitage Field in 1948 had a very unusual configuration with APS-5 radar, two 20mm cannons, and two 11.75" Tiny Tim rockets. *NATIONAL ARCHIVES*

RIGHT: Armitage Field in 1954 with apparent recent runway extensions to accommodate jet aircraft. *NATIONAL ARCHIVES*

NAS Kahului, Hawaii

In early 1942, the Navy surveyed a site on Maui for an air station in addition to the existing one a few miles to the south at Puunene. The Navy leased 1341 acres from the Hawaiian Commercial and Sugar Company and the Kahului Railroad. Construction began in November, but was slowed by the extensive blasting required to level rocky terrain for the airfield. Although the station's commissioning took place on March 15, 1943, another six months passed before the first unit, VC-23, came aboard on September 20. CASU 32, formed out of Puunene's CASU 4, was also present for support.

Throughout the war, approximately 50 additional squadrons, CAGs, and other units spent time at the station. The units conducted final training here before embarking for the combat zone. Every pilot practiced FCLPs, tactics, instruments, strafing, recognition, support of amphibious operations, and night/day carrier rendezvous and break-ups. Further specialty training was also conducted. Fighter squadrons trained in air-to-air gunnery, combat air patrol (CAP), group tactics, and fighter director control. Torpedo pilots made live torpedo drops on Kahoolawe Island, torpedo runs on target ships, glide-bombing, and antisubmarine patrols. Bombing squadrons practiced horizontal bombing, glide bombing, dive bombing on towed spars, mast head bomb runs, and radar bombing. The gunners on the torpedo and bombing aircraft also took flexible gunnery training. An aircraft gunners school conducted ground training with a moving target on the machine gun range. A total of 19 magazines were constructed to handle all the ordnance needed for aircraft and gunner training.

Kahului was twice the size of Puunene with an initial designed capacity for two carrier air groups of 180 aircraft. Two asphalt runways measured 7,000 and 5,000 by 500 ft. Aircraft parking totaled 190,000-sq.-yds. including revetments for 12 bombers and 61 fighters. Three nose hangars plus barracks for 936 officers and 5461 men were part of the station's 166 buildings. The Navy's investment in Kahului totaled $28.5 million by war's end.

In October 1945, the Navy announced plans to make Kahului a permanent installation, but later reversed this decision placing the station on caretaker status in November 1946. The Territorial Government planned to move Maui's commercial airport from Puunene to the larger airport at Kahului. Legal problems with the Navy's lease and the Korean War delayed this move for several years. On June 24, 1952, a new terminal building was dedicated as airlines moved service to Kahului. Today, the airport remains as the commercial airport of Maui.

Avengers at Kahului in late 1943.

SEPTEMBER 1943   NATIONAL ARCHIVES

NAS Kaneohe Bay, Hawaii

NAS Kaneohe Bay was located on the Mokapu Peninsula on the northeast coast of Oahu. The peninsula, once owned by the Hawaiian royal family, was considered sacred ground. During WW I, the Army acquired 322 acres on the peninsula for military use. Following the war, the government leased the Army property for ranching. In 1938, the Hepburn Board chose the location for a patrol plane base initially acquiring 464 acres. Construction began in September of 1939. That same year, the Army reactivated its facility and eventually established Fort Hase for coastal artillery batteries and a radar station. The Navy created an additional 280 acres with 11 million cubic yards of fill, obtained from dredging of channels and seaplane lanes in the bay. The station commission on February 15, 1941, and the first squadron, VP-24, arrived one month later. A 5200 x 1000 ft. runway was used for the first time in July, when the base's C.O. landed in a Grumman J2F Duck.

On December 7, 1941, the Japanese assigned a strike force to attack Kaneohe. At 0750, the first wave strafed the airfield and PBYs moored in the bay for 10 minutes. The bombers arrived 25 minutes later. One of the two Japanese planes shot down was that of the attack's leader, Lt. Iida, who crashed on the station. Kaneohe's personnel suffered 17 fatalities, including two civilians, plus 67 wounded. All the aircraft on the station, including 33 PBYs, were destroyed. Three PBYs, airborne at the time of the attack, survived. CPO John W. Finn USN, later received the Medal of Honor for valor on that day -- the first such award of the war.

The Navy expanded Kaneohe into a major air station and acquired the remainder of the peninsula with the exception of the Army's Fort Hase. The station became the primary Hawaiian base for Navy patrol aircraft. The numbers included five squadrons of 60 seaplanes and several squadrons of patrol landplanes. Initially, these were PV Venturas, later joined by PB4Ys. From October 1942 to August 1945, 64 patrol and bombing, three photo-reconnaissance, and six rescue squadrons passed though the station. HEDRON Two supported the patrol squadrons present. Additionally, Kaneohe served as the base for 90 carrier aircraft that were supported by CASU 1A and CASU 38. An Air Bomber Training Unit trained thousands of enlisted gunners during the war. Schools were conducted in celestial navigation and other patrol plane operations. An instrument training center had 50 link trainers and two bomber mock-ups with 44 instructors and 130 enlisted men.

Kaneohe Bay consisted of 2108 acres. In 1944, the Seabees added a 5,000-ft. runway. That year, station personnel stood at 836 officers, 6584 enlisted, and 1020 civilians while barracks could accommodate 842 officers and 9671 enlisted. Kaneohe's personnel rotated on three month tours to man the NAF at French Frigate Shoals. Station aircraft included two PB2Ys, two PBYs, four TBMs, and one each F6F, J2F, JRB, and NE.

In 1949, the Navy closed Kaneohe Bay and the property remained on caretaker status for the next two and a half years. In 1952, the Marines closed Ewa and commissioned an MCAS at Kaneohe Bay. Improvements over the years included a 7,767-ft. jet runway. In 1997, the station is home to the First Marine Expeditionary Brigade with a population of over 15,000 Marine and Navy personnel. With the proposed closing of Barbers Pt. in 1999, Navy and Coast Guard flying in the Hawaiian Islands will be relocated to Kaneohe Bay.

The 15 Navy men killed on December 7 are buried in a mass grave the next day.   *NATIONAL ARCHIVES*

ABOVE: Six of VF-3's F4Fs are safely tucked away in a concrete revetment. Following the Japanese attack on December 7, revetments were hurriedly constructed at airfields in the islands. *NATIONAL ARCHIVES*

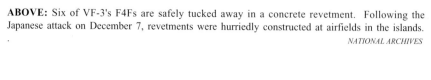

ABOVE LEFT: The *Yorktown's* VF-3 arrives at Kaneohe Bay in May 1942. The Battle of Midway was imminent and photographers were on hand for the momentous occasion. *NATIONAL ARCHIVES*

LEFT: VF-3 prepares to depart for the *Yorktown* and the great battle. Unfortunately, the *Yorktown* sunk on June 7 after being torpedoed by a Japanese submarine. *NATIONAL ARCHIVES*

ABOVE: Kaneohe's crowded ramp in 1945 with SBDs, FMs, SNJs, and a J4F Widgeon. In the background are PBYs, PB2Ys, PB4Y-1s, PB4Y-2s, and PBMs. *NATIONAL ARCHIVES*

ABOVE RIGHT: Another view of Kaneohe's ramp in 1945 with Wildcats of a Composite Squadron, plus a TBM and an SBD. In the background, a PB4Y-2 Privateer touches down on the runway. *NATIONAL ARCHIVES*

RIGHT: Formation of F6Fs from Kaneohe over Hawaii in May 1944. *NATIONAL ARCHIVES*

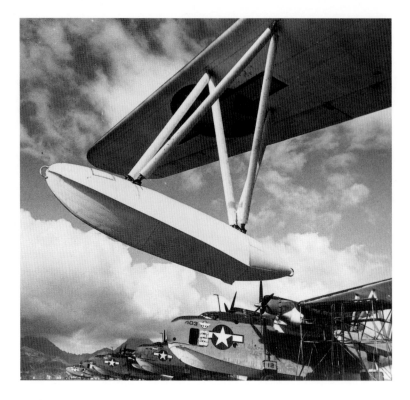

ABOVE AND ABOVE LEFT: Kaneohe's PBM area in February 1944.

NATIONAL ARCHIVES

LEFT: Consolidated PB2Y Coronado is moored at Kaneohe in March 1944. First delivered in December 1940, a total of 219 PB2Ys were built with ten going to the British. Many were converted to transports and hospital aircraft. The Coronado was withdrawn from service before the end of 1945. *NATIONAL ARCHIVES*

OPPOSITE PAGE: PVs at Kaneohe in May 1944. *NATIONAL ARCHIVES*

1945 NATIONAL ARCHIVES

NAAS King City, California

The Army and the Navy rarely saw eye to eye on the same subject -- this included primary training. While the Navy performed the training in-house, the Army contracted the training to civilian operators that formed Contract Pilot Schools (CPS). In 1940, Palo Alto Airport Inc. won a contract and located a school at King City. An agricultural community, 125 miles south of San Francisco, in the San Antonio Valley, King City had a population of 1800 in 1940. The airfield was built on a 249-acre tract owned by the Spreckels Sugar Company and leased to the City that in turn subleased the property to the school. Construction took place during the winter of 1940-1941, the wettest in 25 years. The school, named Mesa del Rey, welcomed the first cadets in March 1941.

By May 1941, five barracks, a hospital, administration building, mess hall, and two hangars were completed. In the fall, a hangar was added -- the investment totaled over $500,000 with an initial annual payroll over $100,000. In October 1941, the City passed a $16,000 bond issue, bought the property, and renewed the flying school's lease. Mesa del Rey accommodated 280 cadets with a staff of 555 civilians and 35 Army personnel. Ryan Recruits and Boeing Stearmans flew 700 hours a day at the peak. In October 1944, the school closed after putting 10,000 cadets through the primary training course. The Army had 59 other CPSs across the U.S. and paid the contractors approximately $1000 for each cadet that completed training.

The airfield had an unusual layout with a dispersal area and revetments -- clearly seen in photograph on the opposite page. Perhaps the airfield was intended as an alternate fighter base. At any rate, the cadets played war games and every night the trainers were moved into the revetments in case of a possible Japanese air attack!

In the spring of 1945, the Navy was attracted to the area by the good flying weather and its nearness to Alameda. The Navy took over the field and commissioned the station on April 6, 1945, as an auxiliary of Alameda. The new Navy C.O., impressed by the facility's well-appointed greenery and rose gardens, proclaimed the station "the prettiest NAAS in the Twelfth Naval District." Four days later, VC-10 arrived from Ventura. By the end of the month VC-20 replaced VC-10 that moved on to Holtville. VC-20's 31 aircraft consisted of Avengers, FM-2 Wildcats, and one SB2C. A detachment of Watsonville's CASU 64 supported VC-20 and oper-ated three FM-2s, two Avengers, and one J2F Duck. The station's aircraft was one GH Howard hospital plane. During the summer of 1945, Navy planes encountered problems with the facility's 4500-ft. runway, taxiways, and ramps when the asphalt surface became soft when hot.

On September 15, 1945, the Navy placed the station on caretaker status and on December 15, 1945, returned the airfield to the City. In 1997, Mesa del Rey, remains as King City's municipal airport. A few of the former base's buildings are in use by a commercial onion and garlic dehydrator.

This is what your aircraft looks like when its rear is chewed up by another aircraft's propeller!   *NATIONAL ARCHIVES*

NAAS Kingsville, Texas

Richard King, a river steamboat captain, came to Texas in 1847 during the war with Mexico. After establishing a prosperous steamboat business on the Rio Grande, King ventured into the cattle business in 1852 by purchasing the 75,000-acre Santa Gertrudis Ranch in Nueces County. King continued expanding the ranch as well as developing the Santa Gertrudis cattle breed and building the Texas-Mexican Railroad from Corpus Christi to Laredo, Texas. After King's death in 1885, his son-in-law, Robert Kleberg, took over management of the ranch. In 1904, the King Ranch became a corporation and at its height encompassed 2,000-sq.-miles or 1.25 million acres -- approximately the size of Delaware. The community that arose around the King Ranch headquarters was incorporated as the town of Kingsville in 1911. In July 1935, the CAA leased 97.2 acres, 2.5 miles south of town, and established the Department of Commerce Intermediate Field #11 on the Ft. Worth to Brownsville lighted airway.

During the development of the Corpus Christi Naval Air Training Center in 1940-41, a delegation from Kingsville led by A. L. Kleberg, the current manager of the King Ranch, tried to interest the Navy in several sites for an air station, but the Navy was non-committal at that time. After Pearl Harbor, the Navy chose a 2850-acre portion of the King Ranch. The locals were shocked since this site had not been offered to the Navy and was considered to be some of the best farmland in the area. Nevertheless, the Navy took over the property and began construction in February 1942, on what was to become the largest auxiliary in the training command. The base was built with the barracks and administration area between two separate airfields -- known as North and South Fields. The Navy built a very similar base at Whiting Field, Florida the next year. The station opened on July 4, 1942, under the most primitive of conditions, a mere four months after ground was

broken. Initially known as P-4, Kingsville was the only auxiliary of the Naval Intermediate Training Command not named in memory of a Naval aviator.

From Mainside, the fighter training squadron, VN-14, moved to North Field. A month later, the dive bomber training squadron, VN-15, transferred to South Field. In January 1943, the station had 316 aircraft aboard -- mostly SNJs, but also including 47 Curtiss SNCs used for dive bomber training. As these squadrons grew in size, they were split into two squadrons each -- VN-14A, VN-14B, VN-15A, and VN-15B. On April 4, 1943, VN-14B transferred to Rodd Field and VN-14C formed to take its place. By mid-1943, Kingsville also added a gunnery school for enlisted crew members. On June 30, Frank Knox, the Secretary of the Navy, inspected the station. This was followed on July 7 by a visit from Franklin D. Roosevelt and the President of Mexico. In late 1943, specialized intermediate flight training ended and all squadrons began teaching a more generalized CV syllabus. By the end of 1944, 628 aircraft were in use at Kingsville.

On April 1, 1945, the slowdown of Naval flight training caused the decommissioning of VN-15A and VN-15B. The void was filled by the forming of night fighter and torpedo operational training units, OTU VFN #2 and OTU VTN #1. The OTUs operated 75 F6Fs, 18 F7Fs, 90 TBMs, 36 SNJs, and 10 SNBs. The units had a student capacity of 150 pilots and 200 air crewmen. The VFN program lasted 12 weeks and the VTN training course six weeks. Training continued for a while after the war, but on August 1, 1946, Kingsville went on caretaker status.

Kingsville had seven OLFs and its two airfields each had four 6,000 x 300-ft. asphalt runways. One of the OLFs was the CAA airfield. In March 1944, station complement stood at 374 officers, 765 cadets, and

3828 enlisted men. Barracks spaces existed for 208 officers, 1176 cadets, and 3821 enlisted. Kingsville also had an Assembly and Repair Department for overhaul and repair.

After the closure of the station, the Navy leased the property to the City of Kingsville for $1 per year. Texas Agricultural and Industrial College of Kingsville utilized the base for its agricultural department and housing for 600 students.

After spending $4.5 million on 8,000-ft. runways for the North Field, the Navy reactivated Kingsville on April 1, 1951. Chosen to be a Navy advance jet training facility, 27 Lockheed TOs (T-33s) of Advance Training Unit Three (ATU-3), a jet transition unit, arrived in August at North Field. At South Field, ATU-6, an antisubmarine pipeline, followed with TBMs and SNJs, as well as ATU-2 with 58 F8Fs. In March 1954, the station's squadrons were operating 99 F9Fs, 76 TV-2s, 4 TBMs, 68 T-28s, 23 S2Fs, and 28 SNBs. In November 1958, ATU-222 was added to give advance jet students a checkout in the supersonic Grumman F11F Tiger. In 1960, the prop antisubmarine pipeline, now VT-27, moved to the newly opened NAAS New Iberia, Louisiana and South Field closed. During the Cuban Missile Crisis in 1962, a few of Kingsville's F11Fs were fitted with Sidewinders and stood air defense alert. On August 8, 1969, the Navy upgraded Kingsville to an NAS.

In 1997, Kingsville is home to Training Wing Two and its three squadrons, VT-21, VT-22, and VT-23. The squadrons operate the North American T-2C Buckeye, the Douglas TA-4 Skyhawk, and the new McDonnell Douglas T-45A Goshawk. Kingsville's airfield is known as Bernhard Field, in honor of VAdm. Alva Douglas Bernhard. The first C.O. of NAS Corpus Christi, Bernhard was instrumental in the establishment of the air station at Kingsville.

Scenes on Kingsville's ramp in November 1942.

NATIONAL ARCHIVES

ABOVE: Excellently composed photograph of student climbing in cockpit of SNJ in November 1942. *NATIONAL ARCHIVES*

ABOVE RIGHT: The target sleeve was twisted and tossed into the air to help the tow aircraft overcome initial drag. *MAY 1943 NATIONAL ARCHIVES*

RIGHT: OLF #20115 was locally known as #42. It appears that the field had a parking area. Perhaps the OLF was a solo check field. *NATIONAL ARCHIVES*

N.A.S. KLAMATH FALLS
KLFL 1566 JULY 17-45
ALT 14,500' (TRUE) FL-12"

600' 1200' 180

JANUARY 1944 NATIONAL ARCHIVES

NAS Klamath Falls, Oregon

Klamath Falls is located 130 miles inland from the Pacific Coast in extreme southern Oregon. A municipal airport was first established five miles southeast of the town in the 1930s. By the beginning of the war, the airport consisted of a small hangar on a 4950 x 2640-ft. parcel of land -- a 4000 x 100-ft. portion of which was paved. In 1942, the Army built a dispersal airfield at the site with 18 hardstands but never used the facility. The airfield was brought to the attention of the Navy by LCdr. William Randle, former manager of the airport. Navy stations near the coast were having considerable problems with inclement weather. Randle pointed out that Klamath Falls had more VFR flying days than any other airport in Oregon. The Navy sent a team from Seattle and entered negotiations with the City and the Airport Commission to lease the airport plus an additional 885 acres. The Army released its claim to the airfield and the Navy began construction on November 1, 1943.

Since the airfield was already in place, construction proceeded rapidly. Navy additions included an 1800 x 400-ft. parking ramp, a tower, four barracks, three BOQs, and a hangar among other buildings. The 100 x 200-ft. steel hangar erected by the Navy was the second largest building in Klamath County and had been originally built at an AAF in Alaska. The Army dismantled the hangar and shipped it to California where the Navy acquired it. In December, VR-5 began using the airfield as a scheduled refueling stop between Seattle and Oakland. However, with a field elevation of 4085 ft., loads had to be reduced when the temperatures rose in the spring, so regular stops were discontinued. The first squadron, VC-82, arrived and began training on January 21, 1944, along with a detachment of Seattle's CASU 7 in support. NAAS Klamath Falls commissioned on February 12, 1944 -- only 74 days after the beginning of construction!

During the year of 1944, various squadrons and CAGs passed through the station including VC-88, VC-97, VC-98, VC-99, and the two squadrons of CVEG 50, VF-50 and VT-50. The station, originally commissioned as an NAAS, was upgraded to an NAS. CASU 50 replaced CASU 7 and later that year, CASU 68 formed out of CASU 50. The Navy made improvements to the airfield including widening of the runways. On May 21, 1944, Klamath Falls opened an auxiliary gunnery station at Lakeview, Oregon, 75 miles to the east.

On January 10, 1945, an F6F of VF-36 shot down a Japanese paper balloon (see Lakeview). During 1945, CAG 36, 37, 38, 60, 7, and 5 all passed through the station. Utilization peaked at Klamath Falls in March of the year, when seven squadrons and a total of 103 aircraft were on board.

Klamath Falls had three asphalt runways -- the longest 7100 ft. Since the climate of the area is semi-arid, gunnery and bombing targets were set up in nearby lakes. The main aerial gunnery ranges were located at the station's one auxiliary at Lakeview. In March 1944, the complement stood at 390 officers and 2603 enlisted men. The Navy eventually built a total of 80 buildings and employed 200 civilians -- many worked in the Assembly and Repair Department.

The Navy closed Klamath Falls on January 1, 1946. The airfield and some buildings were returned to the City and the remainder of the base was taken over by the Bureau of Reclamation. The Air Force took an interest in the site and established an Air National Guard Base in 1957. The airfield was then dedicated as Kingsley Field in memory of Army 2Lt. David R. Kingsley, a B-24 bombardier who received a posthumous Medal of Honor for heroism during the Ploesti oil field raid. In 1997, Kingsley Field is home to the F-16s of the 114th Fighter Squadron of the Oregon National Guard. Among the Navy built structures still in use are the base headquarters, the exchange, and the flag pole.

JANUARY 1944 NATIONAL ARCHIVES

MAY 1942 NATIONAL ARCHIVES

NAS Kodiak, Alaska

Kodiak is a 3,687-sq.-mi. island off the southern coast of Alaska. The town of Kodiak was established in 1792 by Alexander Baranof and served as headquarters for Russian colonists and fur traders. In 1912, the eruption of Mt. Katmi covered the island with a layer of volcanic ash that varied from 18 inches to three ft. with drifts to 20 ft. Kodiak was first proposed for a Naval base in 1927 and interest was renewed six years later. In 1938, Congress allocated the necessary funds with the site being surveyed the next year. Construction began in September 1939 and the station commissioned on June 15, 1941. VP-42 operated from the base from August to October 1941, when replaced by VP-41. The Coast Guard was also present with a complement of 37 men and two PBYs.

Following the outbreak of the war, Kodiak became the Navy's largest base in Alaska and headquarters for the Alaskan sector of the 13th Naval District. The station was the major staging point for the campaign westward to drive the Japanese out of the Aleutians. In addition, the Navy also constructed facilities that supported PT boats and submarines. Kodiak was the base for Scouting Squadron VS-1D13 with Vought OS2U Kingfishers. During early 1942, the Army's 18th Fighter Squadron with P-38s was stationed at the airfield, followed by the 36th Bombardment Squadron. In June 1942, Alameda's VR-2 began regular service from Seattle. Three months later, service rose to eight flights a week with R4Ds. Pan American Airlines' Alaskan Division also served Kodiak with R4Ds under contract to the Navy. VS-1D13 later formed into two squadrons, VS-49 and VS-70. VS-70 transferred to Sitka for a while and a detachment of VS-49 moved to Dutch Harbor.

The importance of Kodiak as an operating base diminished with the opening of Adak and Attu in May and June 1943 -- the headquarters of the Alaskan Sector of the 13th Naval District moved to Adak. Kodiak remained as a major support and administrative base. In the summer of 1943, a Canadian P-40 squadron based at the station for a time. In June, VR-5 commissioned at Seattle and took over NATS service from VR-2.

In April 1944, the Navy created the 17th Naval District to replace the Alaskan Sector of the 13th Naval District; however, the headquarters were established at Adak. In December 1944, VS-49 transitioned to the Douglas SBD Dauntless while VS-70 continued to operate Vought OS2U Kingfishers. By the end of the war, total Navy investment in Kodiak reached $47 million.

Kodiak had three concrete runways of 6000, 5400, and 5000-ft. lengths, as well as two hangars and three seaplane ramps. The station had one auxiliary at Cold Bay and owned 25,482 acres. Complement in March 1944, consisted of 587 officers, 3765 enlisted men, and 181 civilians. Barracks existed for 376 officers and 3942 enlisted men.

Following the war, the headquarters of the 17th Naval District moved to Kodiak. In 1950, the base was redesignated as a Naval Station. The Navy closed Kodiak in June 1972 turning the facilities over to the Coast Guard. Today, Coast Guard C-130s and helicopters patrol Alaskan waters, enforcing U.S. fishing regulations and supplying air/sea rescue service.

Kodiak's seaplane area in May 1942.

N.A.A.F. LAKEVIEW, ORE.
KLFL - 1577   JULY 19 - 45
ALT. 13,000' (TRUE) F.L. -12"
CONFIDENTIAL

JULY 1945 NATIONAL ARCHIVES

NAAF Lakeview, Oregon

Lakeview is located approximately 200 miles east of the Pacific Ocean in extreme southern Oregon. In 1942, the Army built two 5,300-ft. runways, 3.5 miles southwest of the town. The airport was unofficially known as Sult Field -- for a local dentist who was a prisoner of the Japanese. In early 1944, the Navy at NAS Klamath Falls, 75 miles to the west, was attracted to Lakeview by the year-round gunnery ranges in the area. The Navy leased the airport from the City, after the Army's release. On April 1, 1944, the Navy constructed two barracks, a mess hall, and an administration building for a complement of fifty men. The commissioning of NAAF Lakeview took place on May 21, 1944. Over 4,000 people attended an open house celebration.

The gunnery ranges at Klamath Falls were only open from November 1 to April 1. After those dates, the ranges had to be abandoned because of cattle grazing and logging in the area. Since Lakeview had gunnery ranges open all year, aircraft from Klamath Falls came here for an entire day of intense gunnery practice. Lakeview provided rearming and refueling services for those aircraft. The Navy later added shoulders to the runways as well as ammo bunkers and a permanent tower.

On January 10, 1945, a Japanese paper balloon was sighted near the station. A plan had been developed to force one down for examination. An F6F made continuous passes at the balloon making it rock back and forth. This motion caused the balloon to lose some gas and descend to the ground relatively undamaged. Three days later, the device was recovered and sent to Moffett Field for examination. Today, that balloon is in the Smithsonian National Air and Space Museum.

The Japanese balloon attack on the U.S. and Canada was one of the most hairbrained schemes to come out of the war. The first balloons arrived on November 4, 1944. Initially, authorities did not know if they were intentional or by accident. After another 19 arrived by February 10, 1945, the government assumed they were intentional. The balloon was composed of a hydrogen filled envelope, 33 ft. in diameter and made of five layers of glued paper. The lifting capacity was 300 lbs. at an altitude of 30,000 ft. The gondola held a battery, barometric triggers, and usually one 32 lb. anti-personnel bomb plus two 10 lb. incendiary bombs. At the height of the attacks, U.S. intelligence learned that the Japanese propaganda claimed that 10,000 casualties had been incurred and innumerable forest fires started. The last sighting in flight occurred in April 1945. The U. S. government decided not to warn the public. This lack of warning caused the only fatalities of the attacks at Bly Oregon, west of Lakeview on May 6. A reverend's wife and five children on a picnic outing were killed when they set off one of the bombs of a crashed balloon they found.

Following the war, the U.S. discovered that the balloons were a Japanese revenge weapon for the Doolittle raid on Tokyo. A national project involved close to a million people in the manufacturing process. Launched near Tokyo, the balloons were meant to ride the 100-mph plus jet stream winds to North America at 30,000 ft. To maintain the desired altitude, barometric switches released ballast sand bags at night and vented gas during the day. The 6500-mile trip to North America could take from three to eight days. Finally, after all sand bags were released, the bombs would be dropped. The project took the Japanese two years to develop and cost the yen equivalent of $2 million. Of the approximately 10,000 balloons launched between November 1944, and April 1945, less than 300 were known to reach North America. One made it all the way to Michigan and another was discovered as late as 1955 in Alaska! The basic flaw in the Japanese scheme was the fact that the necessary winds for the trip only occur in winter, when damp and cold conditions exist in northwestern United States and western Canada. No forest fires were known to have been started by the balloons.

On November 1, 1945, the Navy closed Lakeview. Ten pilots lost their lives in flight accidents in the area and one enlisted man was killed in an accident on the base. Today, the airfield is known as the Lake County Airport.

The ballon recovered by Lakeview was sent to Moffett Field and later inflated. *MAY 1945 NATIONAL ARCHIVES*

APRIL 1945 NATIONAL ARCHIVES

NAF Litchfield Park, Arizona

The Goodyear Tire and Rubber Company of Akron, Ohio entered the aviation industry in 1911 when the firm began manufacturing balloons and blimps. During WW I, Goodyear produced observation kite balloons, free balloons, and non-rigid blimps for the Navy. Around this time, Goodyear came to Litchfield Park, 18 miles west of Phoenix, and purchased land to grow cotton for its tires. This venture was known as Goodyear Farms. In 1939, the company's aviation interests were split from the parent company with the forming of the Goodyear Aircraft Corporation. After the U. S. entered WW II, the Defense Plant Corporation and the Navy built a manufacturing facility for Goodyear at Litchfield Park. The construction included a 200 x 250-ft. steel assembly building, a 300 x 600-ft. wood assembly building, and two saw-tooth-roof manufacturing buildings with a total of 350,000-sq.-ft. of floor space. At this complex, Goodyear fabricated wings, ailerons, and tail assemblies for Lockheed as well as later modifying Consolidated B-24 bombers to the Navy PB4Y-1 Liberator.

On August 15, 1943, the Navy established an Auxiliary Aircraft Acceptance Unit at Litchfield Park. Prior to completion of the Navy construction, the Acceptance Unit worked out of Goodyear's office spaces and used the small airport one half mile northwest of town. On May 1, 1944, the Navy's facilities, including a barracks and the runway, had been completed. New B-24s were taken directly from the Army production line in San Diego and ferried by civilian Consolidated pilots to Litchfield Park for modification to the PB4Y-1. After the installation of radar and other equipment, the Navy tested and accepted the aircraft. Terminal Island's VRF-3 then ferried the aircraft to operational units. By the end of 1945, Litchfield Park had accepted a total of 585 PB4Y-1 Liberators, 556 PB4Y-2 Privateers, and four Douglas JD-1 Invaders.

Litchfield Park's 491 acres included a 6,000-ft. runway. The number of personnel peaked in March 1945 with 31 officers and 366 enlisted men on board. There was a 30-man BOQ, a 220-man enlisted barracks, and a 150 x 280-ft. hangar. The Navy utilized the Army hospital at nearby Luke Field. Station aircraft consisted of a Lockheed R6O Lodestar and a GH Howard hospital plane.

On February 1, 1946, the Navy reduced Litchfield Park's operational status and designated the station a Navy aircraft storage facility. The next year, the Navy's inventory diminished from a wartime high of 40,912 to 17,600, including those in storage. Besides Litchfield Park, vacant blimp hangars were also used for aircraft preservation. The next year, a Volunteer Reserve Unit from Los Alamitos began drilling at the facility. During the Korean War, Litchfield Park returned 2,000 aircraft from mothballs to flight operations, while using others for the

cannibalization of parts. The use of blimp hangars for storage ended after Korea and Litchfield Park became the Navy's sole aircraft storage site. In 1959, the station had 1621 aircraft on hand. In 1966, the Defense Department consolidated the Navy and Air Force's facilities when a joint Military Aircraft Disposition and Storage Center was established at Davis-Monthan AFB at Tucson, Arizona. Litchfield Park's 800 aircraft were flown or trucked to Davis-Monthan. The base officially closed on January 1, 1967, and was deeded to the City of Phoenix.

In 1997, the Phoenix-Goodyear Airport is home to a Lufthansa German Airlines Training Center. Lufthansa also conducts training for the German Luftwaffe, Swiss Air, All Nippon, and airlines of Taiwan and the Peoples Republic of China. Approximately eight WW II buildings remain including two hangars. The Goodyear plant, closed for some time, is used by other concerns.

Most of the Navy's PB4Y-2s were delivered through Litchfield Park.   *GENERAL-DYNAMICS*

ABOVE: Litchfield Park's ramp is jammed with PB4Y-2 Privateers in the delivery process.
JANUARY 1945 NATIONAL ARCHIVES

ABOVE LEFT AND LEFT: Later models of SNJs and TBMs in storage.

1948 NATIONAL ARCHIVES

TBMs, SNBs, and PB4Ys in storage in February 1948. The Navy's aircraft inventory went from a high of 40,912 in 1945 to 15,147 in 1948. Besides Litchfield Park, vacant blimp hangers were also used for storage at that time. Many of these aircraft were returned to service during the Korean War. *NATIONAL ARCHIVES*

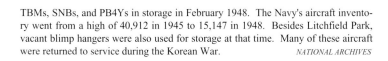

NAS Livermore, California

On August 1, 1928, a Naval Reserve Aviation Base was established at the Oakland Municipal Airport. In 1935, the station began conducting the elimination training course and in 1941, full primary training. Eleven days after Pearl Harbor, the C.O.s of all the NRABs held a conference in Pensacola -- the subject being the increase of primary training at their respective bases. Among the C.O.s with a problem, was Cdr. R. L. Johnson of Oakland. With the addition of Army interceptors at Oakland and the crowded airspace in the area, an increase of primary training would be impossible. After returning to Oakland, Cdr. Johnson and his staff set to work to find a site for a new base.

Surveyors traveled 25 miles east of Oakland, near the town of Livermore, and surveyed the farm of W.G. Wagoner. No one had informed Mr. Wagoner and one day he discovered surveyors on his property. Mr. Wagoner was a patriotic American, but he justifiably objected to the survey crew stomping around in his crops without asking permission. The next morning he pulled up all the surveying stakes and piled them under a tree. When the survey party returned and asked him where the stakes were, Wagoner replied: "They're under that tree. If you want them, get them, and get the hell out of here!" Once the Navy properly contacted Wagoner and stated its intentions, he was very cooperative and willingly sold 629 acres of his farm for $75,260. Construction got under way on January 30, 1942, with a $1.565 million initial allocation. Just 20 days later, an aircraft made a test landing on the proposed airfield. On March 25, training flights from Oakland began using the field on a regular basis. At the end of May, personnel arrived to start operations from Livermore. By the end of November, all primary training activities moved aboard. Since administrative control remained at Oakland, Livermore was not commissioned.

By the beginning of 1943, Livermore was operating 144 N2S Stearmans and 15 N3Ns. The next month, the Navy allocated an additional $1 million for new construction and improvements. Livermore finally separated from Oakland on June 1, 1943, and commissioned an NAS. Aircraft present had risen to 162 Stearmans and 18 Timm N2T Tudors. By the end of the year, the station reached peak utilization with 234 Stearmans and 24 Tudors. During 1944, primary training diminished Navy wide and Livermore was no exception. On October 15, 1944, primary training ended as the last of over 4,000 cadets left the station. On that date, Livermore was placed under the command of Alameda's Naval Air Center. Although, the station's runways had not been designed for carrier aircraft, CAG 33 arrived for operational training with a detachment of Alameda's CASU 6 in support. CAG 40's fighter and torpedo squadrons followed in December with 17 F6Fs and 10 Avengers.

During early 1945, VC-33 and VC-7 passed through the station. In mid-1945, Livermore reached its second peak of operation with the four squadrons of CAG 13 plus VC-77 -- a total of 107 aircraft. One torpedo squadron completed training and received orders to join its aircraft carrier. At the squadron's scheduled hour for departure, their lucky mascot dog could not be located and the squadron refused to leave without it. The situation was beyond the control of the base's C.O. A frantic search was conducted all over the base and the City of Livermore until the dog was found. Once the dog was safely aboard one of the squadron's aircraft, they took off.

The Navy-owned acreage at Livermore totaled 681. The airfield proper consisted of a 3000 x 2700-ft. macadam mat. This unique airfield layout suggests that primary training was meant to remain here throughout the war. There were a total of 12 OLFs

during the station's primary training days. All the OLFs including the CAA Intermediate Field northwest of town were sod. In March 1944, station personnel stood at 228 officers, 800 cadets, 1828 enlisted men, and 25 civilians. Barracks existed for 159 officers, 864 cadets, and 1947 enlisted. The station usually operated a GB Beech Staggerwing for light transport, a GH Howard ambulance plane, and an SNV for proficiency.

Livermore remained in use by carrier units until the end of 1945. For the first six months of 1946, the station served as the Naval Air Reserve facility for the Bay area, until that activity moved to Oakland. On October 10, the Navy inactivated the station opening it to civilian aircraft, although the airfield saw very little use. In early 1947, the airfield was used for a model airplane meet and later for a stock car race. From late 1947 to 1950, the Livermore Elementary School system utilized some of the base's buildings. In 1950, the local community suggested the site for the proposed Air Force Academy. When the Air Force indicated it desired a total of 9,000 acres, the offer was withdrawn.

In late 1950, the U.S. Atomic Energy Commission took over the property for use by the University of California's Radiation Laboratory. Among the atomic weapons developed here over the years were warheads for the Navy's Regulus II, Terrier, and the Polaris missile systems. In 1980, the facility's name was changed by Congress to the Lawrence Livermore National Laboratory in memory of the late Ernest O. Lawrence, former Director of the Laboratory. Lawrence received the Nobel Prize for physics in 1939 for the invention of the cyclotron. In 1995, the laboratory had a staff of 8,000 and a budget of $950 million. Several former Navy buildings are still in use -- the most notable being the drill hall that houses atomic accelerators.

ABOVE: Livermore's drill hall in 1943. The hall has survived to this day and houses the Laboratory's atomic accelerators. *NATIONAL ARCHIVES*

ABOVE LEFT: Cadets march by the base's administration building in July 1943. *NATIONAL ARCHIVES*

LEFT: Cadets mill around the flight schedule board in August 1943. *NATIONAL ARCHIVES*

ABOVE: Seventeen N2T Tudors are present on the ramp along with other types as new hangar is being constructed in July 1943. *NATIONAL ARCHIVES*

ABOVE RIGHT: A rare sight! A formation of nine N2T Tutors in September 1943. The Tudor was manufactured by Timm Aircraft of Van Nuys, California. To conserve critical materials, the aircraft was constructed with a plastic bonded plywood called "Aeromold." Delivered in 1943, the Navy's 262 Tudors were not very durable and most were salvaged by the end of 1944. *NATIONAL ARCHIVES*

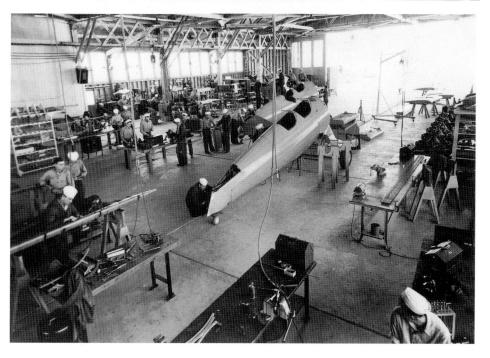

RIGHT: Interior of the Assembly and Repair Department in 1943.
NATIONAL ARCHIVES

Ground crew form a "V" in preparation for a blimp's mooring.   *SEPTEMBER 1943   NATIONAL ARCHIVES*

NAAF Lompoc, California

Lompoc is located 45 miles northwest of Santa Barbara, near Point Arguello and Point Conception. The town was founded in 1874 as a temperance community on the site of Rancho Lompoc and Rancho Mission Vieja. The area eventually became a flower and mustard seed producing region. One of the most infamous episodes in the history of the U.S. Navy occurred 12 miles from Lompoc on the night of September 8, 1923. A navigation error in the fog caused all seven destroyers of Destroyer Squadron 7 to run aground in column on the rocks of Pt. Honda. The Navy lost more combat ships that night than during all of WW I, along with 23 lives. As early as 1920, the development of a municipal airport was considered. Inspired by Charles Lindbergh's flight in 1927, City leaders finally established an airport the next year.

After the completion of the blimp base at Santa Ana in October 1942, the Navy realized that an additional base was needed to provide adequate patrol coverage north of Los Angeles. After conducting extensive weather observations, the Navy chose the Lompoc Airport and leased a total of 65 acres from the City and private individuals. Construction began in December 1942 and when completed, included a 500 x 1000-ft. asphalt mat, two mooring masts, and barracks for 25 officers and 72 enlisted men.

The station commissioned on August 8, 1943. Five days later, tragedy struck the base. In the damp, foggy early morning hours, ground crews were maneuvering ship K-29 for launch from Circle #2. As the blimp's tail pendants approached a high-voltage power line, 11,000 volts arced through the ship. Of the ground crewmen holding the metal handling bars on the bottom of the blimp's cab, four men were electrocuted and a fifth severely burned. Witnesses to the accident reported that the pendants never actually touched the wires. This hazard had been identi-

fied and the line was supposed to have been moved by the local electric power company. For whatever reason, it had not and four men lost their lives. These were the only fatalities at Lompoc during the airport's civilian and Navy use.

After this inauspicious beginning, operations at Lompoc were routine for the remainder of the war. The station was practically identical to Santa Ana's other auxiliary at Del Mar in both physical makeup and operation. One to two ship detachments were maintained at Lompoc by Santa Ana's ZP-31 and Blimp Headquarters Squadron Three. The last Navy

blimp departed Lompoc on September 25, 1945, and the station placed on caretaker status. The Navy had approximately $220,000 invested in the facility. Lompoc remained on the Navy's books for another year, then returned to civilian control.

Located only one half mile north of Lompoc, the airport was overtaken by urban growth during the next 15 years. The City purchased land for a new facility approximately 1.5 miles to the north, and relocated to that site on November 12, 1960. The old airport's property was sold and currently is the location of a high school and shopping center.

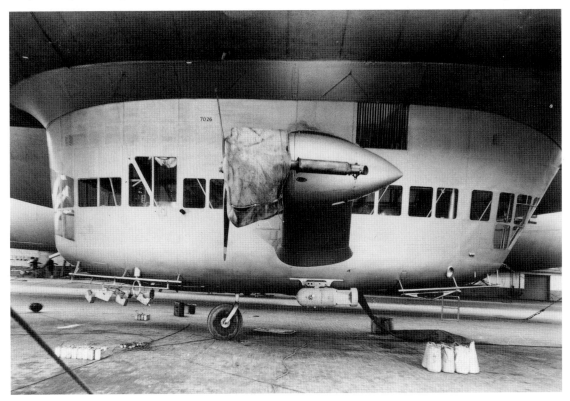

Close-up of this K-ship cab clearly shows the similar metal handling bars that electrocuted four men and severely burned a fifth on the morning of August 13, 1943. Also note the depth charge position. *NATIONAL ARCHIVES*

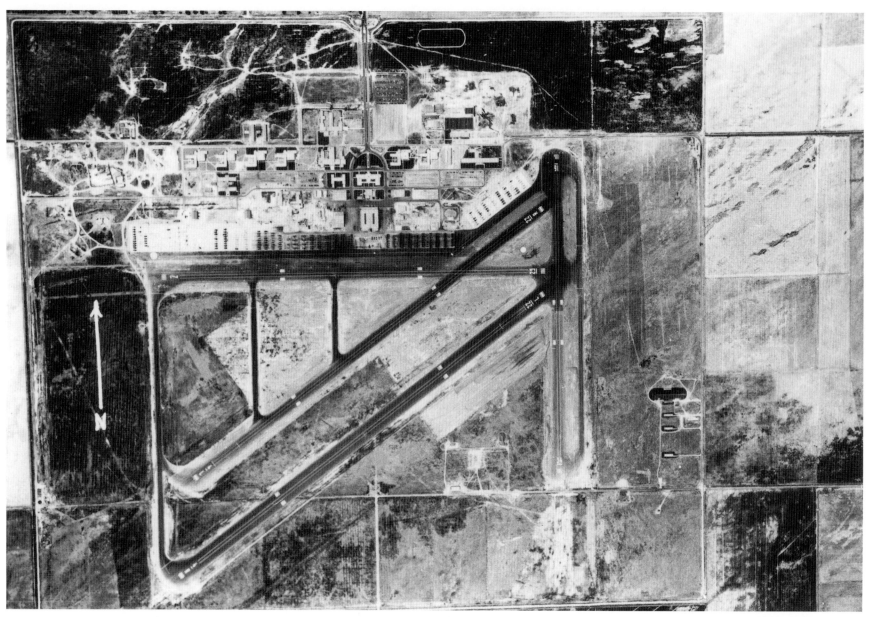

JULY 1945 NATIONAL ARCHIVES

NAS Los Alamitos, California

The historical beginning of Los Alamitos can be traced to the commissioning of an NRAB at the Long Beach Municipal Airport on May 10, 1928. The airfield was later named Daugherty Field in honor of Ltjg. Earl Daugherty, an early member of the NRAB. Because of the station's proximity to Hollywood, it was used for several motion picture productions. In 1931, a portion of the movie *Helldivers* was filmed at the base. In 1934, the late actor Wallace Beery was commissioned as an honorary LCdr. and aviator in appreciation of his efforts to promote Navy Aviation in the prewar days. Long Beach functioned like the other NRABs of the Navy and began elimination training in 1935. With the war on the horizon, Douglas Aircraft expressed an interest in building a plant at the airport. As a result, the City of Long Beach's relationship with the Navy became cold and hostile. The Navy found an acceptable site for a new air station, 17 miles to the east, near the town of Los Alamitos. Although offered $350 an acre, Mrs Suzanna Bixby Bryant sold 715 acres of land for $300 per acre -- her patriotic contribution to the country.

Construction began shortly on a primary training base with the intention of basing fleet units later. All training transferred to Los Alamitos on June 1, 1942, as the Navy leased its facilities at Long Beach to the Army's Ferry Command. NRAB Los Alamitos commissioned on August 1, 1942, and included five OLFs for primary training. To the men assigned there, the new base was nicknamed "Los Al."

Los Alamitos started with just 39 aircraft. By the end of the year, the station had expanded rapidly with 100 aircraft that included 15 N3Ns and 79 N2S Stearmans. A total of 729 cadets had the primary training course with 180 failures and one fatality. Los Alamitos became an NAS on January 1, 1943. Six months later, the station was operating 96 Stearmans and 24 Timm N2T Tudors. Primary training diminished during 1943 and finally ended on August 15, 1943, after 3821 flights had accumulated 5,556 hours during the year.

No time was wasted changing the station over to operational units and the next month three squadrons of CAG 19 and CAG 37 with two squadrons moved aboard for several months of training. CASU 33 commissioned at the station to support the various carrier units present. With the change of mission, Los Alamito's designation changed to an NAAS under San Diego. From August 1943 until September 1945, Los Al hosted two VB, 24 VC, eight VF, two VJ, and five VT squadrons, plus four CAGs, three CASUs, and two ARGUS units. Beginning in late 1944, the primary unit at Los Alamitos was CAG 98. The West Coast's operation training squadron, CAG 98 conducted refresher training to pilots returning from combat and trained replacement pilots. By the beginning of 1945, Navy investment reached $4.8 million.

Los Alamitos during primary training days can be compared to the photo on the opposite page taken near the end of the war. Primary training landing areas consisted of two large rectangular mats orientated in a southwest/northeast direction. With the end of primary training, four runways and taxiways were established obliterating the mats. *AUGUST 1943 NATIONAL ARCHIVES*

Los Alamitos was the largest of San Diego's auxiliaries with the capacity of two large air groups of 180 aircraft. The station's ultimate acreage totaled 1198 with four tarmac runways, the longest 5,700 ft. In March 1944, Los Al had a complement of 414 officers and 2790 enlisted men while barracks existed for 375 officers and 2070 enlisted men. The station operated four to eight aircraft of various types. Utilization of the station peaked during 1945 with almost 300 aircraft on board.

Following the war, Los Alamitos became the Navy and Marine Air Reserve center for the Los Angeles area. In 1947, the station assumed command of the Reserve Unit at Litchfield Park, Arizona. During the Korean War, six of the station's units were activated and participated in the war. In 1972, the Navy closed Los Alamitos turning the facility over to the California Army National Guard that continues to conduct flight operations at the airfield today.

ABOVE: Primary training in July 1942 with the schedule board right on the ramp.

NATIONAL ARCHIVES

LEFT: Cadets in front of their N3Ns in September 1941.

NATIONAL ARCHIVES

ABOVE: During primary, cadets flew three aircraft formation hops that included formation takeoffs and landings. *NATIONAL ARCHIVES*

ABOVE RIGHT AND RIGHT: The Boeing N2S Stearman eventually replaced all other primary types. *NATIONAL ARCHIVES*

APRIL 1943   NATIONAL ARCHIVES

NAAF Meacham Field, Texas

The City of Fort Worth established an airport in 1925 naming it in honor of H. C. Meacham, former mayor of Fort Worth. Airlines began service in 1928. In 1936, paved runways, four large hangars, and a passenger terminal were added. American Airlines, with an operation at the airport, landed a contract on April 1, 1943, to conduct a Naval Transport Transitional School for the Douglas R4D (DC-3) at Meacham.

On May 12, 1943, the Navy commissioned NAAF Meacham Field as an auxiliary of NAS Dallas. Another Meacham Field existed as an OLF to NAS Key West and this duplication caused some confusion -- even in official records. The Navy moved the Naval Air Ferry Command and the NATS servicing unit to Meacham relieving congestion at Dallas. In addition, Navy primary trainers from Dallas also used the airport during wet weather when their grass OLFs were not usable. The Navy's facilities at Meacham consisted of 14.5 leased acres with accommodations for 66 officers and 15 enlisted men.

The 30-day American Airlines' R4D school consisted of a 100-hour ground school, five hours of Link training, 25 hours of flight instruction, 25 hours of observation, and one hour of observation in the control tower with a student capacity of 30 pilots per month. At the end of 1943, the school's student capacity rose to 50 pilots per month. Pennsylvania Central Airlines ran a similar program for the Army at Roanoke, Virginia. When Penn Central's Army contract expired, the Navy entered into an agreement with the airline on December 21, 1943, for an additional R4D school. Both airlines employed eight Navy R4Ds each for flight training. Penn Central's contract ended on January 6, 1945. American's contract was terminated on September 6, 1945, after training over 1300 pilots.

One of the Author's core beliefs, is that it never pays to unnecessarily make enemies. This belief was reinforced by an anecdote related to the Author by a former WW II Naval aviator. During the war, the Navy recruited experienced members of America's civilian aviation community and assigned them an AVT designation. After a military indoctrination course, the AVTs were given an officer's rank commensurable to their age and aviation experience. Most AVTs were used in the training command, NAFC, and NATS. At Corpus Christi, one of the auxiliaries had a regular Navy Lt. as the O. in C. This particular Lt. spent many years as Ens. and Ltjg. in the slow promotion prewar Navy. He resented the immediate rank given to the AVTs, and made life an unmitigated Hell for them -- making quite a reputation for himself in the meantime. Unfortunately, one of his victims was an American Airlines pilot on military leave of absence with a good memory who bore a grudge. Sometime later, the American pilot learned that the Lt. had received orders to American's school. He got word to his cohorts at American and the former tormentor was summarily washed-out of the school -- "What goes around, comes around!"

Airline service at Meacham continued until 1953, then moved to Amon Carter Field. Today, Meacham is a general aviation airport. Several early hangars, in use during the war, have survived.

Details were lacking with this photograph, but it appears that an entire carrier air group was passing through the station. Meacham also served as a designated en route stop for the Naval Air Transport Service and the Naval Air Ferry Command. *NATIONAL ARCHIVES*

APRIL 1945 NATIONAL ARCHIVES

NAS Midway Islands

The Midway Islands, part of the Hawaiian chain, are best known for two reasons: the naval battle of 1942, and as the world's largest nesting grounds of the Gooney Bird (Laysan Albatross). The coral atoll was originally named the Brook's Islands for the Captain of the bark *Gambia* who discovered the islands in 1859. The atoll was formally claimed by the U.S. in 1867 and renamed the Midway Islands -- supposedly for the fact that it was near the 180th meridian, midway around the world from the Greenwich or prime meridian. Midway was made a waypoint of a telegraph cable being laid from Oahu to the Philippines. When the cable was completed in 1903, President Teddy Roosevelt sent the first around-the-world cable on July 4. Alarmed by reports of Japanese bird poachers, Roosevelt placed Midway under the jurisdiction of the U.S. Navy that same year. The next year, 23 Japanese poachers were apprehended in the area with the wings of 200,000 seabirds. U.S. Marines maintained a detachment on Midway from 1904 to 1908.

The Midway atoll is approximately five miles in diameter, encompassing Sand and the smaller Eastern Island. With the Navy's permission, Pan American World Airways built a seaplane facility and hotel on Sand Island as a refueling and rest stop between Honolulu and Wake Island in 1935. Three years later, the Navy provided the Army Corps of Engineers $1.1 million in funds for dredging projects. In late 1938, the Hepburn Board decided that developing an air and submarine base at Midway was second in priority to Pearl Harbor. On Sand Island, the site of the main base, the Navy built a seaplane facility that included a large hangar and four seaplane ramps. Three runways, two hangars, and barracks were also constructed on Eastern Island. NAS Midway Islands was commissioned on August 1, 1941, and Navy PBY squadrons began deployments to the station.

On December 7, 1941, two Japanese destroyers shelled the island, causing considerable damage and three fatalities. The Japanese Pearl Harbor task force planned an attack on Midway during its withdrawal, but bad weather resulted in the cancellation of the raid. On December 17, Marine squadron VMSB-231 with 17 aircraft arrived to reinforce VP-21's 12 PBYs. On Christmas Day, 14 F2A Brewster Buffaloes of VMF-221 flew aboard from the USS *Saratoga*. A Japanese submarine shelled the islands on January 25. Fortunately, all the rounds fell into the lagoon and the sub was driven away by shore-batteries. Two additional Japanese submarines attempted to shell the islands in February, but were thwarted by shore-battery counter fire as well. On March 10, Midway's radar detected a Japanese Mavis flying boat from Wotje in the Marshall Islands and Marine fighters shot it down.

The Navy waged an ongoing, mostly humanitarian, battle with the island's 200,000 Gooney Birds. During initial construction, Washington forbid any harm to the birds, so construction crews spent considerable time shooing the birds out of the way of bulldozers. The crews later ignored this order and began running the birds over. When the stench became unbearable, workers went back to the former practice. After the airfield reached completion, the Navy's aircraft on takeoff and landing often hit the birds with some disastrous results. In frustration and anger, someone in authority ordered the birds on Eastern Island exterminated. Construction workers and Marines clubbed about 1000 to death with no noticeable effect on the population. Cooler heads finally prevailed and the order was rescinded.

In the spring of 1942, the Japanese began an operation to occupy Midway they thought would be a cake-walk. Fortunately, U.S. Naval Intelligence had broken the Japanese code and a Naval carrier task force was waiting in ambush. On the eve of the great battle, Midway's air strength stood at 32 PBYs of VP-23 and VP-44, six new TBFs of a VT-8 Detachment; Marine Air Group 22 with 20 F2A-3s and seven F4F-3s of VMF-221 plus 16 SBDs and 11 obsolete SB2Us of VMSB-241; and four Army B-26s and 19 B-17s. On the morning of June 3, Midway based PBYs located the Japanese fleet several hundred miles to the west and the great Battle of Midway was joined. The next day, the Japanese launched a 108-plane raid against Midway. Alerted by radar, VMF-221 intercepted the Japanese about thirty miles from the island. The Marine fighters shot down several bombers and fighters, but were decimated by the Zeros. Of the 25 fighters of VMF-221, 13 F2As and two F4Fs were lost along with their pilots. The Japanese planes that got through destroyed the hospital, several oil tanks, and other buildings, killing 13 and wounding 18 men. So sure were the Japanese of their victory, they deliberately spared Eastern Island's runways for their use after the capture of the island.

During the course of the four-day battle, Army B-17s and B-26s, operating from Eastern Island, conducted several attacks on the Japanese fleet. Despite claims to the contrary, no Army bombers made any hits and lost two torpedo equipped B-26s in the process. VMSB-241 lost eight of 16 SBDs and at least four of the 11 SB2Us with no hits on the Japanese. Capt. Richard E. Fleming of VMSB-241, was posthumously awarded the Medal of Honor for his attack on a Japanese cruiser. Midway based elements of VT-8 introduced the Grumman TBF Avenger to combat in attacks against the Japanese and fared no better than the carrier-based TBDs. Only one of the six Avengers returned to Midway. The only definite hit by Midway based aircraft during the battle was the torpedoing of a Japanese tanker by a PBY. Carrier-based SBD dive bombers saved the day, The Japanese lost four aircraft carriers, one heavy cruiser, 332 aircraft, and 2500 men -- including many experienced aviators.   U.S. losses included the carrier *Yorktown*, one destroyer, 147 aircraft, and 307 men -- one of the most lopsided victories in history! The Navy learned two important lessons from the battle. First, torpedo planes must have fighter escort and second, the Brewster F2A-3 Buffalo was unfit for combat against Japanese fighters. In a parting shot, a Japanese submarine shelled Midway at 0130 on June 5 without damage.

The next month, construction commenced on an airfield and submarine base on Sand Island. In August 1942, the airfield on Eastern Island was named in honor of Maj. Lofton Henderson, the C.O. of VMSB-241, who lost his life in the recent battle. The Navy continued to improve Midway's airfields and other facilities throughout the war, as the station changed from a defensive, to an offensive, and finally to a support mission.

Useable land at Midway totaled about two-sq.-mi. The station could support a CAG of 90 aircraft plus two squadrons of patrol aircraft. On Eastern Island, the three runways measured 3250, 4500, and 5300 by 300 ft. Two of the three runways built on Sand Island were ultimately 7,500 and 8,600 ft. long. The complement in March 1944 totaled over 500 officers and almost 4000 enlisted men.

Midway closed for a short time in 1950, only to re-open late in the year due to the Korean War. The airfield on Eastern Island was abandoned as aviation activity concentrated on Sand Island's longer runways. Midway played a major role during the Cold War as operating base for the Navy's Airborne Early Warning Barrier Squadron Two's Lockheed WV radar aircraft. Also known as Barrier Squadron Pacific, the squadron flew the Pacific extension of the Distant Early Warning from 1956 to 1965. Collisions between the Gooney Birds and the Navy's aircraft continued. The men took to painting little

birds under the WVs pilot's window to denote Gooney Bird strikes.

When Hawaii became a State of the Union on August 21, 1959, Midway was not included, remaining under the administration of the Navy. During the Vietnam War, Midway became a major refueling point for aircraft and port of call for ships. Peak use occurred during 1968, when over 11,000 aircraft and 313 ships stopped at the island. During the Cold War, Navy patrol aircraft also used the island for antisubmarine missions. Midway closed on September 10, 1993. In 1997, the airfield is manned by a civilian contractor with foreign workers that services a few aircraft each week. The atoll is being transferred to the Department of the Interior's U.S. Fish and Wildlife Service. Midway, closed to the public for almost 100 years, is now available for public visitation. Visitors have the opportunity to observe the bird population, scuba dive, fish, and explore the islands.

Pan Am's hotel on Midway Island has survived to the present day.   *1944 NATIONAL ARCHIVES*

Midway's Eastern Island in April 1944.   *NATIONAL ARCHIVES*

ABOVE: SBD in sand revetment on Sand Island in July 1943. *NATIONAL ARCHIVES*

ABOVE RIGHT: Sand Island in July 1943. *NATIONAL ARCHIVES*

RIGHT: Midway's overhaul and repair hangar in June 1945. *NATIONAL ARCHIVES*

APRIL 1944 NATIONAL ARCHIVES

NAAF Mills Field, California

In 1926, the citizens of San Francisco turned a jealous eye towards Oakland, across the bay. Oakland had recently received service on a newly awarded air mail route. Municipal pride drove the City to establish an airport. Hilly San Francisco is severely geographically restricted so the City traveled south to find an adequate site. Property was leased for $2500 per year from the estate of Darius Ogden Mills, a merchant millionaire from the 1860's Gold Rush days. Mills had established a rancho at the site with the nearby township named Millbrae. Once completed, the airport was named Mills Field.

On November 15, 1940, the Coast Guard commissioned an air station at Mills Field. After the beginning of the war, additional land was created by hydraulic fill and three hard-surfaced runways built -- the longest 8,000 ft. The Army established a sub-base of Hamilton Field, primarily used by the Air Transport Command. Army facilities included an air freight terminal and barracks for 110 officers and 700 enlisted men. The Coast Guard remained at Mills throughout the war conducting patrol and sea/air rescue operations. The Coast Guard's complement numbered 55 officers and 263 men with barracks for 16 officers and 290 men. Aircraft assigned to the Coast Guard peaked in June 1945 with two PBMs, seven PBYs, two PB2Ys, four JRFs, two GHs, and one SNJ.

In September 1942, Pan American Airways began operating under contract to the Navy from the Treasure Island seaplane base. By 1944, growth of Naval activities on and around Treasure Island prompted Pan Am to move its operation to Mills Field. The Navy leased 85 acres at Mills Field and commissioned an NAAF. Pan Am continued to use the facilities at Treasure Island for aircraft overhaul. In the spring of 1945, Pan Am operated four B-314s, 18 PB2Ys, one PBM-3R, and one JRB. Naval presence at the facility was minimal with the C.O. of the Coast Guard station also serving as the NAAF's C.O.

After the Navy placed Pan Am under contract to provide transport services, the airline's Boeing 314s and Martin Clippers were purchased. Pan Am continued to operate these seaplanes plus additional Navy aircraft. Pan Am also had operations at Floyd Bennett Field, New York; Dinner Key, Florida; and Seattle, Washington. In addition, the airline conducted a celestial navigation school at Dinner Key, Florida. Early on, a good and necessary service was provided; however, with the arrival of the Douglas R5Ds (C-54) and the development of modern airfields, transoceananic flying boats had become inefficient, archaic, and redundant. Nevertheless, the contract continued -- Pan Am's pork barrel and payback for services previously rendered. A former NATS R5D pilot recalled his experiences at Oakland to the Author: "We would watch Pan Am takeoff across the Bay. Several hours later, after lunch and flight planning, we also departed for Hawaii. After landing at Honolulu, we would take a nap and get up in time to watch the same Pan Am airplane land. Of course, we came back to the States mostly empty -- all military passengers had to take Pan Am." The minimum flight time between San Francisco and Hawaii for the B-314 was 15 numbing hours -- the R5D could do it in almost half that time!

Following the war, Pan Am operated the last B-314 flight between Hawaii and San Francisco on April 9, 1946, replacing it with DC-4s. However, Alameda's VR-2 continued to operate JRM Mars and R3Y Tradewind seaplane transports on a limited basis until 1958. Today, Mills Field is San Francisco International Airport. The Coast Guard continues a presence with several helicopters.

The Coast Guard and Pan Am area at Mills Field in October 1945.   *NATIONAL ARCHIVES*

NAS Minneapolis, Minnesota

Located over 1200 miles from the nearest ocean, Minneapolis would first appear a very unlikely place to be associated with Naval Aviation; however, during WW I just such an association began when Naval Aviation ground training was conducted by the Dunwoody Institute. An industrial trade school, Dunwoody trained over 5,000 Navy men between 1917 and 1919. Following the war, the local aero club and the National Guard joined to develop an airport. In 1920, they began improvements on a defunct automobile race track between Minneapolis and St. Paul for the new airport, naming it Speedway Field. In 1923, the airport was rededicated as Wold-Chamberlain in memory of the first two local aviators to lose their lives in WW I.

In 1925, Naval aviation returned to Minneapolis when 35 student pilots were trained at the Naval Armory. Three years later, a committee of aviation enthusiasts built an 80 x 90-ft. hangar at Wold-Chamberlain and leased it to the Navy for $1 a year. Naval Reserve Aviation Base Minneapolis commissioned on October 1, 1928. The base continued to grow and began elimination training in 1935 as the airport installed the first hard-surfaced runways. Full primary training began during 1941.

As unlikely as Minneapolis seemed for Naval aviation, the winter weather appeared to make the location even more improbable for primary training. The daily operation of open-cockpit trainers and the problems of orientation by student aviators with snow covered ground during the winter would normally be enough reasons to preclude primary training. However, the Navy took advantage of the facilities already established and began an expansion after Pearl Harbor. At that time, the station consisted of 17 officers, 122 enlisted men, and 68 cadets. One year later, the Navy redesignated Minneapolis as a Naval Air Station and personnel stood at 162

officers, 1,000 enlisted men, and 436 cadets with 128 N2S Stearmans. In the interim, the Navy and the Army cooperated on a Precipitation Static Research Program in a custom built hangar that specialized in reducing environmental static on aircraft communications and navigational equipment. Additional research was conducted on aircraft icing in a separate hangar. George Bush underwent primary training in the dead of winter here from November 1942, to February 1943, and flew as many as four flights a day during good weather. Besides the Stearman, Mr. Bush also flew a few hops in the NP Spartan.

Operations peaked at Minneapolis in early 1944 with over 3,579 personnel including 928 cadets and 266 Stearmans. Thereafter, primary training diminished and ended by the last of 1944, after having trained a total of 4,232 cadets. During 1944 and 1945, the station also served as the U.S. entry point for SBW Helldivers manufactured by Canadian Car and Foundry at Fort William, Ontario. Mechanics also performed engine checks on the SBWs. For the remainder of the war, Minneapolis was transferred to the Naval Air Technical Training Command that conducted training for PB4Y Patrol Service Units (PATSUs).

Group of cadets examine an N2S Stearman.

Wold-Chamberlain had four concrete runways -- the longest 5750 ft. The Army also had a presence at the airport consisting of glider manufacturing, technical training, and a port of embarkation for the Air Transport Command. Minneapolis had six outlying fields. The main OLF at South St. Paul was named Flemming Field, in honor of Marine Capt. Richard E. Flemming, posthumously awarded the Metal of Honor for actions during the Battle of Midway. At Flemming, there were two 1500-ft. circular landing mats -- one sod, the other paved, plus hangars, shops, and barracks. Most cadet solo flying took place here. A plan developed to make Flemming an NAAF was later cancelled.

Following the war, Minneapolis became a Naval and Marine Air Reserve station. In 1963, the station was renamed NAS Twin Cities. After Twin Cities closed in July 1970, a reserve aviation detachment of Glenview remained for a few more years.

ABOVE RIGHT: Flemming Field at South St. Paul had two circular 1500 ft. landing areas -- one paved, one sod. Most of the cadets solo flights took place here. Today, Flemming is a general aviation airport. *JULY 1943 NATIONAL ARCHIVES*

RIGHT: Femming Field had four hangers and enlisted barracks. Cadets were bused to and from Mainside. Flemming was proposed to be made an NAAF, but this later cancelled. At least 73 aircraft are present in this August 1941 photograph.
NATIONAL ARCHIVES

Construction taking place on Hangar #5, the engine testing building, and Hangar #6 in January 1944 with 30 N2S-4s visible. At this time, 192 Stearmans were assigned to the station. *NATIONAL ARCHIVES*

MARCH 1944   NATIONAL ARCHIVES

NAS Moffett Field, California

In the late 1920s, the Navy developed plans to build an airship base on the West Coast similar to Lakehurst. Some 94 communities vied for the base, with the Navy choosing Sunnyvale at the southern end of San Francisco Bay. Even though the country was in the depths of the depression, the community managed to raise $476,000 to purchase 1000 acres for the Navy. When Sunnyvale received official news of the Navy's acceptance, schools closed for a day and a parade was held. On February 20, 1931, President Hoover signed a bill authorizing the Navy to accept title to the land. Construction began in October -- half the $5 million authorized was allocated for construction of Hangar One. On April 12, 1933, the Navy commissioned NAS Sunnyvale. Meanwhile on April 4, 1933, the USS *Akron* crashed off Barnegat Light, N.J. with the loss of 74 lives -- including RAdm. William A. Moffett, Chief of the Navy's Bureau of Aeronautics. Two months later, the station's name changed to Moffett Field in honor of the late RAdm. On October 16, the USS *Macon* arrived at her new home after a 70-hour flight from Lakehurst. The *Macon* operated from Moffett until it crashed in a storm on February 12, 1935, off Point Sur with two fatalities.

In July 1935, VB-2, VF-6, VT-2, and VS-2 operated from Moffett on a trial basis. A proposal then surfaced for the Navy to trade Moffett to the Army in exchange for North Island, California; Bolling Field, Washington, D.C.; and Ford Island, Hawaii. Although the Army opposed the deal, President Roosevelt, nevertheless, ordered the trade. The Army definitely felt shortchanged by the President, considering him an "old Navy man" -- in fact, Roosevelt served as Assistant Secretary of the Navy from 1913 to 1920. The Army took over Moffett in September 1935, and immediately became disenchanted with it, mainly due to the high cost of Hangar One's maintenance. The Army attempted to quit the station, but President Roosevelt would not permit abandonment so the Army remained. Moffett eventually became headquarters of the Army's Western Flying Training Command. In 1939, the Ames Aeronautical Laboratory established. After Pearl Harbor, the Navy desperately needed Moffett back to start West Coast blimp operations. The Army had grown fond of Moffett (probably because the Navy wanted it) and resisted the transfer; however, Washington overruled once again ordering the Army to vacate the base.

The Navy commissioned ZP-32 at Moffett in January, but the squadron had no blimps. Two ex-Army ships, TC-13 and TC-14, had been given to the Navy when the Army abandoned its LTA program in 1937. In January 1942, the deflated blimps, in storage at Lakehurst, were shipped by rail to Moffett and inflated. On February 4, 1942, ZP-32 conducted its first flight. During March and April, Moffett added three L-ships appropriated from Goodyear's advertising fleet. On April 16, the Navy recommissioned the station. The next month, the last Army aircraft finally departed as the headquarters of the Western Flying Training Command moved to Orange County Airport at Santa Ana. Goodyear then began a program to ship new deflated blimps from Akron, Ohio to Moffett for final assembly and inflation. The Navy placed the first airship completed by this program, K-20, in service on October 31. In November, construction began on Hangars Two and Three.

Meanwhile, in October 1942, the first cadets arrived for blimp flight training. During the war, LTA and HTA flight training were completely separate -- Navy blimp pilots were not qualified to fly an aircraft as they were after the war. Prospective blimp pilots were recruited directly from pre-flight schools -- some were former LTA enlisted men. The fact that blimp training only lasted four months, may have motivated some cadets to volunteer. Moffett conducted primary training to relieve the load on Lakehurst. Initially, cadets worked as ground crewmen to learn blimp-handling procedures. A few flights in hydrogen-filled free balloons followed before training in L-ships began. After completing primary, the cadets traveled to Lakehurst for advanced training in K-ships. Blimp flight training later extended to six months.

Moffett was the center for West Coast LTA operations and headquarters for the Commander, Fleet Airships Pacific. Blimp Headquarters Squadron Three also formed at Moffett to provide support for ZP-32. Late in 1942, two additional West Coast LTA stations commissioned at Santa Ana, California and Tillamook, Oregon. On August 6, 1943, Moffett opened two small NAAFs at Watsonville and Eureka, California to provide more patrol coverage of the Pacific coast, north and south of Moffett. Limited HTA operations began at Moffett in December by utility squadron VJ-14.

By the beginning of 1944, the Navy began to scale down on LTA operations -- especially on the West Coast where Japanese submarines had never become a serious threat. In March 1944, primary blimp flight training ended. As a result, Moffett was designated a joint LTA/HTA station. In June, VJ-18 commissioned and was trained by VJ-14. That same month, the Ames Lab dedicated a wind tunnel. In July, VPB squadrons of PV-1 Venturas with Patrol Service Unit 8 - Detachment 2 arrived as VJ-14 transferred. At the end of 1944, four VPB squadrons with a total of 53 PVs plus two utility squadrons, VJ-1 with a mixed bag of aircraft and VJ-18 with nine Martin JM towplanes were on board. Meanwhile, Goodyear's assembly program at Moffett ended after delivering 39 L, G, and K-ships.

During 1945, VPB squadrons received the new PV-2 Harpoons. The Antisubmarine Warfare Training Unit - Moffett formed with 13 aircraft including 10 OS2U Kingfishers. In June, the first M-ship, the largest blimp in Naval service, arrived. The Navy decided to move VR-4 to Moffett from Oakland and a $2.5 million contract began to strengthen the taxiways. The Ames Aeronautical Laboratory continued to grow and by the end of the war, 11 Navy aircraft, including the Ryan FR-1 Fireball, were assigned to that activity.

Moffett had a 7000-ft. runway that was part of a 1.14 million sq. yd. asphalt mat with eight mooring circles. Barracks existed for 290 officers and 2500 enlisted men. The base employed almost 1000 civilians, mostly in the Assembly and Repair Department. In June 1945, the Army transferred the former interceptor field at Half Moon Bay to Moffett for an OLF.

Following the war, Moffett became the West Coast center for NATS and later for the Navy contribution to MATS (still later MAC). Blimp operations ended forever at Moffett in August 1947. The Navy then based carrier squadrons at Moffett and in 1953 designated the station the Navy's first Master Jet Base. Continued urban growth doomed jet operations at Moffett and in the late 1950s, the jet squadrons moved to Miramar, although the Douglas AD Skyraiders remained. In January 1963, Moffett was chosen as the West Coast center for the new Lockheed P-3 Orion. In 1967, VR-7 decommissioned, ending Navy participation in MAC. At its height, P-3 operations totaled nine squadrons -- seven operational, one training, and one reserve.

As a result of the 1993 Base Realignment and Closure Commission's decision, NAS Moffett closed on June 1, 1994, becoming the Moffett Federal Airfield. Moffett's P-3 active duty assets moved to Whidbey Island. The remaining Navy command is now the Naval Air Reserve - Santa Clara. The reserve P-3 squadron, VP-91; Fleet Logistics Reserve Squadron 55 with KC-130Ts; and non-flying reserve units were present in 1996. NASA's Ames Research Facility administers the airfield and has also taken over ALF Crow's Landing.

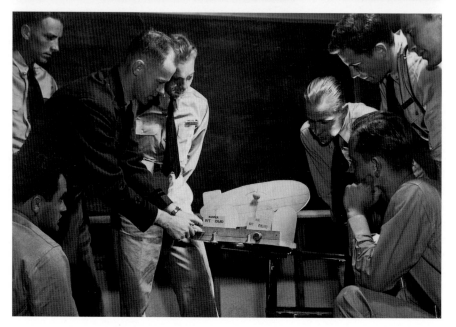

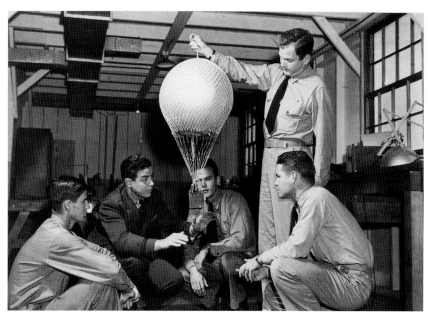

ABOVE: Cadets first learned the principals of powerless flight in free balloons. This was necessary in the event the blimp lost power. Since the balloons were deflated following the flight, hydrogen gas was used due to the high cost of helium.   *FEBRUARY 1944 NATIONAL ARCHIVES*

ABOVE RIGHT: With the aid of a model, an instructor demonstrates the principals of free-flight.
NOVEMBER 1943 NATIONAL ARCHIVES

RIGHT: Initially, cadets learned and participated in the ground handling of blimps.   *USN*

OPPOSITE PAGE: With the help of training aids, an instructor explains blimp aerodynamics.
USN

ABOVE: A 149-ft. long Goodyear L-ship climbs out. The Navy operated 22 L-ships during the war -- five of which were appropriated from the Goodyear advertising fleet. Although used mainly for primary training, at the beginning of the war L-ships were also used for antisubmarine patrols. *GOODYEAR*

ABOVE LEFT: Six K-ships rest in a Moffett hangar. *NATIONAL ARCHIVES*

LEFT: Ten L-ships, almost half the type, over San Francisco Bay.
MARCH 1944 NATIONAL ARCHIVES

ABOVE AND ABOVE RIGHT: On June 11, 1945, M-2 arrived at Moffett. At 310 ft., the four M-ships were the largest non-rigid blimps built in the United States up to that time. The M-ship's 117 ft. long car was built in three articulated sections to match the bending of the envelope. *NATIONAL ARCHIVES*

RIGHT: Blimp primary training ended at Moffett in March 1944. With the wind-down of blimp operations, Moffett was designated as a joint LTA/HTA station. Here are pictured the PV-1 Venturas of VB-142 in February 1944. *NATIONAL ARCHIVES*

NOVEMBER 1944 NATIONAL ARCHIVES

NAAS Monterey, California

The first flights on the beautiful Monterey Peninsula took place from the polo field of the Del Monte Hotel in 1910. For the next 30 years, the nearby area of Tarpey Flats was used for a flying field and eventually consisted of a 1500 x 2500-ft. oiled runway. Finally in March 1941, the local communities formed the Monterey Peninsula Airport District and acquired 455 acres from Del Monte Properties to develop a modern airport. After the start of the war, the Navy leased the airport for $1 per year and the CAA allocated $1.7 million for construction of hard-surfaced runways. The Navy purchased an additional 17 acres for $41,000 on which to build barracks and administrative buildings. Construction commenced in August 1942, and ended with the commissioning of the station on May 23, 1943, as an auxiliary of Alameda.

The primary mission of the base was training of torpedo squadrons and torpedo planes of composite squadrons. For that purpose, the Navy set up a torpedo range at Monterey Bay in cooperation with the local Naval Section Base. Along with Pyramid Lake, Nevada, Monterey was the only other torpedo range in the 12th Naval District and squadrons from other air stations also utilized the range. Torpedoes were loaded at Alameda, 80 miles to the north, and dropped on two target ships at Monterey Bay. The 160-man Field Torpedo Unit at Monterey recovered the torpedoes that were later trucked back to Alameda for overhaul. During the remainder of 1943, 12 squadrons dropped 693 torpedoes and in 1944, 21 squadrons launched 1511 torpedoes -- 71 of which were lost in the bay.

Monterey also served as the base for squadrons that spent several months training prior to shipping out to the South Pacific. During the course of the war, these squadrons included VC-33, 37, 7, 63, and 11, as well as VT-18, 27, 17, and 5. In the spring of 1944, STAG 1 and its units, VK-11 and VK-12, completed final training at the station with TDR drones before deploying to combat. In September and October, STAG 1 conducted a month long demonstration of the TDR assault drone in the South Pacific (see Clinton). Monterey also hosted the electronic advance base elements ARGUS 19, 13, and 54 during the war. In July 1944, a mobile radar intercept unit was set up nearby for the training of fighter pilots. In the last few months of the war, the station supported a detachment of Moffett's Antisubmarine Warfare Training Unit that operated one F6F, 10 OS2U Kingfishers, two SNJs, and one GH Howard. On November 1, 1945, the Navy placed Monterey on caretaker status.

Monterey had a 5,000-ft. and a 4,500 x 150-ft. macadam runway. On September 1, 1944, the station acquired an OLF at San Luis Obispo. In March 1944, complement consisted of 117 officers and 785 enlisted men with accommodations for 120 officers and 928 men. CASU 37 maintained a detachment at the base to support the various carrier squadrons present. NAAS Monterey usually operated two GH Howard ambulance aircraft and one GB.

Opened in 1880, the Del Monte Hotel was billed as the finest luxury resort in the world hosting captains and kings. In late 1942, after facing a dwindling business, Samuel F. B. Morse, the hotel's owner and grand-nephew of the inventor of the telegraph, offered the hotel to the Navy. After leasing the property, the Navy established the Del Monte Pre-Flight School in February 1943. Del Monte fielded an outstanding football team that defeated UCLA and UC-Berkley, ranking eighth in the final 1943 AP national poll. After the pre-flight school closed in December 1944, Del Monte was used for engineering and general line schools. Following the war, the Navy purchased the property moving the Naval Postgraduate School here from Annapolis. The air station reactivated on December 20, 1947, to provide aircraft for flight proficiency by the Navy and Marine aviators at the postgraduate school. Initial aircraft present included 12 SNJs, 12 TBMs, 12 F6Fs, eight SNBs, and two JRBs. The Navy remained at the airport until 1972, when the facility closed. Today, the Naval Postgraduate School remains at Monterey -- one of the most picturesque places in the world. The airport is now known as Monterey Peninsula.

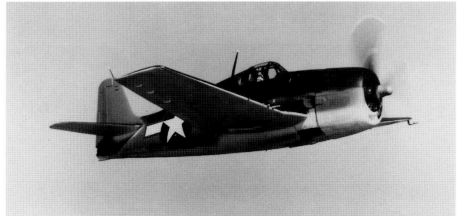

F6F Hellcat *NATIONAL ARCHIVES*

NAS New Orleans, Louisiana

The City of New Orleans donated 182 acres, 4.5 miles north of town near Lake Pontchartrain, to the Navy for an NRAB. The Navy commissioned the base on July 15, 1941, beginning the 30-day Elimination Training Course. After the start of the war, the Navy spent an additional $2 million improving and expanding the base.

In July 1942, New Orleans began a portion of primary training consisting of 33 hours of flying. Only three classes of 179 cadets went through this training before New Orleans began full primary training with over 140 aircraft including the N3N, Stearman, and NP Spartan. On January 1, 1943, New Orleans became a Naval Air Station with facilities for 400 students. A total of 696 cadets received full primary training when the mission of the base changed once again. The Navy decided to merge its three primary instructor's schools into one at New Orleans. The school initially lasted four weeks, but was extended to six weeks in August 1943. Peak load took place in mid-1943 with over 230 N3Ns and Stearmans present. As of December 1944, a total of 11 fatalities had occurred. By this time, aircraft in use had been reduced to 110 N2S Stearmans as primary training lessened. By the end of the war, over 3,000 instructors were qualified.

Besides training instructors, the school also improved teaching techniques and equipment. One innovation involved the elimination of the gosport, a rubber or plastic tube with headphones on one end, used by the instructor to talk to the student. Also called the "Blasphemy Tube" for the verbal abuse instructors sometimes heaped on students, the gosport only allowed one-way communications preventing the student from talking to the instructor. New Orleans developed an electronic intercom for two-way communications in the cockpit greatly improving the training environment.

New Orleans had three asphalt and concrete runways -- the longest only 3300 ft. For that reason, NATS flights used the New Orleans Municipal Airport on the lakefront. New Orleans had eight OLFs including Moisant Airport at Kenner -- today, New Orleans International Airport. Complement in 1944, consisted of 190 officers, 1179 enlisted men, and 62 civilians with barracks capacities for 72 officers and 1190 enlisted. The number of aircraft aboard peaked at nearly 200 including those of the Assembly and Repair Department. VJ-4 usually maintained a detachment of one Avenger and two J2F Ducks. The Commander of the Eighth Naval District based his JRB Beechcraft at the station.

Following the war, the primary instructor's school transferred to Glenview as New Orleans assumed the Reserve mission. By the mid-1950s, the airfield became obsolete with the arrival of jet aircraft in the Reserves. The Navy decided to build a new air station 15 miles south near the WW II OLF, Alvin Callender Field -- named for a New Orleans native, who lost his life in WW I flying for the British. Callender Field was established in the late 1920s, when a landing field was cleared for Charles Lindbergh's nationwide tour. The Navy built a new base southwest and adjacent to the former OLF that included an 8,000-ft. and a 6,000-ft. runway. The Navy opened the new NAS New Orleans on December 13, 1957, dedicating the facility as Alvin Callender Field, four months later.

Today, the NAS is the center of military flying in the New Orleans area. In 1996, the Naval and Marine Reserve operated the P-3, the F/A 18, and the C-130. The station also hosts the Air Force Reserve, the Louisiana Air National Guard, the U.S. Customs Air Operations Branch, and the U.S. Coast Guard. The former air station near the lakefront is now the campus of the University of New Orleans.

The Naval Aircraft Factory produced 1002 N3Ns. The Yellow Peril remained in the inventory until 1961.   *NATIONAL ARCHIVES*

OCTOBER 1944   NATIONAL ARCHIVES

NAS Norman, Oklahoma

In 1938, Mr. Walter Neustadt of Ardmore, Oklahoma donated $10,500 to the University of Oklahoma to establish an airport in memory of his father-in-law, Max Westheimer, a WW I pilot who had passed away earlier that year. An airport was built on 150 acres 2.5 miles northwest of town with additional funds from the WPA, the University, and the City of Norman. Dedicated as the Max Westheimer Flying Field, the airport was later used by the Civilian Pilot Training Program.

After the beginning of the war, the Navy took an interest in the site for a primary training station. The University leased the airport to the Navy for the nominal sum of $1 per year. Additional property was purchased and leased bringing the total acreage to 1650. Construction began in April 1942 with the initial Navy contingent being housed at the National Guard Armory. Coincidentally, Norman was also chosen for a Naval Air Technical Center and construction began on that facility one month later two miles south of town. Locally, the air station was known as North Base -- the technical school, as South Base. In addition, an enlisted aerial gunner's school was established 25 miles south of Norman near the town of Purcell. The air station provided support for these other Naval activities. Norman commissioned on July 31, 1942, although the first cadets would not arrive for another two months. During construction, the Navy mounted a recruiting drive locally. In a practice repeated at many stations, an enlisted boot camp was conducted and new sailors put to work on the base.

On January 1, 1943, a total of 128 aircraft were on the station including the aircraft utilized in support of the technical and gunnery schools. The primary trainers in use totaled 94 Boeing N2S Stearmans, Ryan NR Recruits, and Spartan NPs. By November of the year, Norman completed its 2000th cadet.

On the first of January 1944, the station was operating near maximum capacity. Aircraft present totaled 463, including 301 N2Ss and 80 N2T Tudors devoted to primary training. The technical school's 66 aircraft included just about every example of aircraft in the Navy's inventory including the F6F, F4U, TBF, SBD, FM, SB2C, SB2A, F2A, SBC, and PBY. By the end of 1944, the station reached its peak utilization. With the NRs and NPs retired, primary trainers present totaled 435 Stearmans. In addition, 33 miscellaneous aircraft in operation included 23 SNVs used for instructor instrument proficiency. By mid-1945, the primary training load diminished and trainers numbered 253 Stearmans by VJ-Day. During the war, Norman passed 6461 cadets, washed out 1631, had 721 withdrawals, and suffered 15 fatalities. An additional 22 officers and nine enlisted men were killed in aviation accidents. The station flew 764,381 syllabus hours, 24,612 non-syllabus hours, and 42,495 instructor proficiency hours.

Ultimately, the Navy constructed 91 buildings with a total investment of $9.75 million in the air station. Norman had four 5,000 x 200-ft. asphalt runways and two 2,500 x 2,500-ft. landing mats. The station's 18 OLFs included a hard-surfaced hexagon at Goldsby, south of Norman -- today, a general aviation airport. For a short time, Norman also had one auxiliary at Shawnee. In December 1943, the Chief of NAPT declared Shawnee unsuitable for primary training so Norman never used the field. In March 1944, the air station's complement stood at 353 officers, 1000 cadets, 2164 enlisted men, and 467 civilians. Barracks space existed for 197 officers, 1150 cadets, and 2544 enlisted men. The Naval Air Technical Training Center (NATTC) had 250 buildings with a staff of 416 officers and 1,200 enlisted men with a capacity of 8,000 students every six months. The North and South Base fielded a football team ranking in the top ten in 1944.

At Purcell, the Navy leased 8553 acres for the aerial gunnery school and added barracks for 56 officers and 1160 enlisted men. At one time, the gunnery school had four assigned aircraft -- one NE Piper Cub, two Stearmans, and one Curtiss Seamew.

Following the war, NATTC served as a separation center processing 25,000 men to civilian life. In March 1946, the air station and the NATTC closed. Thereafter, the former Navy facilities were used by the University of Oklahoma -- mostly as housing for married war veteran students. The Korean War necessitated the reopening of NATTC on January 7, 1952. By the end of the year, the staff had risen to 1,938 with 4,352 students. NATTC remained open until June 1959, then closed for the last time. Today, the University of Oklahoma owns the former air station property utilizing it for the Swearingen Research Park and the Max Westheimer Airpark.

NORMAN'S INSIGNA *NATIONAL ARCHIVES*

OCTOBER 1944   NATIONAL ARCHIVES

ABOVE AND ABOVE RIGHT: Undeterminable number of Stearmans are sheltered in Norman's drill hall in July 1943 for an equally undetermined reason.

NATIONAL ARCHIVES

RIGHT: Erco truck-mounted teardrop turret at the Naval Air Gunners School at Purcell, 25 miles south of Norman. *NATIONAL ARCHIVES*

MAY 1945   NATIONAL ARCHIVES

NAAS North Bend, Oregon

In 1936, the City of North Bend, located a few miles from the Pacific Coast on Coos Bay, sponsored the development of a municipal airport. Since most terrain in the area is hilly, land reclaimed from Coos Bay made a suitable site. Begun as a local WPA project, initially all work was done by hand labor. The next year, a dike was constructed and an area for a runway created by cutting down a hill and pumping sand from the bay. The airport eventually opened in 1939. In January 1941, the CAA and the WPA began a major project resulting in three 3,500-ft. gravel and oil-seal coated runways.

Following Pearl Harbor, the WPA lengthened one runway an additional 1600 ft. In the spring of 1942, a detachment of the Army's 406th Bombardment Squadron from Paine Field, Washington operated antisubmarine missions with twin-engined bombers from the field. Later that year, the CAA paved the runways. Meanwhile, the Navy took an interest in the site, leased 618 acres of the airport, and purchased 135 additional acres for an air station. While Navy construction was under way, the CAA extended a runway and paved the taxiways. On May 10, 1943, NAAS North Bend commissioned as an auxiliary of NAS Astoria, Oregon.

The first unit to operate from the station was a detachment of the scouting squadron VS-50 with OS2U Kingfishers. The units that followed, mostly composite squadrons of Avengers and Wildcats, spent several months of fighter and torpedo training prior to combat deployment. However, the first squadron did not appear until October 1943, when VC-11 arrived along with the CASU 7-C detachment from NAS Astoria with four officers and 40 enlisted men in support. The base's blimp facilities welcomed the first visitor on November 10, 1943. The blimp's mooring was supervised by officers from NAS Tillamook, assisted by station and CASU personnel. In December 1943, VC-21 and VC-75 were assigned followed during 1944, by VC-80, VC-84, VC-93, VC-70, and VC-71. Beginning in April 1944, a detachment of ZP-33 from Tillamook began operating from the station flying escort patrol and special coverage for naval vessels. The blimp detachment and its support unit, HEDRON 3, remained at North Bend until October 31, then returned to Tillamook. In May 1944, several squadrons from other bases spent approximately one week at North Bend conducting high speed gunnery training. This training continued through July and included VC-88, VC-97, VC-98, and VC-99. The next month, CASU 55-A with 13 officers and 350 enlisted men relieved CASU 7-C.

In January 1945, VC-65 and VC-68 reported aboard and commenced the fighter and torpedo training syllabus. The same month, a Coast Guard detachment from Port Angeles, Washington also arrived to operate an Air/Sea Rescue Unit. The VF and VT squadrons of CAG 37 were present during March for high speed gunnery training. VC-75 and VC-80 attached to the station beginning in March and April respectively. These squadrons were followed by VC-76 and VC-84. On August 4, 1945, VS-50, that had operated from North Bend since the station's inception, returned to NAS Astoria. At this time, VS-50 operated the SB2C and the SBD. VC-84 and the Coast Guard departed on September 15, 1945, as North Bend went on caretaker status.

North Bend had three asphalt runways -- two 5,000 ft., one 4350 ft. There were also two blimp mooring circles and a seaplane ramp. In March 1944, complement stood at 184 officers and 642 enlisted men with accommodations for 104 officers and 717 enlisted men. The station's maximum aircraft assignment consisted of one GH Howard for ambulance use; another GH Howard and a GB Beech for transportation; two J2F Ducks for rescue; an SNJ for photographic, reconnaissance, and towing work; and an NE Piper Cub for whatever.

The Navy returned the airport to the City in 1947. In 1974, the Coast Guard established an air station. Several Navy buildings have survived including the hangar, fire station, and some barracks.

Utility Squadrons used Martin JM Marauders for high-speed target towing.   *TILLAMOOK PIONEER MUSEUM*

NOVEMBER 1943 NATIONAL ARCHIVES

NAS Oakland, California

On February 5, 1927, the Oakland City Council purchased the 692-acre Bay Farm Island, five miles south of town, to develop an airport. On June 3, the Army informed the City that it wished to use the island as the takeoff point for an attempt to fly to Hawaii. Since a runway did not yet exist, the Army requested that one be graded by the end of the month. Working around the clock for 23 days, crews completed a 7,020-ft. runway -- at that time, the longest in the world. On June 28, 1Lts. Lester Maitland and Albert Hegenberger departed in a Fokker C-2. Twenty five hours and 49 minutes later, they landed on Oahu at the Army's Wheeler Field, completing the first non-stop flight between the Mainland and Hawaii.

Oakland became the departure point for many pioneering flights to Hawaii. In July, Ernie Smith and Emory Bronte, also completed a non-stop flight to Hawaii. On August 16, a group of aviators gathered at Oakland to vie for $35,000 in prizes offered by pineapple magnate James Dole for a race to Hawaii. Six entrants crashed preparing for the race or at the race's start and two disappeared over the Pacific. On August 17, two aircraft completed the flight, with the first prize of $25,000 being claimed by Hollywood stunt pilot Art Goebel and his navigator, Navy Lt. William Davis. Charles Lindbergh was the guest of honor for the dedication of the airport that took place on September 27. On May 31 of the next year, Australians Charles Kingsford-Smith and Charles Ulm departed for Hawaii on the first leg of their epic flight to Australia.

On August 1, 1928, the Navy formed an NRAB at the airport with two aircraft and 1200 sq. ft. of leased hangar space. By 1935, the station began the Elimination Training Course with ten aircraft. Eleven days after Pearl Harbor, the C.O.s of all the NRABs held a conference in Pensacola -- the subject being the increase of primary training at their bases. Among the C.O.s with a problem, was Cdr. R.L. Johnson of Oakland. With the addition of Army interceptors at the airport, the expansion of primary training would be impossible without a new base. After returning to Oakland, Cdr. Johnson and his men selected a site 25 miles away, 3.5 miles east of Livermore. Nevertheless, full primary training began in January 1942. With the imminent departure of primary training, Oakland was chosen to be a Naval Air Transport Service Terminal. In September, VR-3 began scheduled service to the station. By November 1942, all primary flight activities transferred to Livermore; however, administrative control remained at Oakland.

On January 1, 1943, Oakland became an NAS along with most of the other NRABs in the Navy. On March 4, VR-4 commissioned with a complement of 13 R4Ds received from Alameda's VR-2 which then became an exclusive seaplane operation. When Livermore commissioned as an NAS on June 1, Oakland was, in turn, reduced to an NAAS under Alameda. VR-11 commissioned here on September 1. Although the headquarters of VR-11 moved to Honolulu three and a half months later, the squadron maintained a detachment and conducted training at Oakland. Meanwhile, United Airlines had an aircraft mechanics school for the Army at the airport. In 1943, United began training Navy mechanics and completed 1281 during the war.

VR-4's schedule board at Oakland in February 1944 shows the magnitude of NATS's operations. *NATIONAL ARCHIVES*

In April 1944, the station began an expansion program. On June 16, VR-13 commissioned and in the spring of 1945, transferred to Los Negros in the Admiralty Islands. A new NATS passenger terminal reached completion on July 19.

Oakland was situated on 1016 acres of which the Navy owned 65 and leased the remainder. The airfield had four asphalt runways, the longest 6,500 ft. Barracks existed for 253 officers and 4,658 men. The station operated an R5D, a GH Howard, and an SNV. Oakland was a joint-use facility with the Army's Air Technical Service Command that serviced transient aircraft.

Following the war, the Navy began reserve activities at Oakland in 1946, upgrading the station to an NAS. In 1961, Oakland closed and the Reserve mission moved to Alameda. Today, the airport is known as Oakland International.

ABOVE RIGHT: R5D rests outside a hangar.
SEPTEMBER 1945 NATIONAL ARCHIVES

RIGHT: R5D'S propellers being inventoried.
SEPTEMBER 1945 NATIONAL ARCHIVES

ABOVE AND ABOVE RIGHT: Oakland's ramp in September 1945.
NATIONAL ARCHIVES

RIGHT: R5D arrives over San Francisco from Hawaii in September 1945.
NATIONAL ARCHIVES

FEBRUARY 1943   USN

NAS Olathe, Kansas

In the mid-1930s, D. W. Tomlinson, a Trans World Airline pilot in New York and a member of the Naval Air Reserve, transferred to TWA's Kansas City base. Tomlinson missed reserve flying and encouraged the Navy to establish an NRAB at Kansas City. With the help of former Naval Aviator and fellow TWA pilot Jack Frye, as well as the Kansas City community, the Navy opened a Naval Reserve Aviation Base at the Fairfax airport on July 1, 1935. Besides reserve flying, the station also administered the Elimination Training Course that selected cadets for further training. In 1941, full primary training began. When the U.S. entered the war, the Navy realized that Fairfax airport, now the location of a new North American Aircraft factory, was inadequate for expansion. The Navy chose a site 25 miles southwest of Kansas City, near Gardner, beginning construction in February 1942. The CAA had started construction of an airport on the site prior to the Navy's involvement.

Kansas City is about as central a location in the United States as there is. While construction proceeded at Gardner, the Navy chose Kansas City as a division point for the Naval Air Transport Service. VR-3, the Navy's interior transport squadron, commissioned on July 15, 1942, with DC-3 aircraft appropriated from TWA. The Navy also placed the headquarters of the Naval Air Transport Service and the Naval Air Primary Training Command at Fairfax. NRAB Gardner reached completion on October 1, 1942, with Capt. D.W. Tomlinson, who had been recalled to active duty, in command. The primary trainers and NATS moved to Gardner, but the headquarters of the Primary Training Command remained at Fairfax -- apparently the officer in command preferred the creature comforts of Kansas City to rural Gardner. The station's name changed to Olathe shortly after opening and to an NAS on January 1, 1943.

At Olathe, the Navy built facilities for 1000 cadets and 267 aircraft. By January 1943, the 149 trainers on board consisted of 52 Spartan NP-1s, 85 N2S Stearmans, and 12 N3Ns. In May 1943, a tornado struck the base destroying over 100 aircraft. By mid-year, primary training operations had risen to 261 aircraft. The N3Ns had been replaced by Stearmans, but 59 Spartans remained. In January 1944, training peaked with 314 N2S Stearmans, 287 instructors, and over 1000 cadets. By mid-1944, primary training diminished Navy-wide and Olathe's mission was selected to be terminated. On September 10, 1944, training ended after over 4,500 cadets logged 463,220 flying hours. Headquarters of the Primary Training Command then moved to Glenview from Fairfax.

VR-3 began operations with approximately six of TWA's DC-3s redesignated as R4D-1s. The squadron inaugurated weekly transcontinental flights between Alameda and New York on September 8, 1942. VR-3 expanded rapidly and by April 1944, six transcontinental flights operated daily. In September, the squadron's aircraft consisted of 56 R4Ds, six SNBs, and five R5Ds. By the end of the war, the squadron had 75 R4Ds assigned operating an additional six weekly scheduled transcontinental hospital flights. VR-3 also hosted NATS's R4D plane commander school.

The Navy sent all pilots bound for NATS through the Instrument Flight Instructor School at NAS Atlanta -- not to be instructors, but to be proficient instrument pilots. One month R4D schools were operated by American Airlines at Fort Worth, Texas and Penn Central Airlines at Roanoke, Virginia. Without a doubt, NATS was the premier armed service transport operation of the war. NATS was run like an airline by former airline personnel operating airline-type schedules. When NATS and the Air

Force's Air Transport Command combined to form the Military Air Transport Service in 1947, the Navy was the choice to command the new organization. Unfortunately, the Naval "powers that be" rejected this proposal, feeling that MATS would put too much strain on the Navy's resources. According to Colton, "Imitation is the sincerest of flattery;" therefore, NATS became MATS. The professionalism of NATS was further demonstrated by the fact that the Air Force adopted the NATS operating manual practically verbatim! Nevertheless, the Navy participated in MATS on a smaller scale by supplying squadrons and aircraft. The Navy remained a part of MATS until 1967, when eased out by the Air Force -- but that is another story.

Olathe, located on 760 acres, had three 5,000-ft. concrete runways surrounding primary trainer landing mats and five hangars. During primary training days, the station maintained 15 OLFs -- four owned and 11 leased. The four OLFs the Navy owned, #2, #4, #7, and #9, were hard-surfaced. VR-3 utilized the Grandview airport, 16 miles south of Kansas City, Missouri as an OLF. The Navy apparently had plans for Olathe after the war, since the construction consisted of some steel and brick buildings. By 1945, the base had quarters for 6,400 personnel.

Following the war, VR-3 transferred and Olathe became a reserve base. In 1950, the Air Force added air reserve units to Olathe. The next year, two of the station's runways were extended -- the longest to 8,500 ft. In 1954, the Navy established a Jet Transitional Training Unit at Olathe for the purpose of jet transition and/or refresher training for experienced Naval Aviators. "Cougar College's" syllabus consisted of one week of ground school and four weeks of flight training that totaled 10 hours in the Lockheed TV-2 and 20 hours in the Grumman F9F. When the Army located a missile battalion here in

1959, Olathe hosted all four of the military services. In 1962, the airfield was dedicated as Flatley Field, in honor of the late VAdm. James H. Flatley, a former C.O. of the station. The Navy closed Olathe on June 30, 1970, retaining 15 acres and one building for non-flying Marine and Navy reserve units.

Today, the airfield is known as Johnson County Industrial Airport. A group has formed the Old Olathe Naval Air Museum to preserve the memory and history of the station. The museum's address is One Navy Park Drive, P.O. Box 1942, Industrial Airport, Kansas 66031.

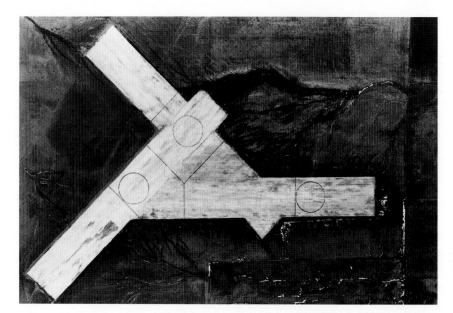

ABOVE: During primary training, Olathe had 15 OLFs -- four owned and 11 leased. The four that were owned by the Navy were hard-surfaced. Pictured here is OLF #2 with an unusual layout.
NATIONAL ARCHIVES

ABOVE: The Naval Air Transport Service's insignia.   *NATIONAL ARCHIVES*

RIGHT: Olathe in February 1943 with the BOQ in the foreground.   *USN*

ABOVE: A NATS Douglas R4D receives a maintenance check. The Navy received 568 R4Ds during the war from Army C-47 production lines. *NATIONAL ARCHIVES*

ABOVE RIGHT: Convalescing sailors boarding a NATS hospital flight. *NATIONAL ARCHIVES*

RIGHT: A Beech JRB Expeditor in NATS livery. NATS used the JRB for instrument proficiency training and light transport. *USN*

AUGUST 1943 NATIONAL ARCHIVES

NAS Ottumwa, Iowa

Ottumwa is located 87 miles southeast of Des Moines. In 1940, the City sent a delegation to Washington to lobby for a munitions plant at their community. When the plant went to another city, Ottumwa then selected 1440 acres of prime farmland 6.5 miles north of town for an air station and offered to lease it to the Navy for the nominal sum of $1 per year. The U.S. entry into WW II started the ball rolling, and in April 1942, a Navy site selection committee visited Ottumwa. The committee recommended the location and in July, the Secretary of the Navy, Frank Knox, approved the plan for a primary training air station. That month, the Ottumwa Airport Commission approved a $200,000 bond issue to purchase the land. The contractor, who had recently completed NAS Bunker Hill, Indiana, broke ground in August. On September 16, two N3Ns flew into the Ottumwa Municipal Airport, also leased by the Navy. The first problem arose when "green," not properly dried, lumber arrived. Due to a nationwide shortage of building materials, the Navy approved a change to hollow tiles, supplied by Ottumwa Brick and Tile Co. Construction crews struggled through the coldest and wettest winter in recent memory.

In January, two N3Ns, two N2Ss and one SNJ used a runway on the base for the first time. On March 10, 1943, the first 21 cadets of a 105-man class from the Pre-Flight School at Iowa City arrived. Three days later, the Navy commissioned the station. During the spring, the station's infirmary encountered several cases of venereal disease. After tracing five of the cases to a local hangout by the name of "The Submarine" frequented by infected females, the station's C.O. placed that establishment "Out of Bounds." By the end of June, Ottumwa had 93 N2S Stearmans in use. On July 1, the station suffered its first two fatalities, when two instructors were killed on an SNJ instrument hop. By August, the station

reached 99% completion. The estimated cost of $10 million had risen to a staggering $16 million due to the weather delays and increased building material costs. By comparison, NAS Pasco, Washington had cost a mere $5 million. By the end of the year, Ottumwa was operating at full capacity with 304 N2S Stearmans.

In the spring of 1944, due to an increased student input and bad weather, 1200 cadets were on the station. Also during the spring, the Navy opened flight training to officers. The Navy selected Ottumwa for officer training and in August the first officer students arrived. By the spring of 1945, the student makeup consisted of 55% officers and 45% cadets. While other primary stations had reductions in training, Ottumwa maintained an average of 300 Stearmans almost to the end of the war. On September 30, 1945, primary training ended and the station's students transferred to Norman, Oklahoma.

Ottumwa trained 6,656 students completing 605,553 flight hours with 17 ground and flight fatalities.

Ottumwa had two 5,000 x 200-ft. concrete runways and two octagonal landing mats. The OLFs totaled 16 -- 14 leased and two owned. On each of the two owned OLFs, #10 and #6, the Navy constructed four 2,000-ft. concrete runways laid out in an unusual square. Today, #10 is the Oskaloosa, Iowa Municipal Airport and #6 is the site of a school. In March 1944, station complement amounted to 356 officers, 1200 cadets, 2430 enlisted men, and 295 civilians. Available billeting accommodated 211 officers, 1160 cadets, and 2080 enlisted men. The station usually operated 36 miscellaneous aircraft including 22 SNVs used for instructor instrument proficiency. James L. Holloway, future Chief of Naval Operations, was a student at Ottumwa and future U. S. President Richard M. Nixon served as an aide to the station's executive officer.

"Mack" a station mascot in March 1943.　　　*NATIONAL ARCHIVES*

Following the end of hostilities, the station served as a Separation Center. In December 1945, the Navy moved the Pre-Flight School at Iowa City to Ottumwa. The Pre-Flight School closed on August 1, 1947, and the Navy deeded the base to the City. Following the Navy's departure, an Army Reserve unit utilized the station's former administration building. Today, as the Ottumwa Industrial Airport, many Navy buildings remain due to their substantial construction. Besides general aviation, the airport is also served by commuter airlines.

Various scenes of N2S Stearmans around Ottumwa in the spring and summer of 1943.   *NATIONAL ARCHIVES*

ABOVE: Formation of Stearmans fly over the station's administration building. When "green," not properly dried, lumber arrived, Ottumwa's buildings were built with tile seen in this photo. The extra expense of the tile and extraordinary bad weather caused the cost of the station to rise from an estimated $10 million to a staggering $16 million! *NATIONAL ARCHIVES*

ABOVE RIGHT: Ottumwa operated 19 OLFs -- two owned and the remainder leased. On the two owned OLFs, the Navy built hard-surfaced squares. Today, one is the site of a school and the other is Oskaloosa, Iowa's municipal airport. *NATIONAL ARCHIVES*

RIGHT: An unusual photo during a night formation flight -- probably with instructor pilots. Night formation flying was definitely not a part of the primary training syllabus. *NATIONAL ARCHIVES*

1945 NATIONAL ARCHIVES

NAS Pasco, Washington

On April 6, 1926, the Pacific Northwest's first contract airmail service began when Varney Air Lines took off from Pasco to Elko, Nevada with a stop in Boise, Idaho. Varney eventually became a part of United Aircraft and Transport Corporation -- today's United Air Lines. In 1932, the Pasco Airport moved to its present location.

On December 18, 1941, the Commanding Officers of all the Navy's NRABs held a conference in Pensacola. The subject of the meeting concerned the increase of primary training. Among the C.O.s that had a problem included LCdr. B. B. Smith of NRAB Seattle. Neither NAS Seattle nor the area's weather would allow much expansion.

Returning to Seattle, the Commandant of the 13th Naval District instructed Smith to find a site for a new station east of the Cascade Mountains. Locations Smith considered besides Pasco included Boise, Twin Falls, and Pocatello, Idaho. Pasco was chosen because it was closest to Seattle, plus the fact that the County and Northern Pacific Railroad offered to sell the Navy the airport and additional land for $1 per acre. The Navy approved the site directing Smith to build a station that could later accommodate carrier-based squadrons. Construction began in March and NRAB Pasco commissioned July 31, 1942, as the aircraft and men of NRAB Seattle moved aboard. Smith had built the station for $5 million -- the least expensive in the Navy. By comparison, Ottumwa Iowa had cost $16 million and Glenview $36 million. Six months later 83 N2S Stearmans and 14 N3Ns were in use.

In December 1942, Pasco had the distinction of being the first Naval station to receive a contingent of Waves. LCdr. Smith was steaming in uncharted waters with this new dilemma. After some deliberation with his subordinates, he laid down one order:

the women were to stay out of the men's barracks and the men were to stay out of the women's barracks -- and left it at that. On January 1, 1943, the Navy upgraded Pasco to an NAS.

At the height of primary training during 1943, Pasco had 189 instructors, 800 students, and 304 aircraft including: 243 N2Ss, 10 N3Ns, 10 N2Ts, three SOCs, seven SNJs, and one J2F. The training program totaled 84 hours of flying time, 38 of which was dual. The syllabus consisted of six stages including acrobatics, formation, and night flying.

The Navy was very pleased with the operation at Pasco. The only other air stations with more VFR flying weather than Pasco were the fields in Florida. LCdr. Smith drew plans and obtained the necessary building material to construct an auxiliary air station at Vista Field, across the Columbia river in Kennewick -- then, one of Pasco's OLFs. Orders from Washington cancelled that plan with no explanation. Later, Smith learned that an official of the *Manhattan Project*, building the nearby Hanford Works, felt that the addition of Vista would over-tax the local facilities.

By the end of 1943, the Navy's primary training requirements diminished. Pasco's location, allowing for establishment of bombing targets and gunnery ranges plus nearness to the West Coast, resulted in the termination of primary training in December 1943. A total of 260,000 hours had been flown with 1878 cadets successfully completing the program. Failures amounted to 568 or an average of 27%. A total of five lives were lost, although the first 25,000 hours were flown with no fatalities.

The Navy transferred the station to the command of Naval Air Center Seattle. Pasco's new mission involved the basing and support of 225 carrier air-

craft and 37 other aircraft. The first carrier units on board consisted of the composite squadrons VC-21, VC-27, VC-81, and VC-83. The newly commissioned CASU 50 also arrived in support. The Seabees installed a catapult and arresting gear at Vista Field. Bombing and gunnery ranges were also established. To the end of the war some units attached to Pasco included: CAG 24, 30, 2, 26, 35, 51, 41, 81, 5, and VC-79. In June 1945, VC-21 and VC-27 returned to the station. By December 1945, air operations ended with the Navy inactivating Pasco on July 1, 1946.

NAS Pasco consisted of 2219 acres. Initially, the station's two landing mats measured 4700 x 1600 ft. and 4700 x 600 ft. The method of the mats construction was unusual. The sandy soil of the station was mixed with cement, watered down, and rolled to obtain a hard and smooth surface. The station had ten OLFs. After primary training ended, the Navy converted nine of the OLFs into targets. Only Vista Field remained for FCLPs. The Navy also leased 270,000 acres for gunnery ranges. In March 1944, station personnel numbered 520 officers, 4382 enlisted men, and 41 civilians. Available berthing space existed for 370 officers and 3700 enlisted men. The number of aircraft on board during this period peaked in June 1945 at 280. The station's ten aircraft included light transports, an ambulance plane, utility, and proficiency types. Pasco's Assembly and Repair Department overhauled the primary trainers of the station and later the carrier types.

B. B. Smith, retired as Captain, settled in Pasco, and became the Mayor before passing away in 1977. Today, the former NAS is known as the Tri-Cities Airport for the towns of Pasco, Kennewick, and Richland, Washington. In 1996, several Navy buildings survived including hangars and the former tower/operations building.

Pasco in September 1943. Landing mats measured 4700 x 1600 ft. and 4700 x 600 ft. Following primary training two sets of parallel runways were laid over the mats.

NMNA

ABOVE: Instructor gives a few final tips to cadet who is about to depart on first solo flight.   *NATIONAL ARCHIVES*

ABOVE RIGHT: Cdr. Basil Smith, Pasco's first C.O., bids goodbye to a group of Waves on March 24, 1944. Cdr. Smith made Pasco his home following the war and later became the Mayor.   *NATIONAL ARCHIVES*

RIGHT: Pasco's Assembly and Repair Department in 1944.

NATIONAL ARCHIVES

NAS Pearl Harbor is in the lower left of the photograph with Hickam AFB in the center background and the adjacent NAS Honolulu in the upper left corner.

FEBRUARY 1945 NATIONAL ARCHIVES

NAS Pearl Harbor, Hawaii

NAS Pearl Harbor, located on Ford Island, was also known as NAS Ford Island during its history. The island was named after Dr. S. P. Ford who acquired the property in June 1866, by marriage. In the years that followed, the Hawaii Insane Asylum and the U.S. Marine Hospital were located here. In 1891, Ford's son sold the island to the Honolulu Plantation Co. to grow sugar cane. At the turn of the century, Congress appropriated funds to open a channel into the harbor and eventually build a Naval operating base across from the island. The first U.S. warship entered Pearl Harbor in January 1911.

With the outbreak of WW I, the Army purchased the island for $236,000. The airfield opened in October 1917 with the arrival of the 6th Aero Squadron. The Army later named the airfield Luke Field in memory of Lt. Frank Luke of Arizona. Luke startled the world by shooting down four airplanes and 14 balloons in 17 days of combat before being killed on September 28, 1918. On December 19, 1919, the Navy established the Pacific Air Detachment at the Pearl Harbor Navy Yard. Initially, the Navy contingent consisted of nine officers and 55 men operating two HS2L flying boats and two N-9 floatplanes.

On January 1, 1923, the Navy moved its flying operations from the Navy Yard to Ford Island with Cdr. John Rodgers, Naval Aviator #2, in command. The Army occupied the west side of the island and the Navy the east. That same year, the Navy built concrete and stone quays around the island that would later become the famous "Battleship Row." In the 1920's, the Navy operated the TS, F5L, H-16, PK, DT, FU-1, VE-7, and VE-9 from the station. The P2Y first arrived in 1933, followed two years later by the PBY. In the mid-1930s, the Navy traded Moffett Field, California, for Ford Island; Bolling Field, Washington, D.C.; and North Island, California. Pan American Airways used Ford Island

as its Honolulu base from 1935 to 1940, when the airline moved to a new facility at Pearl City. During 1936, a 3000 x 4000-ft. hard-surfaced landing mat was added. That same year, Japanese VAdm. Yoshida, on the flag ship *Iwate,* paid a courtesy visit to Pearl Harbor. The information gathered at this time undoubtedly laid the foundation for the attack five years later. On March 19, 1937, Amelia Earhart's first attempted around-the-world fight ended on Ford Island when she ground-looped on takeoff. The Army began construction on Hickam Field in 1938, finally turning Ford Island over to the Navy on November 1, 1939.

Ford Island was the eye of the hurricane during the Japanese attack suffering relatively little damage when compared to the nearby carnage. Although they strafed and bombed the island, the Japanese understandably concentrated most of their efforts on the tempting Battleship Row. On Ford Island proper, ten Navy planes were destroyed and only one man was killed -- a guard at VP-21's hangar. The Navy rapidly built up Ford Island in the ensuing time making it the command and supply center for all air operations in the Hawaiian Islands. An underground command center and gasoline storage tanks were added. On May 1, 1942, the Commander of the Naval Air Force Pacific Fleet moved his headquarters to Ford Island. VR-2 conducted its first flight to the station in September and maintained a detachment there. The next month, the Naval Air Center Hawaiian Islands formed at Pearl Harbor to command the complex of Naval Air Stations in the islands. These stations included prewar Kaneohe Bay, plus Barbers Point and Puunene (Maui) that commissioned during 1942.

Severely geographically restricted with only 334 acres, Ford Island served as the base for utility squadrons and was headquarters for the Commander

of Utility Wing Pacific Fleet. Scout and Observation Service Unit One (SOSU 1) operated similar to a CASU and supported floatplanes of the numerous warships that passed though the harbor. SOSU 1 serviced battleship and cruiser aircraft as well as training personnel in their operation. Since there were no blimps in Hawaii, numerous scouting squadrons stationed at Ford Island patrolled the waters around Oahu. The station had a capacity of 90 carrier aircraft with CASU 1 present for support. During 1943, additional stations opened at French Frigate Shoals, Hilo, and Kahului. VR-10, commissioned at Pearl Harbor on April 10, 1943, with two PBMs from the VR-2 Detachment. VR-10 later became a maintenance squadron. The next year, NAS Honolulu opened and all transport operations moved to that station. For the first six months of 1944, Pearl Harbor used the Army airfield at Barking Sands as an NAAF.

Ford Island had a single 4500 x 450-ft. asphalt runway. In March 1944, complement totaled 823 officers, 6414 enlisted men, and 2759 civilians. Barracks existed for 813 officers and 6382 men. The station supported 90 carrier aircraft, 18 utility, 15 trainers, 24 scout floatplanes, 12 patrol seaplanes, and 13 miscellaneous aircraft. An Assembly and Repair Department existed along with a large spare aircraft pool.

In the years following the war, Ford Island gradually lost its importance as most Navy air operations moved to Barbers Point. Today, the island has remained a Naval reservation. The airfield is a Naval Auxiliary Landing Field and is occasionally used by helicopters from ships in Pearl Harbor. In an arrangement with the State of Hawaii, the Navy allows general aviation aircraft to use the airfield for touch and go landings to relieve the congestion at Honolulu International Airport.

ABOVE: Fleet Air Arm Catalina passes through Pearl Harbor in 1942.

NATIONAL ARCHIVES

ABOVE LEFT: USS *Long Island* is being loaded with aircraft in June 1942. Note torpedo nets in place around the ship. *NATIONAL ARCHIVES*

LEFT: The Navy wasted no time in building revetments in Hawaii.

JUNE 1942 NATIONAL ARCHIVES

ABOVE: The celebrated 10,000th Hellcat produced made its way to Pearl Harbor in 1945. The aircraft was eventually assigned to VBF-87 on the USS *Ticonderoga*. Hellcat production totalled 12,275. *NATIONAL ARCHIVES*

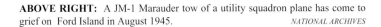

ABOVE RIGHT: A JM-1 Marauder tow of a utility squadron plane has come to grief on Ford Island in August 1945. *NATIONAL ARCHIVES*

RIGHT: An OS2U Kingfisher is tested with a JATO rocket in May 1945. *NATIONAL ARCHIVES*

DECEMBER 1943 NATIONAL ARCHIVES

NAS Puunene, Hawaii

In 1930, the Territory of Hawaii established an airport at Maalaea on Maui. Seven years later, the airfield reached its limitations and work commenced on a more suitable site at the village of Puunene. By February 1939, the Puunene airfield was sufficiently developed so Inter-Island Airways could begin service. The next year, the Navy took an interest in the facility for a utility and experimental station. Construction of the Navy base began in June 1940, as elements of Utility Squadron VJ-3 arrived to tow targets and operate target drones for the fleet. The Navy used barracks at Paukukalo National Guard Camp while completing buildings. Meanwhile, the Army Air Corps also started using the airfield establishing a small support base.

On December 7, 1941, Maui was spared during the attack on Oahu. At that time, military personnel numbered 157 Navy and 202 Army. The next week, plans were drawn up to expand the airport to support a Navy carrier air group and an Army bomber group. On the night of December 15, and again on the 31st, Japanese submarines surfaced in Kahului Harbor and sent several shells in the general direction of the Maui Pineapple Factory. The submarines withdrew when shore batteries counterfired. The Navy commissioned NAS Maui on January 27, 1942. The next month, CASU 4 formed to support the carrier units present. By June, the Navy's facilities had been expanded to support additional units as VF-72 and its F4Fs arrived for training. The airfield quickly became jammed with Navy and Army aircraft.

The Navy became the prime user of Puunene as the Army concentrated most of its forces on Oahu. The Army retained 14 acres and maintained a small servicing detachment. In November of 1942, a second expansion added Link trainers as well as extending and widening the runways. When a second Naval Air Station, NAS Kahului, opened on Maui a few miles to the north in March 1943, the station was renamed NAS Puunene. On July 1, 1945, Navy strength stood at 565 officers, 2798 enlisted men, and 271 aircraft. By the end of the war, a total of 106 squadrons and carrier air groups had passed through the station.

Puunene consisted of 2180 leased and 22 Navy-owned acres. Fourteen acres remained under control of the Army. After several improvements, the two asphalt runways ultimately grew to 6500 x 400 and 6800 x 200 ft. Barracks existed for 539 officers and 4598 men. The Navy leased the former airport at Maalaea as an OLF and the island of Kahoolawe, south of Maui, for a bombing target. Kahoolawe became the most bombed island in the world as squadrons sharpened their skills for combat. Today, Kahoolawe is still Navy-owned -- a sore spot for some Hawaiians.

CASU 4 decommissioned in October 1945. The station was placed on caretaker status shortly thereafter, and released to the Territory of Hawaii in 1947. The airport remained as Maui's commercial airport until 1952, when closed in favor of the former NAS and larger airfield at Kahului.

Flight of Corsairs over Hawaii in 1945.

NATIONAL ARCHIVES

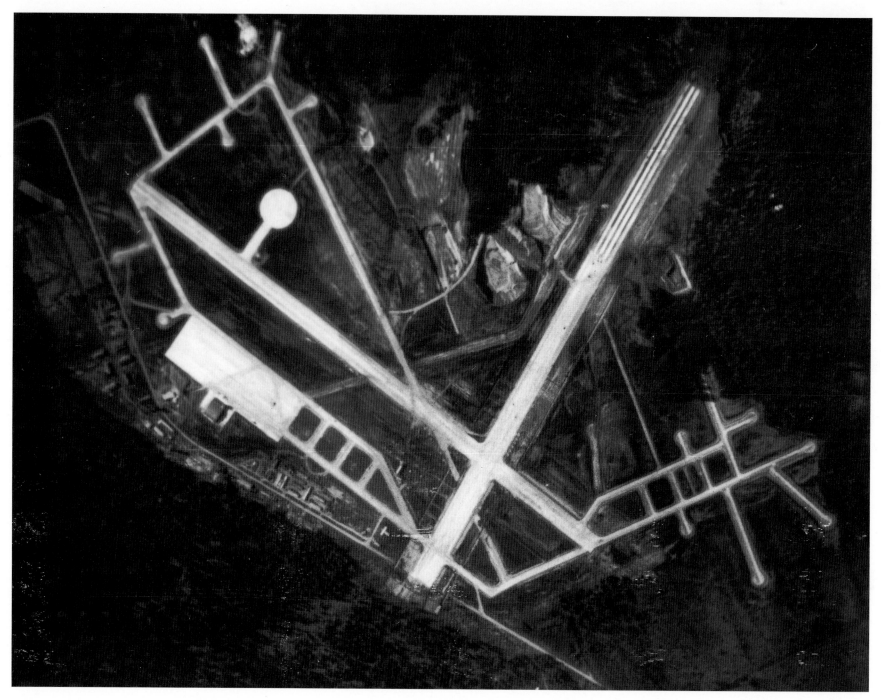

OCTOBER 1944 NATIONAL ARCHIVES

NAAS Quillayute, Washington

Quillayute, located on Washington's Olympic peninsula, is approximately 100 air miles west from Seattle. In October 1940, the Navy recommended building an airfield at the location. An airport existed at the nearby town of Folks, but that location was not adequate for expansion. In May 1941, the Navy purchased 520 acres for $18,000 at a location known as Quillayute Prairie, the only suitable site in the area, and began construction. A county road had to be relocated to accommodate a 4290 x 300-ft. gravel runway. Facilities included a small hangar and the conversion of former farm buildings to house 25 officers and 50 men. Four days after Pearl Harbor, the Army received permission from the Navy to develop the airfield with the stipulation the Navy could also use the improvements. The Army spent $858,000 building a 5000 x 150-ft. concrete runway, hardstands, and a total of 21 buildings that included a 50-man BOQ and a 400-man barracks. In September, the Navy designated the airfield for emergency use.

In early 1943, the Navy planned to build an auxiliary at Mt. Vernon, also an Army improved field. After realizing that Mt. Vernon would further overtax the already overcrowded gunnery ranges in the area, the Navy decided to develop Quillayute instead. The Army approved the proposal and in May, construction began on a second 5,000-ft. concrete runway. This required the relocation of the county road for the second time. The Navy commissioned the facility on June 1, 1943, to support a CV group of 90 aircraft, two 12-plane patrol squadrons, and two blimps. Barracks for 40 officers and 330 enlisted men were added to the existing Army barracks. In December 1943, however, the station's complement only numbered four officers and 33 enlisted men.

Initially, the Navy did not use the base a great deal. The main reason being the generally poor flying weather. The area has received as much as 100 in. of rain in the winter. The secondary reason was the available electricity. Quillayute at that time was quite isolated and sparsely populated -- mostly by lumber men and Quillayute Indians. The only power plant in the area at Folks was unable to supply the electrical needs of the Navy. Due to other higher priorities, a new power plant was not available. In desperation, two used Atlas diesel/electric power generators were located and moved to the station. These generators, designed in 1908 and built in 1914, served for 25 years at Casper, Wyoming before being retired. When the first generator was started, it ran for five minutes and quit. By February 1944, the longest time one of them had run was five hours -- later, the longest either one of them ran was 24 hours. The generators required three mechanics, on duty 24 hours a day, to keep the bearings lubricated. The bearings sprayed oil all over the power plant and on the worst occasion, used 200 gals. of oil in a 24-hour period. Finally, the base received a new Worthington Power Plant. When the Navy mechanic received the signal to pull the switch on the Atlas for the last time on September 15, 1944, he remarked: "Now you can go to Hell."

An additional amusing situation developed early on at Quillayute with the station's bus. On Friday and Saturday nights, the enlisted men took liberty in the seaside town of LaPush -- 1940 population of 200. The men made their way to town at different times; however, when the saloons closed at midnight, they all wanted to come back to the base at the same time. This proved to be difficult since the station's one bus could take as much as three hours to get everyone back. Meanwhile, the men left waiting in town caused considerable mischief amusing themselves, creating friction with the locals and complaints to the base C.O. This situation improved with the arrival of a second bus.

On January 4, 1944, blimp K-39 got caught in a storm and crashed into trees one mile north of the station. Although the blimp was a total loss, no fatalities were suffered by the crew. With adequate electricity available and the winter weather nearly over, the station was deemed ready for carrier squadrons. On March 23, 1944, the first squadron, VC-96, arrived with TBMs and FM-1s with Detachment G of CASU 7 in support. The next month, a blimp detachment from Tillamook also arrived. On June 5, a blimp from the station crashed in the mountains of British Columbia while looking for a downed RCAF airplane. Fortunately, there were no injuries. The airfield received permanent lighting in August. On September 9, VC-96 departed and VC-72 arrived. The next month, two VC-72 airplanes had a midair with the loss of one pilot. That month, the Army officially transferred its facilities at the base to the Navy. On October 10, blimp operations were secured for the winter.

On January 11, 1945, VC-3 arrived for three months training followed by VC-78 in April. The same month, two Army P-38's staged at the station to intercept Japanese balloons (see Lakeview). During 1945, the base added a gunnery-training building, a radio localizer, and a 600-acre rocket range. The station maintained a crash-boat facility in LaPush and an emergency seaplane facility on Lake Ozette. VC-86 arrived on June 2, only to be decommissioned in less than a week. VC-82 was present at the base from June 13 to August 4. Two days later, VC-85 arrived remaining until the station went on caretaker status September 15, 1945.

Following the war, NAS Seattle used the airfield as an OLF into the 1950s, before releasing the facility to the State of Washington. Today, the airport is known as Quillayute State Airport. Several WW II buildings have survived.

NAAS Ream Field, California

During WW I, the Army took over North Island at San Diego for primary training. The Army then established an auxiliary named Aviation Field, 11 miles south at San Ysidro. Once the Army changed North Island to pursuit and gunnery training, the facility was renamed the Oneonta Gunnery School Field. On October 5, 1918, the name changed to Ream Field, in honor of Major William Ream, killed in an aircraft accident during a Liberty Bond drive in Indiana. Major Ream was the first Army flight surgeon to be killed in an aircraft accident. The Army investment at the field totaled $148,000 including several hangars. Following the war, the Navy leased the field's 140 acres from the civilian owners for an OLF. The property remained in use as an OLF through the 1920s and 1930s. In October 1942, the Navy allocated $1.2 million to develop an auxiliary at the site. Initially, San Diego maintained administrative control of the station. Commissioning eventually occurred on July 17, 1943, with the completion of construction. Surprisingly, the Navy retained the designation, Ream Field -- previously named for an Army officer.

From July 1943, to June 1944, a total of 13 VC squadrons based at the station with CASU 17 in support. A detachment of San Diego's CASU 5, later replaced CASU 17. In July, the station embarked on an expansion project including installation of an HE-5 catapult and arresting gear system -- the only one in the San Diego area. In October, CASU 65 commissioned remaining at the station to the end of the war. In late 1944, and early 1945, units on board included the light CAGs 32 and 38 as well as VT-9, VF-12, and VBF-12. After the expansion program had been completed in early 1945, the station hosted large carrier air groups. CAG 14 trained at Ream in the spring and the war ended with CAG 80 on board. Meanwhile, a Fleet Airborne Early Warning Training Unit also operated from the station in June.

Ream had expanded from the original 140 to 630 Navy-owned acres. The airfield had one 5,000 and three 2,500-ft. x 500-ft. asphalt runways. In March 1944, personnel stood at 324 officers and 2567 enlisted men while barracks existed for only 254 officers and 1800 men. Station aircraft usually consisted of a GH Howard or a GB Staggerwing Beech and a J2F Duck.

In June 1949, the Navy inactivated the field making it an ALF of San Diego. The Korean War brought renewed activity as the first helicopter squadron arrived in October 1950. Ream eventually became home base for all helicopter squadrons of the Pacific Fleet and was known as "Helicopter Capital." The station was redesignated NAAS Imperial Beach in July 1955. The Vietnam War brought modernization with additional construction including a new hangar and a 500-man barracks.

On January 1, 1968, the Navy upgraded the station to an NAS. The end of the Vietnam War caused Imperial Beach to be disestablished on December 31, 1974, and the facility became an ALF once again. Today, Imperial Beach is used by helicopters from North Island and as a Navy Supply Center.

Motley dressed group of ground crewmen and pilots holding an informal debriefing on ramp following flight. *NATIONAL ARCHIVES*

JANUARY 1944 NATIONAL ARCHIVES

NAAS Rodd Field, Texas

Construction on P-1, an initial auxiliary of the Corpus Christi training complex, began in August 1940. The site, located five miles west of Mainside, consisted of 860 acres of farm land and pasture. Construction also included a 2.75-mile spur of the Texas-Mexican Railroad and an all-weather road to the other auxiliaries, Cabaniss and Cuddihy. On June 7, 1941, the airfield opened at the station as the primary training squadron, VN-11A, transferred from Mainside. The Navy named the station in honor of Lt. Herbert C. Rodd who lost his life in a 1932 aircraft accident at Norfolk. Lt. Rodd had previously received the Navy Cross for his role as radio officer of NC-4 on the transatlantic flight in 1919. One month later, the station added a second primary training squadron, VN-11C. On August 25, 1941, Rodd became home for Corpus Christi's Instructor School, at that time training instructors for primary and intermediate training.

At the outset, the station opened with a minimum of facilities -- the perimeter fence was not completed. Part of the land the station occupied had been used for the grazing of goats which remained on the adjacent property. The first time aircraft were left on the station overnight, the goats wandered onto the airfield. Attracted by the glue used on the fabric, the goats, to the Navy's dismay, chewed some of the fabric off the airplanes. Guards were posted at night until completion of the fence.

The station commissioned an NAAS on October 12, 1942. Up to then, Rodd had been administratively under the command of NAS Corpus Christi. On March 15, 1943, primary training ended at Rodd. In the place of VN-11A and VN-11C, the Navy commissioned basic training squadron VN-12F the same day -- only to decommission the squadron sixteen days later. Then, squadron VN-18C moved aboard with SNBs and the multi-engine land syllabus. VN-18C formed at Corpus Christi on February 22, 1943, with PBYs. In conjunction with the multi-engine syllabus, a celestial navigation school was also added including the construction of six Celestial Navigation Trainer towers. On April 4, 1943, VN-14B, a fighter training squadron, transferred aboard from Kingsville. Fourteen months later, VN-14B moved to Mainside.

In January 1945, VN-18C instructed 250 cadets with an aircraft complement of 100 SNBs. At the same time, the Instructors School had 90 prospective instructors. In May 1945, VN-18C decommissioned. In the course of the squadron's existence, VN-18C graduated 4121 multi-engine students while 91 failed and three were killed. The Instructor School closed three months later.

Initially, Rodd had two circular landing mats for primary trainers. Later, four 5,000-ft. asphalt runways were built over the mats to accommodate SNVs, SNJs and SNBs. The station had eight OLFs assigned. Complement in March 1944, numbered 371 officers, 364 cadets, and 1179 enlisted men. Available billeting could accommodate 253 officers, 670 cadets, and 1439 enlisted. At its peak, multi-engine training utilized over 100 SNBs, while the Instructor School operated over 120 aircraft including SNBs, SNJs, SNVs, and N2Ss. Although the N2S Stearmans were not a specific part of Intermediate Training, they were used for certain maneuvers such as the inverted spin checkout.

On August 15, 1945, VN-14A commissioned at Rodd and instructed the CV syllabus. VN-14A remained on board until decommissioned in February 1946. The station then became home for basic training with the reformed squadrons VN-1A and VN-1B. In March 1947, the station implemented Project X-ray, which experimented with giving primary training in the SNJ. The Navy found that more students failed primary training; however, the overall flight training failure rate remained essentially the same. In this respect the program was a success, since the weak student failed sooner in the program -- a benefit to the Navy and the student.

A group of South American cadets enjoy a volleyball game.   *MAY 1943 NATIONAL ARCHIVES*

On June 24, 1947, all flight operations ended. The station closed four months later. Rodd then became an OLF for Corpus Christi. With the beginning of the United States' space program in the 1950s, NASA took over the field for a space surveillance radar site remaining here through the 1970's. In 1997, the property is owned by the City of Corpus Christi. A public park, presently here, has several athletic fields and a radio-controlled airplane facility, as well as other recreational activities.

Both N2S Stearmans and N3Ns were being used at Rodd in November 1942. Students were organized into Morning and Afternoon wings. The Morning Wing flew in AM and attended classes or other activities in the PM. The Afternoon Wing did the opposite. *NATIONAL ARCHIVES*

ABOVE AND ABOVE RIGHT: Additional scenes at Rodd in November 1942. Enlisted men act as taxi guides into Rodd's crowded ramp to avoid accidents. Aircraft in use at this time were a mixed bag of N2S Stearmans and N3Ns. The novice often mistakingly refers to the N3N as the Stearman. The distinguishing features are the N3N's larger front wheel hubs, rounded vertical stabilizer, and double rear wing struts.

NATIONAL ARCHIVES

RIGHT: Officer monitors flight operations in case of an accident. Primary training was conducted without the use of two-way radio communications. *NATIONAL ARCHIVES*

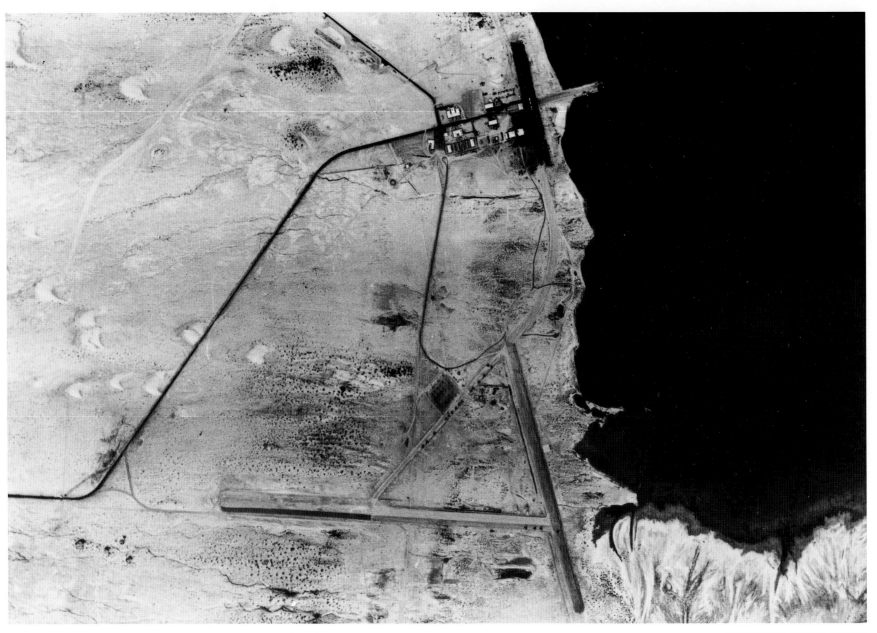

DECEMBER 1944 NATIONAL ARCHIVES

NAAS Salton Sea, California

The Salton Sink was a depression in the Imperial Valley of California, 280 ft. below sea level, containing salt marshes and seasonal shallow lakes. In 1905, during the construction of irrigation canals, the Colorado River broke through dikes flooding the Sink. By the time the Colorado was returned to its original course two years later, a lake 42 miles long, 10 to 16 miles wide, with a maximum depth of 93 feet, had been created. The lake, known as the Salton Sea, receded until 1920, when it stabilized to the size of 30 miles long, 8 to 10 miles wide, with a maximum depth of 37 ft.

The Navy first came to the Sea in 1939, when the northeast corner of the lake was used as a seaplane operational area with bombing targets and for emergency landings. Navy crews utilized Eiler's Salton Sea Resort, near Mecca, California for overnight lodging. Eiler's employees provided a boat to bring the Navy crews ashore from the moored seaplanes. In 1940, the Navy and the Coast Guard agreed to share the cost of constructing a facility at a better location. After the outbreak of war, the Navy constructed a seaplane base on the southwest shore commissioning an NAF there on October 8, 1942. Planned as a training base for 12 seaplanes, the first four PBYs arrived three weeks later. The Navy also used the facility as a seaplane ferry stop and as a weather alternate for seaplanes when San Diego became fogged in. Later that year, Paramount Studios built a 4,000-ft. clay airstrip at the site for the filming of the motion picture *Wake Island*.

A change of mission occurred in March 1944, when VT-20 deployed to the base for rocket training. An additional 56 squadrons received rocket training. Along with the carrier squadrons came a detachment of CASU 53 from Holtville in support. Meanwhile, the station upgraded to an NAAS and added another runway. In July 1944, the Navy conducted the test-ing of rocket assisted takeoffs (JATO) at the base. Rocket training continued to the end of the war. In December 1944, B-29s of the 509th Composite Squadron from Wendover AAF, Utah made over 150 drops at the facility, testing the prototype atomic bomb shapes. The Navy finally disestablished NAAS Salton Sea on November 13, 1946; however, an emergency seaplane facility consisting of a radio beacon, a light beacon, a boat house, and a lighted 10,000-ft. seadrome was manned and maintained. The facility was active until 1967 -- as long as seaplanes remained in the Naval inventory.

With a field elevation of 245 ft. below sea level, Salton Sea was the second lowest elevation airfield in the U.S. with a 4,000 by 200-ft. and a 4,900 by 300-ft. clay runway. In March 1944, base personnel numbered 85 officers and 465 enlisted men with barracks for 72 officers and 566 men. The station operated a Piper AE ambulance plane, a GH Howard transport, a Grumman J2F Duck rescue amphibian, and 12 crash boats. CASU 53 used one SBD and up to 13 TBMs in its rocket training support role.

Following the Navy's departure, the base was taken over by the Atomic Energy Commission and used to test inert nuclear weapons drops from 1946 to 1961. NAF El Centro then took over the facility using it for parachute tests of the manned space program and other military systems until 1979. In the meantime, the Marines and Navy Seals also conducted training exercises at the location. Today, the former base is abandoned and will probably become a wildlife refuge in the future.

Salton Sea's landplane area -- 57 squadrons received rocket training here. *DECEMBER 1944 NATIONAL ARCHIVES*

ABOVE: Salton Sea's seaplane ramp was long and narrow -- resembling a runway. After someone probably landed on the ramp, a large "DO NOT LAND HERE" was added.

MARCH 1944 NATIONAL ARCHIVES

ABOVE LEFT AND LEFT: The first amphibious PBY-5A was delivered prior to the beginning of the war. PBY operations were greatly simplified since the aircraft could enter and exit the water without the aid of beaching crews. However, the extra weight of the landing gear caused a performance penalty. *NATIONAL ARCHIVES*

Operations with non-amphibious PBY models required crews to attach and remove beaching gear. By the end of the war, most non-amphibious versions had been retired with the exception of those in the Training Command. *NMNA*

MAY 1944 NATIONAL ARCHIVES

NAAS San Clemente Island, California

San Clemente Island, located 75 miles west of San Diego, is 25 miles long and two to five miles wide. The 56 sq. mi. island received its present name when sighted by the Spanish explorer Vizcaino on November 25, 1602, Saint Clement's Day. During the 1800s and the early 1900s, the island, used for sheep grazing, was also frequented by fisherman and smugglers. San Clemente, under the jurisdiction of the Navy, had a fleet training facility at Wilson Cove. A small crushed rock and shell air strip, built in 1933, was also used by the Marines. These two facilities were connected by a six-mile macadam road. In late 1938, a project began to improve the existing airfield. The WPA and a civilian contractor built a 3000-ft. and a 2000-ft. runway plus a hangar. The runways were available for use in December 1939. The remainder of the project reached completion in July 1941.

In January 1942, a Marine scouting squadron with 19 Vought SB2U Vindicators and one J2F Grumman Duck operated from the airfield. The next month another project commenced to extend the runways and make additional improvements. In March, a 200-man Army detachment set up two radar stations on the island. Two months later, the Marines returned for flight operations with the establishment of an antiaircraft machine gun training unit. The Marines utilized J2F Ducks for target towing.

In February 1943, the Navy commissioned NAAF San Clemente Island. The location was evaluated for blimp operations and deemed, at that time, to be unsuitable due to strong and unpredictable winds. In March, the Bureau of Ordnance came to the station for a two month period to test 1600-lb. bombs. VJ-7 supported the project with two PBY-5As. In July, the Navy formed a Combat Information Center (CIC) - Team Training Unit. The unit's syllabus consisted of a three-week course training 589 offi-

cers and 1914 men during its existence. The next month, this unit trained the first of seven ARGUS units. ARGUS was a shore-based radar unit that provided the CIC mission for island bases. Airborne radar targets for training were provided by VJ-7 with two PBY-5As and 12 SBDs.

In January 1944, Seabees built two permanent radar installations on the island. The next month, the Navy upgraded San Clemente to an NAAS. Beginning in April, fighter components of VC squadrons started using the station for gunnery training. A total of 10 groups of 10 to 15 FM-2s, supported by San Diego's CASU 5, trained at the base during 1944. In June, the Navy established a Special Projects School for Air that taught radio and radar countermeasures. The School utilized 15 SNBs and trained 44 teams during the war.

In early 1945, the Navy rebuilt the runways. On April 15, an Airborne Early Warning Training Unit began operations from the station. In June, this unit operated one SNJ, three TBM-3Es, and nine TBM-3Ws. Also that month, LTA began operations at San Clemente, as blimps from Santa Ana and Del Mar averaged three landings a week.

San Clemente had three asphalt runways -- the longest 5,000 ft. On the northern tip of the island was Castle Field, a dirt strip used for emergencies. In March 1944, station personnel numbered 117 officers and 749 men with barracks for 100 officers and 600 men. The station usually had a J2F Duck, but in mid-1944 also had a GH ambulance plane.

Following the war, San Clemente became an ALF to San Diego and remains so to this day. The Navy has since abandoned the WW II station site and built an 8,000-ft. runway at the former Castle Field. In 1961, the Navy named the facility Frederick Sherman Field in honor of the three-time winner of the Navy Cross and carrier task group commander during WW II.

The TBM-3W, similar to the above aircraft, was equipped with the APS-20 search radar. *NATIONAL ARCHIVES*

APRIL 1944 NATIONAL ARCHIVES

NAS San Diego, California

North Island lies between San Diego Bay and the Pacific Ocean southwest of the city. In the winter of 1910-1911, Glenn Curtiss set up winter quarters for his flying school on the island. Navy Lt. T. G. Ellyson, the first student of Curtiss's new class, crashed on January 18, 1911, when he inadvertently became airborne during taxi practice. This inauspicious beginning was the first aircraft piloted by a Navy man. Lt. Ellyson would go on to become Naval Aviator #1. Another first occurred here on January 26, when Glenn Curtiss made a successful hydroplane flight. In January 1912, Curtiss offered to donate facilities for a Naval aviation base. The entire Navy aviation contingent consisting of Ellyson, John Rodgers, John Towers, and Victor Herbster remained at North Island for three months before moving to Annapolis, Maryland.

In November 1913, the Army Signal Corps established an aviation school on North Island. With the United States' entry into WW I, the government purchased the property. The Army named the base Rockwell Field on July 20, 1917, in honor of 2Lt. Louis Rockwell killed in an aircraft crash in 1912. The next month, the Army changed the mission of the base from primary to pursuit and gunnery training. In November, the Navy took over the former Curtiss facilities and commissioned NAS San Diego. During WW I, the Navy conducted training for mechanics and preliminary training for pilots, starting a new class every two weeks.

The Army and Navy continued joint occupancy of North Island following the war -- the Army controlled 725 acres and the Navy 550. Hap Arnold served as the Army C.O. on two occasions. During the 1920s, many aviation firsts and records made history here. On September 5, 1922, the Army's Jimmy Doolittle landed after setting a transcontinental record flight of 22 hours and nine minutes. The

next June, Naval aviators set several world seaplane records. In October 1924, the dirigible *Shenandoah* paid a visit to the station with RAdm. Moffett on board -- 25,000 people gathered for the occasion. Later that year, the first night catapult launch took place, followed the next year by the first night carrier landing. Charles Lindbergh departed from North Island in the Ryan *Spirit of St. Louis* en route to New York for his attempted solo flight across the Atlantic. In 1935, President Roosevelt approved an agreement in which the Navy traded Moffett Field to the Army in exchange for Rockwell Field; Bolling Field, D.C.; and Ford Island, Honolulu. After taking over the Army's facilities, the Navy gradually built up the station. The first big contract for construction was let on July 6, 1940, including additional hangars, a carrier pier, and runway paving.

After the beginning of the war, the Navy built up San Diego into one of the largest, if not the largest, NAS in the U. S. Navy's establishment. The headquarters of the Commander of the Naval Air Forces - Pacific and the Commander of Fleet Air West Coast were located at San Diego. In 1942, NATS established a terminal on the station. During 1942, San Diego opened auxiliaries at Los Alamitos and the Salton Sea. On October 12, the Naval Air Center San Diego was created to command the Naval aviation complex in Southern California. The largest growth of the Air Center took place in 1943 as the training command and aircraft manufacturers reached full production. During the year, auxiliaries were added at Camp Kearny, Brown Field, Ream Field, San Clemente Island, and Holtville. The next year, the Navy took over the former Army airfields at 29 Palms, Ventura, and San Nicolas Island. In early 1945, San Diego opened its last auxiliary of the war at Thermal, also a former Army airfield. The war ended with the F8F Bearcat equipped VF-18 and VBF-18 aboard.

The activity at San Diego during the war can be judged by some of the statistics -- the numbers speak for themselves. The tower logged an average of 1400 to 1800 takeoffs per day for a wartime total of 1,203,032 takeoffs and 1,196,837 landings. An average of 1200 aircraft were on board at any time with 2538 present on VJ-Day. A total of 30,269 aircraft were ferried to/from the station and 13,891 loaded on ships. An estimated 350,000 men received training on the station. These included 16,000 enlisted air gunners and 4,000 pilots.

The station grew in proportion. The airfield had the world's largest paved landing area including two 6,000-ft. heavy duty concrete runways. By the end of the war, San Diego had four aircraft carrier piers, 20 hangars, and one of the largest Assembly and Repair Departments in the Navy. Peak Naval personnel reached over 14,000 plus an additional 8,000 civilians. NATS occupied two hangars with the capacity to handle six transports at one time. The total investment reached $57.5 million.

Following WW II, San Diego maintained its prominent role in Naval aviation. In 1955, the station was renamed NAS North Island. In 1961, to resolve an in-house dispute between Pensacola and San Diego concerning the early days of Naval aviation, the House Committee of the Armed Services passed a resolution recognizing North Island as "The Birthplace of Naval Aviation." Pensacola had to settle for "The Cradle of Naval Aviation."

In 1996, North Island was home to 23 squadrons and 50 other commands. The station serves as homeport for the USS *Kitty Hawk* and USS *Constellation* as well as headquarters for Naval Air Force Pacific and Third Fleet. The Naval Aviation Depot employs over 3,800 civilians. When all ships are in port, base population reaches over 30,000.

ABOVE: Portion of seaplane ramp in April 1944.   *NATIONAL ARCHIVES*

ABOVE LEFT: The aircraft pool at San Diego in April 1944.   *NATIONAL ARCHIVES*

LEFT: Photograph taken during the filming of the motion picture *Dive Bomber* at San Diego in the early 1940s.   *NATIONAL ARCHIVES*

ABOVE: VD-1 conducts recognition training at San Diego in July 1942.

NATIONAL ARCHIVES

ABOVE RIGHT: Truck-mounted upper turret. Over 16,000 enlisted gunners were trained at San Diego during the war. *NATIONAL ARCHIVES*

RIGHT: VF-66 Ryan FR Fireball at San Diego in July 1945. With a Wright R-1820 in the nose and a General Electric J-31 turbojet in the tail, the Fireball was the Navy's first jet. The 66 produced were used on an experimental basis providing the Navy with jet aircraft experience. *NATIONAL ARCHIVES*

JANUARY 1945   NATIONAL ARCHIVES

NAAS San Nicolas Island, California

San Nicolas Island, approximately nine miles long and four miles wide, lies in the Santa Barbara Channel 75 miles west of Los Angeles. The island, first discovered in 1543 by the Spanish explorer Ferrer, received its present name when sighted by Vizcaino on Saint Nicholas's Day, December 6, 1602. Local Indians were present until 1835 when they were moved to the mainland by the government. During the 1800s, smugglers used the island to avoid custom duties. The island was also used by fisherman, as well as for sheep and goat grazing. Although low scrub oaks originally covered the landscape, most were destroyed by the goats.

In the 1920s or early 1930s, the CAA built two emergency dirt landing strips 2300 and 2100 ft. long. In January 1933, the CAA relinquished the airstrips as the Navy took over ownership of the island. In 1939, a Naval weather station was established issuing daily weather reports to NAS San Diego.

In late 1942, the U.S. Army Air Corps determined a requirement to build an interceptor base for the air defense of Southern California. The Navy gave the Army permission to build the base providing the Navy could also use the facility. By the time construction reached completion, the Army no longer had a need for the base turning it over to the Navy. Used for patrol aircraft, training, and other activities, the station commissioned on September 26, 1944, an auxiliary of NAS San Diego. In November 1944, ACORN 46 trained at the station followed by ACORN 45. The ACORNs, Seabee units from Port Hueneme, built and operated small advanced air bases. PB4Ys from Camp Kearny used the base for training and staging until the end of the war. Carrier aircraft from Southern California stations also utilized the airfield for training.

NAAS San Nicolas consisted of the island's entire 13,370 acres. The airfield's single Army-built 6250 x 150-ft. runway had several hardstands. Station complement numbered 121 officers, 312 enlisted men, and nine civilians with barracks for 100 officers and 346 enlisted men. A 30-man dispensary and an auditorium with a 300-person capacity also existed. The station aircraft were usually a Grumman J4F Widgeon amphibian and a TBF Avenger.

Following the war, the Navy decided to locate all testing of pilotless aircraft and missiles on the West Coast. The site chosen was Pt. Mugu, 65 miles northwest of Los Angeles. San Nicolas Island was a major factor in this choice since it was an ideal location for placement of radar and telemetry equipment to observe missile testing in Pt. Mugu's 100-mile long range. Initially, the Navy spent $5 million upgrading the facilities. San Nicolas was officially disestablished as an NAAS on December 15, 1946, becoming an Auxiliary Landing Field of Pt. Mugu.

Today, San Nicolas is an integral part of the Pacific Missile Range. In the intervening years, the runway has been improved and extended to 10,000 ft. Besides radar and telemetry facilities, the island also has several target sites used in missile testing.

PB4Ys from Camp Kearny used San Nicolas for training.
NATIONAL ARCHIVES

One of the station's aircraft was a Grumman J4F Widgeon.
NATIONAL ARCHIVES

JULY 1943 NATIONAL ARCHIVES

NAS Santa Ana, California

The Navy's Lighter-than-Air master plan called for three blimp bases on the West Coast -- one north of the existing Moffett and one to the south. Congress appropriated funds for the stations in July 1941. In southern California's rural Orange County, a 1606-acre site was chosen 35 miles southeast of Los Angeles and 10 miles inland. Modeled on South Weymouth and Weeksville, construction began in April 1942, three and a half miles southeast of the town of Santa Ana. The property had been cultivated for years so little was required to prepare it for construction.

Although the hangars had not been completed, the station and ZP-31 commissioned on October 7, 1942, only six months after ground breaking. On October 19, L-8 of Moffett's ZP-32 became the first blimp to land. Incidentally, L-8 had previously distinguished itself as the infamous "Ghost Ship" (see Treasure Island). ZP-31 received its first blimp on November 11, with the arrival of K-20, the first ship assembled on the West Coast (see Moffett). On November 28, 1942, an Army P-38 from the nearby Orange County airport crashed into a concrete door pylon of an unfinished hangar, killing the pilot.

The building of two wooden blimp hangars was aided by a movable scaffold, mounted on 18 railroad flatcars. The location was considerably less than ideal for blimp operations, since the area was subject to strong desert winds, coincidentally known as "Santa Anas." Twice during construction, erected hangar trusses were felled. On January 23, 1943, an 85-mph gust of wind blew down a truss. Two weeks later, another gust moved the scaffold train pulling down three more trusses.

In 1943, Santa Ana realized the need for two auxiliary facilities. In May 1943, the station sent 14 men to establish an auxiliary at Lompoc, California, 140 miles northwest of Los Angeles near Pt. Auguello. One month later, a similar complement was sent to Del Mar, another auxiliary just north of San Diego. On August 16, 1943, VJ-8 with nine officers and 66 enlisted men arrived at Santa Ana establishing a target drone school. The next month a detachment of Blimp Headquarters Squadron Three formed to support ZP-31.

The year of 1944 was somewhat uneventful. VJ-11 replaced VJ-8, and by September had a complement of 14 officers and 148 men. At this time, VJ-11 operated one JRF, 2 SNBs, one SNJ, eight TDC drones, 11 TD2C drones, and 70 SO3Cs. Due to the unsatisfactory performance of the SO3C Curtiss Seamew, the Navy converted many into radio-controlled drones, finding a use for the aircraft.

On May 5, 1945, K-51 experienced an in-flight fire that killed eight of the nine-man crew. K-51 had dumped fuel in preparation for landing and inadvertently descended into the gasoline vapor subsequently ignited by the engines. MCAS El Toro is only seven miles southeast of Santa Ana and in June, a Marine fighter replacement squadron, VMF-462, was on board the station with 21 Corsairs. Also in June, ZP-31 received its first new "M" ships. During the war, Metro-Goldwyn-Mayer used the station to make two motion pictures -- a Navy training film and the commercial production *This Man's Navy*. In September, Lompoc and Del Mar closed.

Santa Ana initially cost $11 million to build. One-half of that cost went for the two 1000-ft. wooden blimp hangars. The airfield amounted to a 2,000-ft. diameter circle asphalt landing mat with six-mooring circles. Although the base originally had billeting for a total of 456 men, by March 1944, barracks had grown to accommodate 152 officers and 1242 enlisted men. The maximum number of blimps present reached 14 K and L ships. The station usually operated one GB Staggerwing for transport.

Following the war, all blimp squadrons decommissioned except two which included Santa Ana's ZP-31 renamed ZP-1. Santa Ana also became an aircraft storage facility in November 1945. Finally in August 1947, the Navy relocated ZP-1 to Weeksville, N. C. and all blimp operations on the West Coast ended. On June 6, 1949, Santa Ana decommissioned becoming an OLF. For a time, the hangars were used by advertising blimps.

The station reopened during the Korean War. Blimp operations staged a brief resurrection when the Navy established a two-blimp Naval Air Reserve Training Unit (NARTU) on April 1, 1951. The Marines arrived the next month establishing a helicopter air facility. West Coast blimp operations ended for good in June 1956, when the Navy disestablished the NARTU. In 1969, the Marines elevated Santa Ana to an MCAS only to change the name to Tustin the next year. In 1975, Malcolm Forbes used a hangar for his attempted balloon flight to Europe. The same year, Universal Pictures used the station for the filming of *The Hindenburg*.

The 1993 Defense Base Realignment and Closure Commission has recommended the closure of Tustin and El Toro. Both stations, in the country when built 50 years ago, are today surrounded by the urban growth of Orange County. Tustin and El Toro are scheduled for relocating to Miramar and other stations during 1997. The two blimp hangars are still in existence, but reportedly in need of repairs that is estimated to cost $10 million initially, plus a continuing annual maintenance expenditure of $500,000. Although designated as National Historic Landmarks, the hangars razing is also being considered -- at a cost of $5 million.

MAY 1944 NATIONAL ARCHIVES

NAAS Santa Rosa, California

In 1942, the Navy traveled to Sonoma County, northwest of San Francisco Bay, and purchased property to build a main station and an OLF. Construction of the proposed NAAS began in November 1942, near the small town of Cotati, eight miles south of Santa Rosa. The next month, work began on an OLF 2.5 miles southwest of Santa Rosa. When drainage problems were encountered at Cotati, the Navy reversed the plans developing Santa Rosa as the main station and Cotati as the OLF. NAAS Santa Rosa commissioned on June 29, 1943, an auxiliary of Alameda.

Beginning on August 6, the station's first tenant, CASU 13, arrived for training prior to embarking for the South Pacific. CASU 13, departed on September 20, and four days later, CASU 18 arrived. CASU 18's stay lasted less than a month when it also departed. On October 20, CASU 36 commissioned and was permanently based at the station to support the carrier squadrons present. For the next few months, several squadrons were aboard including VT-2, VB-2, VB-11, VF-28, and VC-4.

Starting in January 1944, the first of three shore-based support squadrons arrived for several months of operational training. These squadrons, VB-301, VB-302, and VB-303, operated SBDs -- the last one departed May 3. CAG 6, reformed at Alameda in April, transferred to Santa Rosa on May 10, and conducted operational training for the next six months. About the same time, an expansion program doubled the station's aircraft capacity. In September, the first unit of CAG 5, VT-5, came aboard. After CAG 6 left in November, CAG 5's remaining squadrons, VF-5 and VB-5, transferred in. The next two months, Marine fighter squadrons VMF-452 and VMF-214, assigned to CAG 5, joined the air group at Santa Rosa for training. CAG 5, along with the Marine squadrons, embarked on the *Franklin*

February 8, 1945. CAG 19 replaced CAG 5 later in February with a new VBF bomber/fighter squadron of F6Fs. VF-19 received the Navy's first F8F Bearcats in May. The war ended before the Bearcats reached the combat area. Santa Rosa finished out the war with CAG 11's and VBF-151 aboard.

Santa Rosa's 498 acres had two 7,000 x 200-ft. concrete runways plus a catapult and arresting gear system. Total Navy investment in the facility topped $4.5 million. In a rather mundane matter, the Navy sold hay cut on the property in May 1945 for $51. The station had two OLFs -- Cotati and Little River OLF in Mendocino County to the north. The Navy leased the airport at Little River in January 1945, as an emergency field for the numerous flights between Santa Rosa and the rocket training station at Arcata.

Santa Rosa's status changed from an NAAS to an OLF of Alameda in 1947. The station saw renewed activity during the Korean War by ADs, F4Us, and F9Fs. Following the Korean War, the Navy deeded the facility to the City of Santa Rosa. The airport was known as the Santa Rosa Air Center and remained open until 1993. In 1996, the property was in the hands of developers. The airfield at Cotati is also no longer in existence -- the property is occupied by a K-Mart and industry. During the war, the Army developed Santa Rosa's existing municipal airport, seven miles northwest, as an AAF. Today, that airfield, Sonoma County, serves as Santa Rosa's municipal airport.

Open House for the public at Santa Rosa after VJ-Day, 1945.   *USN*

NAS Seattle, Washington

Seattle's City fathers first realized the need for a municipal airport during WW I, when Army aviators on a war bond drive had to land on a golf course. It was not until 1920, however, that King County purchased property to develop an airport. The land consisted of a 268-acre peninsula in Lake Washington, a former picnic area 6.5 miles north of town, known as Sand Point. The County had been further motivated by the needs of the Boeing Company. Boeing, created in 1916, had only built seaplanes up until this time. With a contract for Army landplanes in hand, Boeing needed an airfield.

In June 1920, the airfield opened as King County Airport. That same year the Navy inspected the site to determine the feasibility of establishing an air station. The County was agreeable and proposed to deed the land to the Navy, provided it was developed as an air station. After Congress failed to provide funding for the Navy, the Army leased the airport from the County and built a hangar. In 1922, Congress finally appropriated $800,000 for the Navy to develop the airfield also to be used by the Army. The station was slow growing with the first hangar reaching completion in April 1924. The first leg of the Army's epic around-the-world flight departed on April 6. The Army returned after circling the globe 175 days later! During 1927-29, funds were appropriated to further develop 400 acres and build a railroad spur. On November 22, 1928, the Navy commissioned NAS Seattle with Naval Reserve Aviation Base (NRAB) Seattle as a subordinate command. Beginning in November 1935, VP-35 was based at the station. The commissioning of VP-17 took place in January 1937.

Meanwhile, the station continued to serve as Seattle's municipal airport. On August 3, 1938, a Pan American Sikorsky S-43 amphibian began air mail service to Alaska. This service was provided by Pacific Alaska Airways, a Pan American subsidiary. Also in 1938, the station added another 31 acres spending $300,000 on improvements. In July 1940, construction began on a $4 million project including the first paved runways. In October 1941, civilian activities at the station ended as Pan Am moved to the modernized Boeing Field. Meanwhile, the activities of NRAB Seattle continued with the conduction of the Navy's Elimination Training Course. In 1941, the NRAB began full primary training. In September, two Russian PBYs with 38 men visited the station.

With the beginning of the war, Seattle continued to grow in size and importance. The NRAB, finding expansion of primary training impossible due to congestion and weather, moved to Pasco, Washington on July 31, 1942. During 1941 and 1942, the NRAB trained 500 cadets. On October 12, 1942, Naval Air Center Seattle was created and vested with the command of all Naval aviation activities in Washington and Oregon. As location for headquarters of the 13th Naval District, Seattle also commanded all Naval activities in Alaska. Alameda's VR-2 provided NATS service to Alaska through the station. On November 2, 1942, CASU 7 commissioned to provide support for the carrier squadrons on the base.

In May 1943, the station added another 16 acres at a cost of $18,000. On June 24, VR-5 formed out of a VR-2 Detachment taking over the routes previously flown by VR-2 to Alaska. VR-5 aircraft complement consisted of 16 R4Ds and four R5Ds providing service between San Diego and Attu, Alaska. A $600,000 NATS hangar was also built. In April 1944, the creation of the 17th Naval District for Alaska relieved Seattle's 13th District of some command and administrative duties. By September 1944, 48 squadrons and CAGS had passed through the station. Three months later, the base grew to

1880 officers and men plus 2480 civilians who were mainly employed by the station's Assembly and Repair Department. By the end of the year, Naval investment at Seattle topped $20 million.

During the course of the war, the station had served as homeport for 36 VC squadrons, four CAGs, 11 VPB squadrons, VR-5, CASU 7, three utility squadrons, three scouting squadrons, the Fleet Air Wings, and two headquarters squadrons. Pan American was also present on contract to the Navy with 13 aircraft, mostly R4Ds. Seattle ultimately had five runways, the longest 5,000 ft. plus seaplane facilities. The station had three auxiliaries at Arlington, Quillayute, and Shelton, Washington. Of the 478 acres, the Navy owned 471, leasing the remainder. On VJ-Day base complement stood at 211 officers, 2850 enlisted men, and 2435 civilians. Aircraft present totaled 443 including CASU 7's pool of 222, the Assembly and Repair Dept.'s pool of 123, and 19 miscellaneous types operated by the station.

Following the war, Seattle continued as the base for various fleet air units while adding Naval reserve flying. Eventually, the station became strictly a Naval reserve base also commanding small reserve units at Spokane, Washington and Salem, Oregon. By the end of the 1960's, the geographically restrained station had become expendable, since its runways were inadequate for jet aircraft. On July 1, 1970, all reserve flying transferred to Whidbey Island and Seattle became a Naval support facility.

In 1997, the Naval Support Activity Seattle and the National Oceanic and Atmospheric Administration are located on the property, although the majority of the former air station is a public park and marina. A 1996 overfly of Sand Point by the Author indicated that the runways have been removed, but most of the former base's buildings and hangars remain.

ABOVE: Pan Am Boeing B-314 at Sand Point in June 1938. Civilian aircraft operated from the station until October 1941. *NATIONAL ARCHIVES*

ABOVE LEFT: The ramp at Sand Point in July 1943. *NATIONAL ARCHIVES*

LEFT: The raging U-boats offensive off the U.S. coast prompted the Navy to order the Boeing PBB-1 Sea Ranger in June 1940. The Navy built a factory for the PBB at Renton south of Seattle. The prototype took to the air in July 1942. British success with land-based patrol bombers and the desire of the Army for additional B-29 manufacturing facilities, prompted the Navy to reach an agreement with the Army. In exchange for B-24s, B-25s, and B-34s from the Army, the Navy cancelled the PBB and turned the Renton plant over for B-29 production. The single XPBB, dubbed the "Lone Ranger," visited NAS Seattle in February 1943. *NATIONAL ARCHIVES*

OPPOSITE PAGE: Flight of F6F-3s from Seattle in September 1943. National insignia has the red border used from July to August 1943. The F6F-3s are easily distinguished from later models by the extra window behind the cockpit. *NATIONAL ARCHIVES*

ABOVE: R3D with Mt. Rainier in the background in November 1944. Douglas only built 12 DC-5s. The Navy and the Marines operated eight during the war as the R3D. *NATIONAL ARCHIVES*

ABOVE LEFT: A VR-5 R4D in olive-drab paint over the mountains. *JULY 1943 NATIONAL ARCHIVES*

LEFT: Prospective Naval Aviation Cadets, called "Tarmacs," drill at Seattle while awaiting assignment to Pre-Flight School. *FEBRUARY 1944 NATIONAL ARCHIVES*

ABOVE: Tired PBYs from the war at Seattle in August 1944.
NATIONAL ARCHIVES

ABOVE RIGHT: Seattle's ramp in December 1944.
NATIONAL ARCHIVES

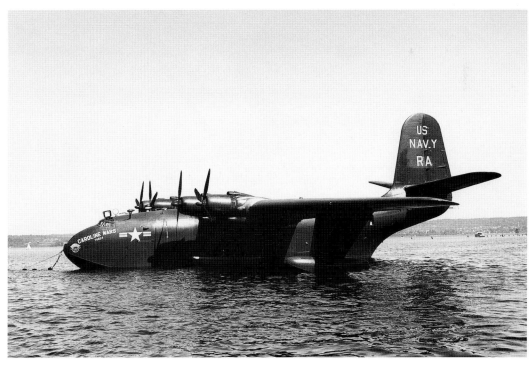

RIGHT: The last JRM produced, the *Caroline Mars,* visits Lake Washington in the late 1940s. *NATIONAL ARCHIVES*

NAS Shawnee, Oklahoma

The land on which NAS Shawnee would be located began its days in public service, as the pasture for horses of Shawnee's horse-drawn fire engine. The City retained the 80-acre tract after obtaining a motorized fire engine and established a landing field on the property in the 1920s. In the early 1940s, Regan Flying Service operated a Contract Pilot School for the Army with J-3 Piper Cubs.

In December 1942, the Navy chose the airport, 2.5 miles northwest of town, as location for a Marine Corps glider base. The Navy leased the 361-acre airfield from the City and purchased an additional 92 acres for $16,000. The Navy insisted the Regan Flying Service move, so the City purchased land eight miles north of Shawnee for Regan and established an airfield there known as Shawnee Municipal Airport #2. The Navy began construction on Shawnee in April 1943, spending a total of $1.7 million to complete the station. Meanwhile, the Marine glider program cancelled.

The station commissioned as an NAAF of NAS Norman, Oklahoma on August 31, 1943, under the command of the Naval Air Primary Training Command (NAPT). Four N2S Stearmans from Norman landed for the commissioning ceremony. Initially, the Navy planned to transfer aircraft from NRAB Squantum to Shawnee. Furthermore, the base was planned to eventually accommodate 200 primary trainers. However, the Navy never used the station for that purpose as the Chief of NAPT declared the station unsuitable in December 1943.

Intended for gliders, and then primary training, the airfield retained its grass runways. In early 1944, the Navy added hard-surfaced runways. Shawnee transferred from the NAPT to the Naval Air Operational Training Command in March 1944. The Naval Air Navigation School (NANS) moved aboard from Hollywood, Florida with 30 SNBs. One month later, the station upgraded to an NAS. In the summer of 1944, the Navy faced a shortage of multi-engine pilots. Since the Navy employed pilots as navigators on its multi-engine aircraft, the shortage could be alleviated by training non-pilot navigators. Due to the cutback in the blimp program, former blimp pilots were also trained. During the winter of 1944-1945, the NANS planned to expand navigator training to 300 a month. Since facilities for 300 students did not exist at Shawnee, the Navy proposed establishing an additional ground school at Oklahoma A & M University in Stillwater. In the spring of 1945, R4Ds began to replace the SNBs. In March, the Navy changed the plan moving the entire NANS to NAS Clinton, Oklahoma. All training ceased on March 20, with Shawnee placed on caretaker status. The closure of Shawnee was somewhat of a curiosi- ty, since air stations were then being added on the West Coast. Why close an existing station containing a substantial monetary investment? One explanation could be location and/or the lack of gunnery and bombing ranges in the area.

Shawnee had three 4200 x 150-ft. asphalt runways. In March 1944, station personnel numbered 96 officers, 200 students, and 472 enlisted men. Berthing at that time was available for 50 officers, 232 students, and 678 enlisted men.

Today, the Shawnee Municipal Airport is a general aviation field with light industry. Very few Navy buildings have survived. The main gate house and columns of the gate with Naval wings embossed in the concrete remain. Someone has painted the wings blue, making them very noticeable.

Celestial navigation trainer had a moving map display for drift meter observations and a star projection on the ceiling on which a sextant could be used. The trainer was housed in a silo type building. *NATIONAL ARCHIVES*

MAY 1945 NATIONAL ARCHIVES

NAAS Shelton, Washington

Shelton is located 40 miles southwest of Seattle. In 1927, county commissioners set aside a portion of the local fairgrounds for a municipal airport. The airfield was named Sanderson Field, in honor of Marine pilot 1Lt. Lawson Sanderson. Born in Shelton, Sanderson was one of the area's most renowned athletes who starred for the University of Montana and Mare Island football teams. Sanderson went on to become a Major General in the Corps.

In July 1942, the Navy purchased 1098 acres including the airport for $16,000. In October, the Army and the Navy reached an agreement whereby the Army would develop the airfield with joint Navy use. The Army spent $500,000 constructing two 5,000-ft. runways, hardstands, and facilities for 50 officers and 400 enlisted men. The Army intended using the airfield for interceptors; however, by the time the airbase reached completion in March 1943, the threat of a Japanese invasion diminished and the Army need no longer existed. In July, the Navy took control of the base, reimbursing the Army for its monetary investment. The Navy agreed to allow Army use of the base if the need arose. The Navy added blimp facilities and commissioned NAAS Shelton on July 7, 1943, an auxiliary of NAS Seattle.

On August 14, 1943, the first squadron, VC-66 arrived on the station with a detachment of CASU 7 in support. VC-69 and VC-15 followed. Shelton was one of the foggiest airports in Washington. Weather remained a constant concern with the exception of the height of summer. This weather situation was not conducive for training of carrier aircraft squadrons. The last VC squadron departed on December 15, 1943, and for the remainder of the war, VJ utility squadrons made Shelton their home.

VJ-12 had arrived at Shelton on November 14, 1943, and VJ-13 commissioned at the station on January 3,

1944. After training VJ-13, VJ-12 departed in March 1944. The main mission of Shelton's utility squadrons was target towing, providing service for aircraft, ships, and an antiaircraft gunnery school. The primary customer was Pacific Beach, Washington, Antiaircraft Gunnery School that required four to seven missions a day, six days a week. The squadron, at times, also maintained detachments at Whidbey Island, Astoria, and Hoquiam Washington. The predominate aircraft for normal towing duties were SBDs and TBMs. The squadrons also employed Martin JM Marauders for high-speed towing missions. Aerial photography was a secondary mission provided. On one occasion, VJ-13 photographed a large portion of eastern Oregon. The squadrons also used a few other aircraft including one PBY, one JRC, and two J2F Ducks.

On September 13, 1944, VJ-10 joined VJ-13. K-71 of ZP-33 struck the mooring mast and deflated in

November. After training VJ-10, VJ-13 departed for the South Pacific leaving its aircraft behind for VJ-10 that remained on board to the end of the war.

Shelton had two 5,000 x 150-ft. asphalt runways and 25 Army-built hardstands. One hardstand was utilized as an aircraft bore sight and gunnery range. The Navy used two others for the station's tennis courts and a badminton/volley ball court. Shelton's complement reached a maximum of 150 officers, 1000 enlisted men, and 100 civilians. Barracks existed for 120 officers and 640 men. The station operated one GB Staggerwing Beech for light transport and a GH Howard hospital aircraft.

The Navy closed Shelton on December 15, 1945, eventually returning the airport to the County. In 1997, the airport is still known as Sanderson Field. The former barracks and administrative area has reverted to the Mason County Fairgrounds.

Shelton's ramp in July 1944.
NATIONAL ARCHIVES

SEPTEMBER 1942 NATIONAL ARCHIVES

NAS Sitka, Alaska

The Russians established a fort here in 1799, although the local Indians destroyed it in 1802. The Russians rebuilt the fort as New Archangel three years later. Sitka served as the capital of Russian America until Alaska was purchased by the U.S. in 1867. Sitka remained the capital of the Alaskan territory until 1906 when the government moved to Juneau. In 1890, the U.S. military acquired Sitka harbor's Japonksi Island and the Navy established a coaling station. During WW I, the Navy opened a small seaplane facility and commissioned an NAS for a short time.

Sitka reopened as an advanced seaplane base in 1937, as NAS Seattle's patrol squadrons deployed to the WW I facility. The Hepburn Board realized the strategic importance of Sitka and a contract was let on August 29, 1939, to build a modern air station and Naval operating base. The next month, on September 12, Sitka recommissioned as an NAS.

The Navy opened the Sitka section base here on September 24, 1941, only to redesignate it as a Naval operating base on July 20, 1942. Following the beginning of the war, Sitka opened auxiliaries at Annette Island, Port Althorp, and Yakutat. VS-70 moved to Sitka from Kodiak in March 1943. As the focus of the Alaskan campaign moved west to the Aleutians, Sitka lessened in operational use as well as strategic importance. On May 31, 1944, the Navy closed Sitka and its auxiliaries. The Navy's investment in the Sitka area was estimated at $32 million.

Sitka had three concrete ramps and two hangars. The station supported 12 observation floatplanes, 24 PBYs, and 18 carrier aircraft on an emergency basis. A 1500-ft. runway was laid out across the parking apron with an arresting gear to be used by carrier planes. Barracks had a capacity for 135 officers and 1113 enlisted men.

On October 19, 1977, the Coast Guard air station, located at Annette Island, moved to Sitka. In 1996, the station was home to three helicopters, 21 officers, and 103 enlisted men.

The Martin PMs of VP-17 at Sitka in November 1937.

NATIONAL ARCHIVES

Sitka's ramp is virtually deserted in September 1942.

NATIONAL ARCHIVES

NAS St. Louis, Missouri

On June 18, 1920, Major Albert Bond Lambert leased a 160-acre tract, 11 miles northwest of downtown St. Louis, for an airfield. Major Lambert, heir to the Listerine fortune and aviation enthusiast, experienced his first aircraft flight with Orville Wright. He was taught to fly by Arch Hoxsey and was the first person in St. Louis to obtain a pilot's license. Hoxsey had also given a flight to ex-president Teddy Roosevelt on October 10, 1910, at St. Louis. Teddy Roosevelt became the first ex-president to fly -- 30 some years would pass before a president in office, FDR, would take to the air. Lambert's lease included an option to buy which he exercised in 1925. Lambert promoted his airfield to become St. Louis's municipal airport. This was realized on June 12, 1930, when RAdm. Richard Byrd dedicated the airfield as the Lambert-St.Louis Airport. The City first leased the airport and later purchased it from Lambert for a nominal fee.

Navy reservists formed an aviation unit at St. Louis in 1925. The reserves rented aircraft until 1928, when Major Lambert donated an aircraft to the unit. In 1931, after the City of St. Louis funded the construction of a hangar and other buildings, the Navy established an NRAB. In 1935, the NRAB began the Elimination Training Course for Naval Aviation Cadets. In January 1941, the station expanded by 21 acres to begin full primary training.

OPPOSITE PAGE: Lambert Field in March 1945. The Navy's area at the airport is the lower right of the airfield.
NATIONAL ARCHIVES

By this time, Curtiss-Wright, McDonnell, and Robertson were all manufacturing aircraft and aircraft sub-assemblies at Lambert. The Army also had a presence with a transient aircraft servicing unit. In spite of this congestion, the Navy remained at the airport expanding the base by 40 acres to accommodate additional personnel. The station now consisted of a North and South base with the Navy spending almost $4.5 million in construction. The main OLF, Smartt Field, was located 12 miles to the north. The Navy built a 2,000-ft. octagon landing mat, a hangar, and other buildings at a cost of nearly $250,000. Initially known as Neubeiser for the former owner of the property, the field was later named in honor of Ens. Joseph G. Smartt, who lost his life on December 7, 1941, during the Japanese attack on NAS Kaneohe Bay, Hawaii.

On January 1, 1943, St. Louis became a Naval Air Station and at that time, operated 115 primary trainers including Naval Aircraft Factory N3Ns, Spartan NPs, and Boeing N2S Stearmans. St. Louis, one of the smallest stations in the primary training command, had a capacity of 400 cadets. Peak operations occurred in mid-1943, with over 160 trainers on board. When Grosse Ile ended the primary training of British cadets in March 1944, the British were sent to St. Louis for completion. Primary training ended here in August 1944, so British cadets on board were sent to Bunker Hill and American cadets to Glenview. From January 1, 1943, the station trained 2501 American cadets and from March 1944, 732 British students.

After the end of primary training, the Ferry Service Unit at Adams Field, Little Rock, Arkansas moved to the vacant St. Louis. Shortly thereafter, the Advance Base Aviation Training Unit (ABATU) also transferred aboard from Norfolk. The ABATU trained enlisted men for CASUs, ACORNs, and AROUs. CASUs were carrier aircraft service units that performed maintenance on carrier squadron aircraft, provided instrument proficiency aircraft, trained squadron's enlisted men, maintained a pool of spare aircraft, and towed targets among other duties. ACORNs built and maintained advance airbases, while AROU were advanced aircraft repair and overhaul units. At the peak, ABATU operated 40 aircraft that included F4Us, F6Fs, TBMs, SB2Cs, PVs, PB4Ys, and JMs. The ABATU conducted much of its flying operations at Smartt Field, but closed down on September 1, 1945.

Navy holdings only amounted to 62-owned acres, 45 leased and seven OLFs. Lambert had a total of six runways -- the longest 6,000 ft. In March 1944, complement stood at 200 officers, 400 cadets, 1083 enlisted men, and 100 civilians. Available berthing accommodated 98 officers, 592 cadets, and 1478 enlisted. The station operated approximately six miscellaneous aircraft plus the aircraft assigned to the Bureau of Aeronautics Representative of the aircraft factories at the airfield. During the war, Lambert Airport's factories produced over 3,000 aircraft including the Curtiss R5C Commando (C-46) and 900 Curtiss A-25 Helldivers (SB2Cs). Over 400 of the Army's A-25s, with non-folding wings, found their way to the Marines as the SB2C-1A.

In September 1945, the Navy used the station as a demobilization center to process Naval personnel out of service. In 1946, St. Louis became a base of the Naval Air Reserve also operating auxiliary units at Springfield, Illinois, Cape Girardeau, Missouri, and Evansville and Terre Haute, Indiana. Smartt Field became a general aviation airport. St. Louis fell victim to the Naval base closings of the late 1950's. The station disestablished on February 1, 1958. Following the Navy's departure, the Missouri Air National Guard took over the former Navy base.

ABOVE: The Navy's holdings at Lambert Field consisted of 45-leased acres and 62-owned acres. Wartime growth of the station took place to the south of the airport and across a public highway. Locally, the two facilities were known as North and South Base.

MARCH 1945 NATIONAL ARCHIVES

OPPOSITE PAGE: Stearmans and what appears to be an SB2C Helldiver in St. Louis's hangar in February 1944.

NATIONAL ARCHIVES

The self-explanatory photographs on this and the next page capture behind the scenes work necessary to keep primary trainers in the air. *JUNE 1944 NATIONAL ARCHIVES*

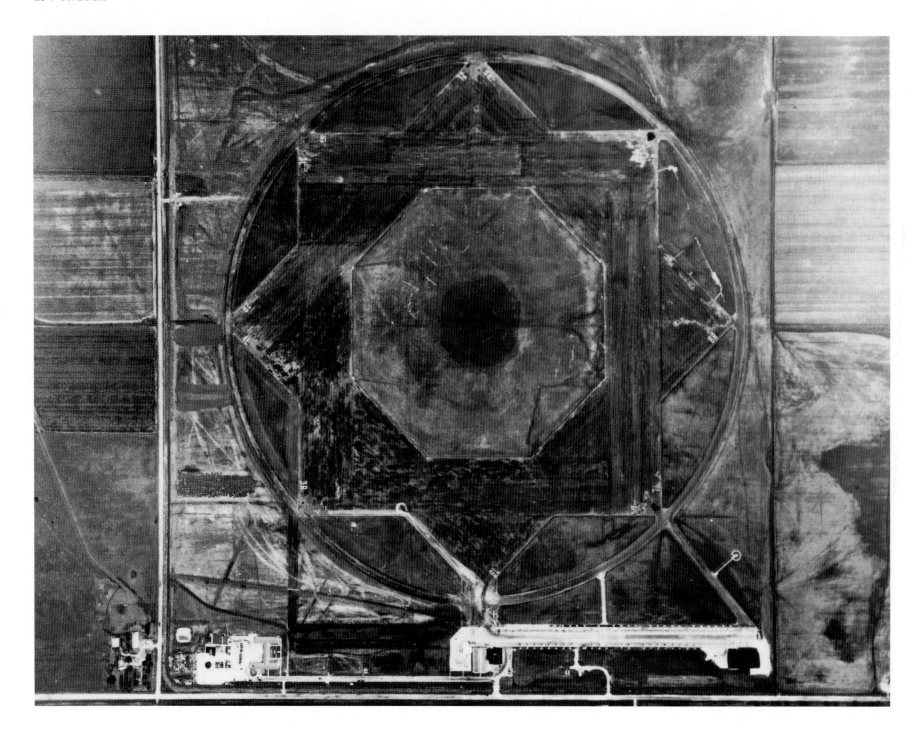

ABOVE: An ABATU F6F Hellcat makes a low pass. ABATU's flight operations also took place at Smartt Field. *MAY 1945 NATIONAL ARCHIVES*

ABOVE RIGHT AND RIGHT: Cadets receiving training on synthetic gunnery trainers in November 1943. *NATIONAL ARCHIVES*

OPPOSITE PAGE: Smartt Field. A large portion of St. Louis's primary training took place here. The field was named in honor of Ens. Joseph Smartt, killed at Kaneohe, Hawaii on December 7, 1941. *MARCH 1944 NATIONAL ARCHIVES*

APRIL 1945 NATIONAL ARCHIVES

NAS Terminal Island, California

Long Beach and San Pedro serve as the harbor for the greater Los Angeles area. During WW I, the Navy established an operating base at San Pedro that remained in use through the 1920s and 30s. In 1935, a need arose for an aviation facility to support the floatplanes of battleships and cruisers. The harbor's sand-filled Terminal Island was leased for no charge from the City of Los Angeles. The WPA provided initial construction of the break water, a seaplane ramp, a concrete parking mat, and three runways that reached completion in June 1937. Work continued with the addition of hangars, barracks, and other facilities in the fall. The station commissioned on March 1, 1938, as NAS San Pedro, and went through a series of name changes before finally settling on Terminal Island.

In early 1939, the Navy began construction of a training facility nearby, named Roosevelt Base, and a shipyard. On October 1, 1941, the Navy formed an Aircraft Delivery Unit (ADU) at the air station. Shortly after the attack on Pearl Harbor, the Army stationed P-40 and P-38 interceptors at the airfield with the permission of the Navy. In January 1942, VS-46 began operating the inshore patrol mission from the base with 12 OS2U Kingfishers. The same month, the Army built eight concrete revetments on the airfield to protect its aircraft. The primary mission of the air station became the major West Coast Aircraft Delivery Unit. In the last six months of 1942, the ADU commissioned 200 aircraft a month from the Douglas and Lockheed factories in the area including the SBD, SNV, PV, and the A-24 (SBDs for the Army). Meanwhile NATS's VR-2, began three flights a week.

During 1943, activity continued to rise. VR-2's service increased to daily with VR-3 beginning two daily transcontinental flights. Scouting squadrons continued operating from the station and from August to December of the year, VS-52 conducted operational training with SBDs. During the year, the ADU's deliveries averaged 434 aircraft a month including Culver TD2C drones, PB2Bs, PB2Y-3R transports, Canadian produced SB2Cs, and PBYs from Consolidated's new plant in New Orleans. Terminal Island reached the limit of its capacity; therefore, an Auxiliary Aircraft Acceptance Unit opened at Litchfield Park, Arizona, to accept the PB4Ys Liberators from San Diego. On December 1, the ferry squadron, VRF-3, commissioned at Terminal Island. Army continued to operate interceptors and added antiaircraft guns plus barrage balloons. During 1944, the station started performing aircraft modifications. At the end of 1944, the ADU began receiving the new Lockheed PV-2 Harpoon. VJ-12 also arrived and remained to war's end.

Terminal Island had three asphalt runways with the longest 4900 ft. In March 1944, personnel totaled 341 officers, 1274 enlisted men, and 420 civilians. Billeting was available for 171 officers and 1054 men. Peak utilization of the station occurred in the spring of 1945, with over 300 aircraft on board. VRF-3 operated 18 aircraft -- mostly light transports. The station proper had approximately 20 aircraft assigned. An Assembly and Repair Department maintained an aircraft pool that reached over 100.

Terminal Island closed in 1947, and its property assigned to the Bureau of Yards and Docks. Growth of the Long Beach Naval Shipyard eventually obliterated the former airfield's runways. The 1995 Base Realignment and Closure Commission recommended closing the shipyard.

Kingfishers of a scouting squadron execute a formation takeoff.   *NATIONAL ARCHIVES*

APRIL 1945 NATIONAL ARCHIVES

NAF Thermal, California

During the first year of U.S. involvement in WW II, the Army hurriedly established a training center in the California desert, 25 miles southwest of Palm Springs. General George Patton trained his army here in preparation for *Operation Torch* -- the invasion of North Africa. Known as Thermal Ground Support Base, the 2553-acre facility had two 5,000-ft. runways. Between March 1943, and May 1944, the Army attached several liaison and tactical reconnaissance squadrons to the airfield. Thermal had been inactive for six months when the Navy requested permission to occupy the base on December 2, 1944. Things were done quickly in those days and the Army gave verbal approval five days later. ACORN 29 and CASU 11 arrived aboard on December 7, and began readying the station. On December 12, the Commanding General 4th Air Force gave the Navy official authorization to take over the airfield with the stipulation that the Army could reoccupy with 30-days notice.

Initially known as Naval Air Bases Detachment Thermal, elements of CAG 98 arrived in late December and flight operations began. Besides flying operations, the station also served as a pre-embarkation training center for ACORNs, CASUs, and Seabee units. The Navy officially commissioned NAF Thermal on February 1, 1945. A Ferry Service Unit was established for use by VRF-3. CASU 70, the last CASU created during the war, commissioned in March to support CAG 98.

The base's facilities were in rather poor condition. During the first few months of the Navy's occupancy, the ACORNs and Seabees made extensive improvements. Spread over four miles of desert, the usual Army tar paper shacks were repaired and brought up to "Navy standards." The runways and taxiways had to be repaired and additional aircraft parking ramps installed. The Navy leased a recre-ation center, 2.5 miles from the base, with a swimming pool and dance hall for enlisted men. In addition, a local citizen supplied a house and swimming pool at a nearby ranch to the Navy. The house became the Commanding Officer's residence. Officers and their wives were allowed to used the pool. The ACORN, CASU, and Seabee training program ended on April 20, 1945, after ten such units had passed through the station.

CAG 98 was an operational training unit that administered refresher training -- similar to the East Coast's CAG 97. CAG 98 also maintained units at Los Alamitos and Ventura. Activity of CAG 98 peaked between June and September 1945, when 375 pilots received rocket, gunnery, and bombing training. Aircraft strength reached 115 including the F6F, F4U, TBM, SB2C, and SBD. Station aircraft consisted of a J4F, an N2S, an NE, and a GB.

Located in the Coachella Valley 150 feet below sea level, the place was named Thermal for a reason. Daily summer temperatures reached 120F in the shade soaring much higher on the concrete ramp. Conducting training here was not easy and summer flight operations took place from 0300 to 1300. In the heat of the day, the ground crews simply could not service the aircraft. At those temperatures, just touching hot aluminum would blister the skin!

The Navy closed Thermal on November 1, 1945, returning the field to the Army two months later. Today, Thermal is a municipal airport serving general aviation. Among the WW II buildings surviving is a hangar that is presently used by the local Fixed Base operator.

Tiny Tim rocket is readied for use.   *NATIONAL ARCHIVES*

NAS Tillamook, Oregon

In the summer of 1941, the Army Corps of Engineers, the CAA, and Tillamook County developed a plan to build an airport. A site was chosen four miles south of the town of Tillamook and $410,000 allocated to build two 4,000 x 150-ft. runways. Shortly after the start of the war, the Navy selected the site for an LTA base. The location, sheltered from winds by hills, was also the northernmost site on the West Coast where snow and icing conditions were not a major concern. The U.S. Army relinquished its option on the airport in April 1942. The County followed by donating 600 acres to the total of 1965 acres required by the Navy. Construction got under way in July, with grading and construction of a railroad spur, continuing through the severest winter in years. Over 18 inches of rain fell in November and over 19 in December -- the most in 25 years. The Navy commissioned NAS Tillamook on December 1, and the station's squadron, ZP-33, ten days later. Two months would pass before the first blimp arrived.

Nature's onslaught continued with over 15 inches of snow in January, 1943 -- the first snowfall in 30 years! The next month, the first blimp arrived and moored in the open, since the blimp hangars were still under construction. On March 27, 1943, a strong gust of wind blew K-31 from the mooring mast to its destruction. The first blimp hangar reached completion in July, followed one month later by the second. In September, Headquarters Squadron 3 (HEDRON 3) commissioned to support ZP-33 with maintenance and other services. Routine operations continued until November 20, when ship K-71 made a forced landing at Long Beach, Washington. The crew intentionally ripped the blimp's envelope to prevent further harm. Although the car and engines suffered damage, no injuries were incurred by the crew. The first of 1944 started badly for ZP-33, when ship K-39 make an emer-

gency landing at Quillayute, Washington. The landing ripped the bag, but no injuries were suffered by the crew.

The Navy continued to make improvements to Tillamook's airfield as well as constructing additional buildings. In March, Tillamook was approved for heavier-than-air operations as 45 aircraft of VC squadrons were assigned aboard. Tillamook also began refueling and rearming other station's squadrons conducting aerial gunnery training off the coast. Another injury-free accident occurred on June 5, when K-83 crashed in mountainous terrain on Vancouver Island, British Columbia while searching for a downed RCAF aircraft. In August, K-111 experimented with the servicing of a blimp from an aircraft carrier. The demonstration lasted a total of 72 hours with the crew being changed every 12 hours. Ironically, K-111, temporarily deployed to Delmar, California, by HEDRON 3, crashed in fog on Santa Catalina Island, on October 17. The ship's depth charges and gasoline tanks exploded and six of the crew of eight were lost -- the only Tillamook aircrew fatalities of the war. That month, a memorial service was held for the Tillamook-based crew.

On March 18, 1945, another blimp from Tillamook crashed as K-103 fell into Tillamook Bay with no injuries. In April, the station began long-term storage of airships and aircraft. Beginning with 10 L-ships, the next month, the first FM-2 Wildcats also arrived for storage. Following VJ-Day, blimp operations began to wind down. On August 27, the station reduced to a functional status. The decommissioning of ZP-33 and HEDRON 3 took place on November 10, 1945. The blimps present were flown to Moffett and Santa Ana.

On January 1, 1946, 11 L-Ships and 107 FM-2 Wildcats were in storage. Station manning stood at

200 Naval personnel and 100 civilian employees. One year later, aircraft in storage totaled 433. The next year, the Navy decided to close the storage facility and all aircraft were removed from mothballs and flown out. The decommissioning of Tillamook took place on July 1, 1948. The County leased the airport from the Navy until 1963, when it took over title to the property.

Tillamook had two 5,000 x 150-ft. asphalt runways and four blimp mooring circles. In March 1945, personnel numbered 74 officers, 859 enlisted men, and 120 civilians. Available barracks could accommodate 154 officers and 950 enlisted men. ZP-33 operated a maximum of eight airships and also deployed detachments to Astoria and North Bend, Oregon as well as Shelton and Quillayute, Washington. The station operated a J4F Widgeon for rescue, a GH Howard for ambulance, and a GB Beech for transport. Tillamook was responsible for the maintenance of the OLF at Newport, Oregon.

Following the war, plywood manufacturers used the old blimp hangars until 1982. The hangars have also been used for various LTA projects. Each hangar was 1072-ft. long, 296-ft. wide, and 192-ft. high with over seven acres of floor space each. Approximately two million board feet of fire-retardant treated Douglas fir timber went into each hangar. They were the largest clear span all-wood buildings in the world and listed in the Guinness Book of World Records. In August 1992, Hangar A, that was being used for storage of straw, burned to the ground. Arson was suspected, but never proven. In 1996, Hangar B housed a commercial blimp. The history of the station is remembered by the Tillamook County Pioneer Museum that maintains a photographic and memorabilia collection of the base, as well as the NAS Tillamook Museum, with an aircraft collection, in Hangar B.

ABOVE: Blimp night flight.   *TILLAMOOK PIONEER MUSEUM*

ABOVE LEFT: K-31 was the first blimp to land at Tillamook on February 15, 1943.

TILLAMOOK PIONEER MUSEUM

LEFT: K-71 was the first blimp to be docked in a hangar on August 18, 1943. Until the hangars reached completion, blimps were moored in the open.   *TILLAMOOK PIONEER MUSEUM*

ABOVE AND ABOVE RIGHT: Blimp is readied for flight. *TILLAMOOK PIONEER MUSEUM*

RIGHT: FM-2 Wildcats at Tillamook awaiting preparation for storage in 1945.
TILLAMOOK PIONEER MUSEUM

Treasure Island looking south in April 1942. Built for the 1939-1940 Golden Gate Exposition, the island was slated to become San Francisco's municipal airport. Pan Am's seaplane operation was located at the far side of the island and an airfield on the near side. The Navy used the island for blimp operations early in the war and a blimp is present in this photo. Growth of the Naval base during the war took over the airfield and prompted Pan Am to move its operation to Mills Field, now San Francisco International Airport.

NATIONAL ARCHIVES

NAF Treasure Island, California

In 1937, a project began to build a man-made island in San Francisco Bay for the 1939-1940 Golden Gate International Exposition and a base for Pan American Airways. Following the Exposition, the island was to become San Francisco's municipal airport. The Army Corps of Engineers oversaw the project with $4 million in funding provided by the WPA. Construction included a terminal building with two hangars on the southside of the island and an airfield on the northern end. On January 23, 1939, Pan Am moved to new quarters on Treasure Island from Alameda. Pan Am's operation was a part of the Exposition and featured a spectator's gallery in one of the hangars to view the airline's maintenance and overhaul work. With the beginning of the war everything changed. The Navy placed Pan Am under contract in September 1942, and commandeered its aircraft. The Navy also took over the island commissioning an NAAF.

Early in the war, Treasure Island was involved in one of aviation's great mysteries. ZP-32 from Moffett Field used Treasure Island as a forward base for antisubmarine patrols of the approaches to San Francisco Bay. This arrangement saved flight time to and from Moffett. On August 16, 1942, Lt. Cody and Ens. Adams departed Treasure Island at 6 A.M. on a round-robin patrol to the Farallon Islands, Pt. Reyes, and back to Treasure Island. The blimp used was L-8 that had been pressed into Navy service from the Goodyear advertising fleet. The pilots radioed Moffett at 7:38, four miles east of the Farallons, reporting that they were investigating an oil slick. Two hours later, the blimp drifted ashore and hit a glancing blow to seaside cliffs knocking off the depth charges that fortunately, did not explode. The blimp finally came to rest in the middle of a street in Daly City, south of San Francisco -- with no one on board! The door was locked open with the safety bar down. The radios and ignition were on and the only missing equipment consisted of two life-preservers. A search of the patrol area failed to find any trace of the missing pilots. One year later, the Navy declared the pilots dead. Meanwhile, L-8 was repaired, placed back in service, and eventually returned to Goodyear following the war. The public quickly became intrigued by this incident as journalists dubbed the airship "The Ghost Blimp." Whatever happened to the pilots is anyone's guess!

Pan Am operated its Martin M-130 China Clippers and Boeing 314s, as well as Navy supplied Consolidated PB2Y-3Rs. The two M-130s used out of Treasure Island, the *China* and the *Philippine Clipper*, operated between Treasure Island and Honolulu. On January 21, 1943, the *Philippine Clipper*, inbound from Hawaii, struck a mountain northeast of San Francisco with the loss of all on board. The *China Clipper* labored on until October 1943, when it was returned to Pan Am after having made 88 trips to Hawaii and back in a year's time. Naval ship traffic became so heavy that in 1944, Pan Am moved its operations to Mills Field -- today's San Francisco International Airport. Treasure Island remained an NAAF as Pan Am continued to use the facility for seaplane overhaul.

Naval construction eventually took over the airfield. The primary mission of the base was processing of personnel to and from the Pacific Theater. At the peak, 12,000 men a day passed through the station. Treasure Island also served as headquarters of the Twelfth Naval District.

Following the war, the Navy traded land at Mills Field for the island. In the ensuing years, Treasure Island housed various activities to support the Naval and Marine forces in the San Francisco Bay area. Pan Am's former terminal housed the Commanding Officer of the Treasure Island Naval Base, the Commandant of the San Francisco Naval Base, and the Navy/Marine Corps Museum. Treasure Island was selected for closure by the 1993 Base Realinement and Closure Commission.

L-8, the "Ghost Blimp," repaired and restored to service, was eventually returned to Goodyear following the war. *NATIONAL ARCHIVES*

APRIL 1945 NATIONAL ARCHIVES

NAAS Twenty Nine Palms, California

In November 1941, a U.S. Army Contract Pilot School was established at Twenty Nine Palms, 125 miles east of Los Angeles in the Mojave Desert. Twenty Nine Palms Air Academy conducted primary training for prospective Army glider pilots from January 1942, until April 1944, when it closed.

Attracted by excellent flying weather and bombing/gunnery ranges in the area, the Navy requested and received permission to take over the base from the Army. After Seabees readied the facilities, an NAAS commissioned on August 1, 1944. NAAS Twenty Nine Palms consisted of 1600 acres of leased land with barracks for 164 officers and 2146 enlisted men. The base was located on Mesquite Dry Lake, north of town. The landing area, previously known as Condor Field, was an 1800 x 3000-ft. mat used during wet weather. Normal air operations took place from the dry lake bed.

The Army did the Navy no favor by releasing the base. The Navy intended to use the facility for PVs and PB4Ys; however, the field had been built to accommodate primary trainers and the mat was not stressed for heavy aircraft; therefore, carrier squadrons were sent aboard. Even carrier aircraft broke through the pavement and the mat deteriorated to the point that Seabees had to lay 1,459,000 sq. ft. of Marston Matting. Built on a dry lake bed, the field was also subject to flooding during heavy rains. Once a dike broke in the station's sewage treatment plant flooding the base. Besides bringing flight operations to a halt, everyone must have had a very unpleasant experience. An additional problem was extremely high desert temperatures during the summer of 1945 that reduced flight operations here and at other stations in the desert. In spite of these handicaps, a total of 51 squadrons completed gunnery, rocket, and bombing training. ACORNs, CASU,

and Seabee units also received pre-embarkation training at 29 Palms. A detachment of CASU 45 initially supported the carrier squadrons. By June 1945, CASU 69-F commissioned, replacing CASU 45. The Navy closed Twenty Nine Palms in October 1945, returning the airbase to the Army that in turn released the airfield for use by San Bernardino County in February 1946.

The facility lay idle for six years. In 1952 during the Korean War, the Marines took over the property establishing a Marine Corps Base. The Marines continued to expand their presence over the years and in 1976, an 8,000-ft. Expeditionary Airfield was completed, capable of handling a C-5 Galaxy. In 1979, the Marines redesignated the base as the Marine Corp Air Ground Combat Center. Today, the Center encompasses 932 sq. mi., and is home to over 10,000 military and 1,300 civilian employees.

Tiny Tim rocket, with what appears to be an inert warhead, is loaded on a Corsair in June 1945.
NATIONAL ARCHIVES

Built on a dry lake bed, Twenty Nine Palms was subject to flooding.
AUGUST 6, 1945 NATIONAL ARCHIVES

NAAS Ventura County, California

Oxnard is located approximately 50 miles northwest of Los Angeles. In 1935, the WPA built a 1980-ft. runway on 35 acres one mile west of town. The airport's dedication was celebrated on July 4, 1935, with an airshow. The airport was later enlarged to 242 acres and the runway extended to 4517 feet. In June 1940, Cal-Aero Corporation, with headquarters at Glendale's Grand Central Airport, opened the Mira Loma Flight Academy, a primary training Contract Pilot School for the Army. The barracks and administration buildings were built in a very unusual circular layout. The Academy closed on June 28, 1944. The primary cadets present at that time were transferred to another Cal-Aero facility, the Polaris Flight Academy at Lancaster.

The Navy was attracted by the airport's proximity to the Advanced Base Depot at Port Hueneme, only five miles away. The Navy requested to take over the base and the Army obliged. The Army caretakers vacated the airport on July 7, 1944, and an ACORN Assembly and Training Detachment arrived six days later. The base was used for training of ACORNS, CASUs, and Seabees. On August 8, CAG 98 transferred aboard. CAG 98 conducted refresher training for pilots returning from combat, as well as training replacement pilots. On December 4, the bulk of CAG 98 departed for Los Alamitos, but a detachment remained at Ventura. CASU 47-F was present during December with 19 SB2Cs and 2 SBDs. During 1945, Ventura hosted VC-5, 10, 41, and 3 in addition to the detachment of CAG 98. Naval holdings totaled 203-leased acres with barracks for 554 officers and 2190 enlisted men.

Ventura's activity ended quickly after the war and the station disestablished on February 1, 1946. In October 1946, the Navy traveled 10 miles to the south and built NAS Pt. Mugu for a missile test center. Pt. Mugu did not exist during the war. Today, the Ventura County Airport serves general aviation in the Oxnard area.

The very unusual circular layout of the barracks and administrative area. *USN*

Ventura County's ramp in January 1945. *NATIONAL ARCHIVES*

MAY 1944 NATIONAL ARCHIVES

NAAS Vernalis, California

In late 1942, the Navy started work on two auxiliary stations in the San Joaquin Valley near the small and isolated communities of Vernalis and Crows Landing. At Vernalis, 16 miles west of Modesto, 700 acres were purchased for $33,300 to build a base to support two multi-engine patrol squadrons. The Navy commissioned NAAF Vernalis on June 8, 1943, as an auxiliary of Alameda with one 4,000 x 500-ft. tarmac runway.

In November, a project began to extend the existing runway to 7000 ft., as well as add buildings and gasoline storage capacity. In the meantime, Vernalis's designation changed to an NAAS. During this time, VB-148 and VB-150 were aboard. In the spring of 1944, the Navy realized that Crows Landing, 18 miles to the southeast with concrete runways, would be better suited for the heavier multi-engine types. The two stations swapped missions. Thereafter, Vernalis hosted carrier squadrons. With the arrival of carrier units, Vernalis added a 160 acre dive bombing range and commissioned CASU 63 in support. Due to the limited crosswind landing capability of Navy carrier aircraft, $240,000 was spent on the addition of a 4000 x 150-ft. crosswind runway. Further improvements included $16,000 in permanent runway lighting and a Seabee installed catapult and arresting gear. At a strafing range on the Diablo Mountain Range to the west, a silhouette of a submarine was painted on rocks for strafing practice.

Vernalis proper consisted of a single country store that also served as a Post Office. One local resident remembers that a visitor once walked out of the store and asked: "How do you get out of town?" -- the supreme insult! To keep the sailors entertained, Vernalis ran a liberty bus service to Modesto. German POWs arrived late in the war, constructed an Olympic-sized swimming pool, and worked on local farms. The base had a quarter-mile field track and an ice hockey team that played in Modesto.

Vernalis had daily afternoon logistic aircraft service from Alameda that brought mail, personnel, and aircraft parts. One morning, the passenger manifest for the afternoon flight, received by teletype, listed Admiral Dewey Bluitt as a passenger. The C.O. alerted the troops, who policed the base, neatly parked the aircraft in one direction, and decked out in dress uniform for the occasion. The C.O. and an honor guard met the flight when it arrived. Off the PBY stepped Admiral Dewey Bluitt -- a black Seaman First Class! Presumably, Bluitt's father had been a Navy man who named his son after the famous Admiral Dewey.

After the war, Vernalis initially was chosen to remain open; however, Crows Landing received the nod due to its concrete runways. On October 15, 1945, Vernalis was placed on caretaker status and abandoned three months later. In the 1950's, the Air Force used the airfield to launch 300-ft. diameter balloons that carried electronic equipment for experiments in the stratosphere. In recent years, the property has been used for sun-drying of agricultural products and the storage of cannery waste that is subject to spontaneous combustion. Locals claim the former base is haunted by a ghost, known as "the Colonel." The ghost is alleged to be a former military man who was murdered and dismembered on the base. Another explanation might be a tragic accident that occurred during the war. A cable broke on the catapult and arresting gear system killing two men -- decapitating one. The decapitated man was working in place of another man who had a date. Could this man be the ghost in question?

Vernalis's ramp is deserted in May 1944.

AUGUST 1944 NATIONAL ARCHIVES

NAAS Waldron Field, Texas

In late 1942, the Navy decided to build an additional auxiliary at Corpus Christi. Initially an OLF known as #21305, the site was located on a magnetic bearing of 213 degrees and five miles from the main station on a portion of the Chapman Ranch. Since the Navy planned to utilize the base for the torpedo training syllabus, the station was named in honor of LCdr. John C. Waldron on commissioning day, April 1, 1943. LCdr. Waldron, the C.O. of VT-8, had been killed in the Battle of Midway on June 4, 1942. All fifteen TBD Devastators of VT-8 were shot down during the squadron's attack on the Japanese fleet with the loss of 29 crewmen. The sole survivor was the late Ens. George Gay.

VN-16, commissioned at Corpus Christi, moved aboard and began instruction. Since the barracks lacked completion, all hands were initially bussed daily from Mainside. On August 23, 1943, VN-16 split into two separate squadrons -- VN-16A and VN-16B. The same month, the torpedo syllabus changed to a more generalized CV course. The CV syllabus consisted of an eight-week course with approximately 75 hours of flying including five hours of familiarization, six hours of instruments, 12 hours of formation, six hours of night flying, seven hours of navigation, four hours of primary combat, and 35 hours of gunnery. Cadets also received ground school classes on engines, navigation, recognition, meteorology, Naval regulations, and other subjects. Other activities involved Link trainer flying, physical training, code/blinker training, and gunnery ground training. Gunnery training included target practice with the pistol, shotgun, .30 cal. machine gun, and instruction in the Gunairstructor.

In the first 18 months of operation, VN-16A flew 174,231 hours and graduated 1375 students. Seventeen students were dropped and the five fatalities included two South American students. Up to December 31, 1944, VN-16B flew 165,512 hours with 1276 graduates, 18 drops, and five fatalities. On January 1, 1945, VN-16A aircraft included 127 SNJs, three N3Ns, and two N2S Stearmans. VN-16B, on the other hand, operated 133 SNJs, one N3N, and two Stearmans. The Stearmans and the N3Ns were used for the inverted spin checkout and other duties. On January 28, Cdr. David McCampbell, the Navy's top ace with 36 victories, paid a morale boosting visit. McCampbell had received the Medal of Honor for shooting nine Japanese planes down in a single engagement -- the record for American fighter pilots!

Waldron had four 5,000 x 300-ft. asphalt runways and four OLFs. In March 1944, personnel totaled 166 officers, 232 cadets, and 1488 enlisted men. Available berthing could accommodate 100 officers, 432 cadets, and 1150 enlisted. The station operated a Howard, an SNB, and two Piper Cubs.

Shortly after the war on August 25, 109 Waldron aircraft were evacuated to Dallas to avoid a hurricane. On October 1, 1946, Waldron closed becoming an OLF to NAS Corpus Christi. The Author practiced FCLPs here in January 1963 in the twin-engine Grumman S2F while in VT-28. Called the "Flying Speedbrake" by the students because of the assorted appendages the Navy attached to it, or the "Stoof," the S2F was not the favorite Navy aircraft flown by the Author. During the Author's stint at Corpus Christi, two students on a solo flight, one an acquaintance of the Author, were killed when they failed to handle an S2F engine loss following a touch-and-go landing at Mainside. Waldron remains an OLF to Corpus Christi in 1997.

Typical temporary wooden-wartime tower cab found in the training command -- usually mounted on corner of hangar.
CURTISS SILVERNAIL

NOVEMBER 1943   NATIONAL ARCHIVES

NAAS Watsonville. California

Naval Aviation at Watsonville during WW II consisted of two facilities. The new CAA built airport became a carrier aircraft station as an auxiliary of Alameda. The Navy never liked mixing heavier-than-air operations with blimp operations if avoidable. Therefore, the local airport was taken over and an NAAF for blimp use established -- this facility was an auxiliary of Moffett.

NAAS Watsonville

In 1939, the CAA offered to build an airport at Santa Cruz, the largest city in Santa Cruz County and the county seat, if the necessary land was provided. After Santa Cruz turned down the proposal, the CAA then approached the City of Watsonville -- the second largest city in the county. A small airport existed four miles SSW of town, but it was inadequate for the modern facility planned by the CAA. Watsonville floated a bond issue for $125,000 to purchase 330 acres, 2.5 miles northwest of town. The CAA completed its initial work by the end of 1941. During 1942, the CAA made additional improvements spending a total of $740,000 on the project that resulted in a 4500 and a 4000-ft. macadam runway. In mid-1943, the Navy leased the airport's 288 acres from Watsonville and purchased 35 additional acres to build administration and barracks buildings. Navy construction began in July 1943, and the station commissioned on October 1.

In October, VB-18 with 36 SBDs arrived along with a detachment of CASU 19 in support. On November 14, VF-28 and 24 F6Fs flew into Watsonville for a two week stay. On December 9, VB-18 departed for Crows Landing, replaced by VF-26's and VF-27's 48 F6Fs. In December, the station suffered its first fatality in the crash of a VF-27 F6F. That month, CASU 35 relieved CASU 19.

RIGHT: An FM has crashed and burned.   *NATIONAL ARCHIVES*

In February 1944, VF-26 and VF-27 moved to other stations as VT-28 and VF-28 arrived. The CASU merry-go-around continued as CASU 37 relieved CASU 35. From March to July 1944, CAG 22's VF-22 and VT-22 trained aboard. CAG 23's fighter and torpedo squadrons were present from July to October. On July 16, an F6F of VF-23 hit the tower of the local radio station. The pilot later died of injuries. During the year, the Navy spent $1.2 million enlarging the station to accommodate 90 aircraft. Improvements included a new administration building, four barracks and a BOQ, and a Gunnery Training building. In November, the CASU situation stabilized with the forming of CASU 64 that absorbed the personnel of CASU 37. The end of the year found VC-33 and VOC-2 at the station. VOC-2, an observation composite squadron, had a complement of 23 FM-2s and six TBM Avengers.

On January 15, 1945, CAG 8, the first large air group arrived after reforming at Alameda. CAG 8's 96 aircraft consisted of VF-8 with F6Fs, VBF-8 also with F6Fs, VB-8 with SB2Cs, and VT-8 with Avengers. On May 17, CAG 8 departed for Alameda prior to embarking for Hawaii. Shortly thereafter, CAG 4 came aboard with a similar make-up excepting that its VBF squadron was equipped with Corsairs. The diverse Corsair squadron consisted of F3As, FGs, and F4Us. CAG 4 departed for Groton, Connecticut after VJ-Day. On October 15, 1945, the station went on caretaker status.

The airport was opened for civilian use and the Navy finally turned over all facilities to the City in March 1947. Until 1963, some of the former Navy buildings were used as a school. Today, the airport is used by general aviation.

NAAF Watsonville

The first airport was established in Watsonville in 1930. A group of investors and aviation enthusiasts formed a corporation known as the "Watsonville Airport, Inc." The corporation issued 5,000 shares of stock, mostly purchased by local citizens. With the funds raised, 85 acres were bought four miles SSW of Watsonville. Although Watsonville is located in Santa Cruz County, the property purchased was across the county line in Monterey County -- the most reasonably priced land available at the time. An aircraft carrying California Governor James Rolph made a low pass cutting a ribbon, officially opening the airport on May 9, 1931.

In 1942, the Navy leased the airport and established an auxiliary blimp base of Moffett. The station opened August 6, 1943. Moffett's ZP-32 usually maintained a detachment of one to two K-ships at the base that conducted patrols of the Monterey area. The facility had three asphalt runways -- the longest 2300 ft. and three blimp mooring circles. Apparently the entire airfield was paved or oiled. Peak complement consisted of nine officers and 96 enlisted men with barracks for 15 officers and 101 men. The Navy utilized the existing 60 x 60-ft. hangar on the airport. Although the NAAF was officially a separate command, facilities were minimal at best and NAAS Watsonville was undoubtedly relied upon for much of its administrative support as well as supply of the 1001 items needed to operate an airbase. As far as is known, nothing unusual or of note occurred at the facility during the war.

Following the war, the Navy returned the 87 acres to the corporation. When the heavier-than-air station northwest of town was deeded to the City, the former blimp facility was abandoned. In May 1947, the corporation sold the property to an individual who used it for a cattle feed lot.

ABOVE: An L-ship, used early in the war for patrol, comes in for a landing.

NATIONAL ARCHIVES

LEFT: For transportation of helium to remote sites such as Watsonville, the Navy utilized special built trucks. Helium was normally shipped via railroads.

NATIONAL ARCHIVES

AUGUST 1943 NATIONAL ARCHIVES

OCTOBER 1943 NATIONAL ARCHIVES

NAS Whidbey Island, Washington

Whidbey Island is a 40-mile-long narrow island in Puget Sound, beginning 25 miles north of Seattle. The island was named for Joseph Whidbey who discovered it on June 2, 1792. Whidbey was master of the HMS *Discovery* and part of George Vancouver's fleet. In 1940 and 1941, the Navy chose the island for a second major air station in northwest Washington. Construction included a seaplane base near the town of Oak Harbor and an airfield four miles north of Oak Harbor at an area known as Clover Valley. With $3.8 million earmarked for the station, work began on January 15, 1942. The population of Oak Harbor in 1940 was only 200; therefore, an immediate problem arose in obtaining skilled labor at the isolated location. Temporary quarters for 1000 single workers were created as well as low-cost housing for married workers.

At Oak Harbor, initial plans called for minimum facilities to support seaplanes; however, once the war began the project expanded. The seaplane facility was built on a peninsula between Oak and Crescent Harbors. Construction included three seaplane ramps, a 240 x 320-ft. hangar, barracks and dredging of sea lanes. Administration and other facilities were provided at Clover Valley. During clearing, workers unearthed 142 Indian skeletons that were re-buried on the nearby Indian reservation. The Navy named streets at the seaplane facility for WW II battles.

During construction, no mess facilities had been planned. Higher authorities, appraised of this fact, directed that personnel could eat at NAS Seattle. Mess facilities were quickly provided when it was pointed out that the men would have to travel 130 miles round trip, three times a day.

The airfield and main base were located at the 4,200-acre Clover Valley site. The streets here were named for aircraft carriers. On August 28, 1942, the first aircraft landed on the airfield's runways. The commissioning occurred on September 21, 1942. The airfield at Clover Valley was named Ault Field, in honor of Cdr. William Ault who lost his life in the battle of the Coral Sea. At the outset, Whidbey was planned as the base for two CAGs, two PV squadrons, and three seaplane squadrons. VC squadrons were the first landplane squadrons to arrive and PBYs the first seaplanes. On September 1, 1943, OLF Coupeville, located a few miles to the south, opened with a tower and an HE catapult and arresting gear. By late 1943, the first F6Fs arrived and the next summer, the first PBMs.

By the fall of 1944, numerous other air stations opened in the Northwest. Whidbey was then chosen to be an exclusive multi-engine patrol plane base so the station converted for these types. In October, the first PB4Y squadrons transferred aboard. The next month, the station began rocket training for PV squadrons. Rockets, loaded at OLF Mt. Vernon on the mainland, were fired on the Lake Hancock range. The airport at Mt. Vernon had been acquired by the Navy and improved by the Army early in the war. In October 1943, Mt. Vernon was designated as a Navy OLF. In April 1944, the Army totally released the field to the Navy. Mt. Vernon, used for transition landings and instrument practice, had barracks and other facilities. Whidbey also operated two torpedo ranges for the Puget Sound area that included the target ship USS *Hatfield*. The station added a torpedo shop in February 1944. By January 1945, a total of 4264 torpedo drops had been made as new Lockheed PV-2 Harpoons and PB4Y-2 Privateers began to arrive. By the end of the war, Whidbey Island had become the main training and operational base of the Seattle Naval Air Center. The station had a 7,000-ft. and a 5,000-ft. runway, five hangars, and accommodations for 5,900 personnel. A sophisticated gunnery training facility for enlisted multi-engine gunners also existed with rail-mounted turrets and targets.

One might think with the wet maritime weather of the Puget Sound area, Whidbey would not have particularly good flying weather. However, the location is somewhat of a meteorological abnormality in that the sun shines about 75% of the time. Average rainfall is 17 in., but in 1943 the station only received 10.11 in. followed in 1944 by a mere 8.15 in. Compare this to the 100 in. of rain that fell during one year at Quillayute 100 miles to the west. One C.O. claimed that Whidbey Island has more VFR flying days than San Diego.

Following the war, the Navy reduced Whidbey in operational status putting its fate in doubt. In 1949, the Navy decided to make the station the main Naval air base in the Northwest. The seaplane base remained open as the new Martin P5M Marlin arrived in the early 1950s. The Lockheed P2V Neptune was the main aircraft in use at Ault Field. In 1953, the Navy designated Whidbey as a Master Jet Base. Two new 8,000-ft. runways were built for the arrival of new Douglas A3D Skywarriors. All A3D squadrons in the Pacific fleet were based here. In 1966, the first Grumman A-6 Intruders also came to the station followed later by the EA-6 Prowler electronic countermeasure aircraft. The next year, the Navy ended seaplane operations, closing the Oak Harbor seaplane base, but retained the property. Today, Oak Harbor is location of the base exchange, commissary, and some family housing. In 1970, when NAS Seattle closed, Whidbey began reserve activities. Whidbey survived the base closing in 1993; however, Moffett did not and its P-3 assets moved to Whidbey. The last A-6 Intruder squadron was retired in 1997, but the EA-3s will remain on board for the foreseeable future.

ABOVE: View of F6Fs from Hangar 4 in November 1943.   *NATIONAL ARCHIVES*

ABOVE LEFT: OLF Mt. Vernon was purchased by the Navy and improved by the Army. The Navy contemplated developing Mt. Vernon into an NAAS, but developed Quillayute instead due to the already crowded gunnery ranges in the area. Whidbey Island used the OLF for transition landing, instrument practice, and rocket loading. Mt. Vernon had barracks and a small contingent of men stationed there.

NATIONAL ARCHIVES

LEFT: Ault Field's tower and operations building.   *NATIONAL ARCHIVES*

ABOVE: View of Ault Field's ramp in December 1945.

NATIONAL ARCHIVES

ABOVE RIGHT: View from Hangar 1 in December 1945.

NATIONAL ARCHIVES

RIGHT: Lockheed PV-2 Harpoon in January 1946 at Ault Field.

NATIONAL ARCHIVES

ABOVE: Captured Japanese Kawanishi H8K2 "Emily" at Oak Harbor in December 1945. With an endurance of over 24 hours, the aircraft was one of the best flying-boats of the war. Armed with five 20mm cannons in powered turrets, allied fighter pilots treated the "Emily" with respect.

NATIONAL ARCHIVES

ABOVE LEFT: PBMs at Oak Harbor in August 1945.

NATIONAL ARCHIVES

LEFT: Whidbey Island's Oak Harbor seaplane base in October 1943.

NATIONAL ARCHIVES

Whidbey Island had a sophisticated gunnery training range. Both guns and moving targets were rail-mounted. *JUNE 1943 NATIONAL ARCHIVES*

ABOVE: Alaska's quick changing weather can catch up with the most competent and cautious aviator. A PBY-5A of VPB-43 suffered a forced landing at Atka Island in June 1945. *NATIONAL ARCHIVES*

ABOVE LEFT: Many of the Navy's flight facilities in Alaska were small, such as this floating hangar at the Ketchikan Section Base.

MAY 1942 NATIONAL ARCHIVES

LEFT: When the weather is good, the view in Alaska is incomparable. This PBY-5A extended the landing gear to prevent the aircraft from drifting onto the rocky shore incurring damage. *NATIONAL ARCHIVES*

Minor Alaskan Stations

By anyone's standards, Alaska is a big place. At 586,000 sq. mi., the State, twice the size of Texas, was a U.S. Territory during World War II. With freezing temperatures, mountainous terrain, and arguably the world's worst weather, the area is very inhospitable to aviation. Alaskan weather is unpredictable and changes fast. Due to the terrain, space for airfields is in very short supply. The Japanese invaded the Aleutians in June as a diversion for the primary target of Midway not planning on remaining through the winter. After the staggering defeat at Midway, the Japanese High Command claimed, for home front propaganda, that Midway was a diversion for the Aleutians campaign extending their planned stay. Later, the Japanese anticipated an American invasion from the Aleutians and decided to reinforce their garrisons. In the campaign to expulse the Japanese from the Aleutians, the Army and the Navy worked closely together building bases along the Aleutian chain. Since the Navy had its hands full with seaplane and harbor facilities, the Army assumed responsibility for constructing most of the airfields. The Navy established a string of bases along Alaska's southern coast from Annette Island in the east to Attu Island in the western Aleutians stretching a staggering 2600 miles -- travel another 1500 miles southwest of Attu and you reach Tokyo. The histories of the NASs at Sitka, Kodiak, Adak, Dutch Harbor, and Attu have been addressed earlier. The minor facilities featured here, for the most part, served as emergency/weather alternates and weather stations.

NAAF Afognak Island

Located 50 miles north of Kodiak, Afognak opened as a small seaplane base/radio station in March 1942, an auxiliary of NAS Kodiak. Although used mainly for administration purposes, two years later the base opened a recreational facility for hunting and fishing. All personnel at Kodiak were allowed a two-to-three day recreational and rest trip to the facility. Afognak disestablished in 1944, but remained for recreational use by NAS Kodiak. The facilities were renovated in the mid-1960s. Today the island is part of the Chugach National Forest.

NAAF Amchitka

After the Japanese invaded Kiska and Attu on June 7, 1942, the U.S. needed an advanced base to operate closer to the two islands. The nearest island that could accommodate an airfield was Amchitka, 90 miles to the southeast of Kiska. Army engineers built a 5000 and a 3000-ft. gravel and steel mat runway for joint use with the Navy. NAF Amchitka commissioned on February 24, 1943. The Navy's area at the base consisted of 575 acres and barracks for 140 officers and 919 enlisted men. The mission of the base was to support a 12-plane PBY squadron and a 12-plane PV squadron that used the Army's airfield. Seaplane facilities consisted of a 50 x 150-ft. seaplane ramp, a 60 x 115-ft. parking apron, and nine shops. Additional Navy facilities on the island supported a PT boat unit. Amchitka closed in October 1945. The island was used for underground nuclear testing in the 1960s and 1970s. Today the airfield is a U.S. Fish and Wildlife facility.

NAAF Annette Island

Annette Island opened on March 1, 1943, as an auxiliary of NAS Sitka, 200 miles to the northwest. Initially, the station was known as NAAF Metlakatla for the nearby town and was the southernmost Navy air station in Alaska. The mission of the base was to support three observation aircraft and service aircraft en route from Alaska to Seattle. A seaplane facility only, the station also used the nearby Army field. Complement consisted of 16 officers and 95 enlisted with barracks for 32 officers and 86 enlisted men. The Navy departed Annette Island on May 31, 1944. The Coast Guard then took over the facility. The initial Coast Guard air detachment consisted of one officer, six enlisted crewmembers and one aircraft. The Coast Guard remained at Annette Island until 1977, when it moved the station and three helicopters to Sitka. Today, the airfield is a private airport owned by the Metlakatla Indians.

NAF Atka

Atka Island is located 100 miles east of Adak in the Aleutian Islands. The Navy PBYs operated from the island's Nazan Bay early in 1942. After the Japanese invasion at Kiska, the seaplane tenders were withdrawn to the east. The Navy sent a seaplane tender back to Atka on July 19. On August 3, the tender *Gillis* and the destroyer *Kane* were attacked by Japanese flying boats from Kiska without suffering any hits. Another Japanese attack took place the next day; however, this time Army P-38s from Umnak were waiting in ambush and shot down two four-engine Kawanishi 97 Mavis flying boats. On August 30, the Japanese submarine RO-61 slipped into the bay and torpedoed the *Casco* then present. The *Casco's* captain beached the ship which was later repaired. PBYs from Dutch Harbor damaged the submarine that was later sunk by an American destroyer. The Navy continued to use the facility for PBY patrols establishing an NAF in November. The Army, meanwhile, added a runway while the Navy built a 50 x 80-ft. nose hangar for use by its landplanes. Atka also served as a weather station. Barracks existed for 15 officers and 160 men. With the opening of Adak, activity lessened at Atka. Following the expulsion of the Japanese from the Aleutians, NAF Atka closed on September 1, 1943, but the weather station remained. Today, the facility is an unattended airport.

NAAF Cold Bay

Cold Bay, on the western end of the Alaskan Peninsula, first became a Naval reservation in 1929. Seabees built a section base at the location in mid-1942, and the Navy established an NAAF seaplane base there on July 14, 1942. The Army also built an airfield with three 5,000-ft. asphalt and steel runways. The mission of the facility, an auxiliary of NAS Kodiak, was to support a squadron of PBY amphibians. The air station's personnel consisted of 87 officers and 482 enlisted men with barracks available for 36 officers and 408 enlisted men. In November 1944, the air station closed. The Naval base continued to serve as a training and transfer point for small vessels going to the Soviet Union as part of the Lend Lease Program. Cold Harbor trained 9,000 Soviets and transferred 149 vessels the Soviets sailed across the Bering Sea.

NAAF Kiska

The Navy acquired control of Kiska in 1908. Inhabited by a ten-man Navy weather station, the Japanese occupied the island in June 1942. The Japanese stationed seaplanes and floatplanes at Kiska defending the island from American bombers that pounded it for the next year. Japanese fortifications were extensive including numerous antiaircraft guns plus a railroad gun captured from the British at Singapore. After the Americans invaded Attu, the Navy blockaded Kiska. Japanese forces on the island were isolated in an untenable position. Reconnaissance flights suggested the Japanese had withdrawn from the island. Nevertheless, a 34,426 Allied invasion force assaulted Kiska on August 15, 1943, only to discover the Japanese had successfully evacuated their 6,000-man garrison. Friendly fire killed 24 and wounded 50 American and Canadian troops. An additional four men were killed by Japanese booby traps.

The Navy established a small seaplane base there on September 11, 1943. The station's complement of 35 officers and 139 enlisted men supported six observation type floatplanes. Facilities consisted of a 30 x 150-ft. nose hanger, a 30 x 150-ft. seaplane ramp, and a steel mat apron. A small airstrip, built by the Japanese, was taken over by the Army. One year later, the Navy closed the facility on September 19, 1944. Today, the former facility is abandoned.

NAF Otter Point

On Umnak Island, 75 miles west of Dutch Harbor, the Army built an airstrip in March 1942. The Navy established a seaplane base that commissioned on October 22, 1942. The Navy facility consisted of 100 acres, one hangar, and a complement of 100 officers and 489 enlisted men. Barracks were built for 200 officers and 600 enlisted men. The base mission was support of a squadron of 12 PBYs and six observation floatplanes. The Navy's landplanes and amphibians used the Army field at nearby Ft. Glenn which had three 7,000-ft. cinder packed runways. Umnak was the western most Aleutian airfield at the time of the Japanese invasion and the primary Army airfield until the opening of Adak. Otter Pt. decommissioned in November 1944. Today, it is an abandoned airport.

NAAF Port Althorp

The Navy built a section base at Port Althorp, on Chichagof Island 70 miles north of NAS Sitka, in July 1941. In March 1943, an NAAF seaplane facility commissioned as an auxiliary of Sitka. The complement of 15 officers and 98 enlisted men supported five observation floatplanes. Available barracks built at the facility accommodated 16 officers and 50 men. The Navy placed the facility on caretaker status May 31, 1944.

Primitive PBY and Kingfisher operations in the Aleutians during June 1943.   *NATIONAL ARCHIVES*

NAAF Port Armstrong

In July 1941, the Navy established a section base at Port Armstrong. Located on Baranof Island, 50 miles south of Sitka, Port Armstrong opened a small seaplane base as an NAAF in March 1943. The Navy built the air facility on the site of a former commercial oil company's station. Barracks were built for 50 officers and men. Used as an emergency alternate for Sitka, the facility closed in July 1943.

NAAF Sand Point

The Navy built a section base at Sand Point, in the Shumagins Islands, in June 1942. Located south of the Alaska Peninsula, the station became NAAF Shumagin on April 1, 1943. The name later changed to Sand Point. The facility also had a radio range navigation aid, a weather station, and accommodations for 410 personnel. Since Cold Bay, a larger facility existed only 90 miles to the west, the station became superfluous and closed in late 1943.

NAAF Seward

Seward is located 80 miles south of Anchorage and is the southern terminal for the Alaska Railroad. The deep water harbor remains open all year and is Alaska's principal port. The City was named for Secretary of State William Seward, the driving force in the purchase of Alaska from the Russians in 1867 for $7.2 million or two cents per acre. In 1919, the Navy first established a Naval reservation at the port. In July 1942, the Navy opened a section base and on April 1, 1943, an NAAF at the port. On July 29, 1943, the Navy had no further use for the facility, turning it over to the Coast Guard.

NAAF Shemya

During the battle for Attu, the Army built an airstrip on the island of Shemya, 40 miles to the east. The Navy opened an auxiliary on the island in June 1943. VP-43 operated from the base beginning in October 1943. The Navy facility amounted to six acres on which was situated a seaplane ramp and barracks for 12 officers and 132 men. The complement of eight officers and 79 enlisted men supported a 12-plane PBY squadron. The Army used the airfield for operations against Japan and built a 10,000-ft. runway. Following the war, Shemya closed. In 1954, the base was turned over to the CAA. Northwest Airlines leased the airfield and used it as a refueling stop on flights to Japan. In 1958, the Air Force reopened the base and built a radar station to monitor Soviet rocket launches. The airfield was used by RC-135 reconnaissance aircraft. MAC aircraft also utilized Shemya for refueling during the Vietnam War. In 1993, the air base was named in honor of Col. W. O. Eareckson, the WW II commander of the Army's Aleutian bomber forces. F-15s of the Alaskan Air Command occasionally deployed to the base. In 1995, the Air Force closed the base turning it over to a civilian contractor that maintains the airfield for emergency landings.

NAAF Tanaga

The Navy opened an airfield 50 miles west of Adak in July 1943. The airfield consisted of a 5000 x 200-ft. steel mat runway used as an emergency landing field. Five hardstands and revetments were also added. The 1500-acre facility had a complement of eight officers and 86 enlisted men with barracks for 15 officers and 120 men. The Navy closed the base in October 1945. The airfield remains in use today.

NAAF Yakutat

Yakutat is located northwest of Sitka on the Gulf of Alaska. The Navy established a seaplane facility on September 5, 1942. As an auxiliary of Sitka, the base supported three observation floatplanes and four seaplanes. The Army had a large airfield at Yakutat also used by Navy landplanes. The Navy's complement of 16 officers and 95 enlisted men had barracks for 20 officers and 72 men. The Navy placed Yakutat on caretaker status May 31, 1944. Today, the former Naval facility is abandoned.

FEBRUARY 1943 NATIONAL ARCHIVES

BARKING SANDS

SEPTEMBER 1944   NATIONAL ARCHIVES

Minor Hawaiian Stations

Unlike Alaska, the weather in Hawaii is outstanding. The problem is the shortage of land suitable for airfields. The Army and the Navy cooperated very well in the islands to alleviate this problem.

NAAF Barking Sands

Barking Sands is located on the western end of the island of Kauai. English Captain James Cook became the official discoverer of Hawaii when he first set foot on the islands at Waimea, nine miles southeast of Barking Sands on January 18, 1778. Cook named the islands the Sandwich Islands, in honor of the First Lord of the Admiralty, the 4th Earl of Sandwich, John Montagu. The same Montagu was also the namesake of our popular snack convenience, the sandwich, allegedly concocted by him as to not let meals interfere with his gambling.

In the late 1800s and early 1900s, the area was used for the grazing of cattle. Barking Sands played a pivotal role in the epic Kingsford-Smith flight of the *Southern Cross* from the U.S. to Australia in 1928. On the first leg of the flight, Kingsford-Smith landed at the Army's Wheeler Field on Oahu. Since Wheeler Field was not long enough for the fully fueled aircraft to get airborne for the second leg, another site had to be found. Level land for an airfield in mountainous Hawaii is in short supply. Volunteer local workmen quickly prepared a 4300-ft. strip on the flat coast plain at Barking Sands to which the *Southern Cross* was ferried. On June 4, 1928, the *Southern Cross* departed from Barking Sands and landed at Suva, Fiji, 34 hours and 24 minutes later, completing the 3,180-mile flight — the longest over water flight up to that time.

During the 1930's, Inter-Island Airways, later Hawaiian Airlines, served the airport. In 1940, the Army acquired the airfield's 549 acres naming it

Mana Airfield, after the nearby town. The next year, the Army acquired additional acreage, bringing the total to 2,058 acres and the WPA began a project to improve the airport. Initial plans called for grass runways, but were changed to hard-surfacing after Pearl Harbor. Construction included a 6400 x 200-ft. asphalt runway, a 6360 x 200-ft. crushed rock runway, and a 1600 x 300-ft. apron, suitable for heavy bombers. The Army added 14 barracks and four mess halls. For the next two years, the Army continued to improve the airport by adding 23 revetments for heavy bombers and permanent accommodations for 1500 men. In spite of all these improvements, the Army did not use the base to its full capacity. although Navy and Marine aircraft occasionally utilized the airfield. When the Navy needed additional aircraft facilities in late 1943, the Army turned a portion of the base over to the Navy on January 1, 1944.

The Navy commissioned a temporary NAAF at Barking Sands in the spring of 1944. The only Navy units assigned to the station were VF-28 with 24 F6Fs, VT-28 with nine TBMs, and VC-66 with 12 FM-2s and nine TBMs. CASU 45 supported the squadrons present. Reclaiming the base on June 15, 1944, the Army formed an Air Combat Replacement Center and also used the airfield as a staging base for B-24s. The Navy and the Marines, however, continued to use the airfield. The Marine's commissioned Towing Detachment One (later VMJ-1) at Barking Sands on March 21, 1945, that would remain there through the end of the war.

In 1946, the base suffered severe damage from a tsunami. Hawaiian Airlines continued to use the airport until 1949, when the Lihue Airport opened on the other side of the island. In 1954, the airfield was officially renamed Bonham AFB. Two years later, the Air Force turned over 37 acres on the base to the

Navy for Regulus I operations. During the next few years, the Navy became the principal user of the airfield. In 1962, the Navy officially commissioned the Pacific Missile Range Facility, Barking Sands and two year later, the Air Force transferred the ownership of the property to the Navy.

In 1995, Barking Sands operated the world's largest training range for the Navy, the other services, and NASA as part of the Pacific Missile Range Command. The range consists of 42,000 sq. mi. of air and surface space plus a 1500 sq. mi. underwater range. The facility, manned by 900 military and civilian personnel, is capable of tracking subsurface, surface, airborne, and space vehicles simultaneously. Aircraft in use were six Sikorsky UH-3A Sea King helicopters and two Beech RC-12F Hurons.

NAF French Frigate Shoals

Located 550 miles northwest of Honolulu, French Frigate Shoals is a crescent-shaped atoll of small islands and reefs, 18 miles in diameter. The atoll's La Perouse Pinnacle is named for the French navigator who explored the area in 1786. The Navy first used the atoll in the early 1930s for training exercises. Prior to the war, PBYs occasionally operated from the area, although facilities were minimal consisting of a few shacks. The atoll played a major role in the Japanese campaign to conquer Midway in 1942. Since Japanese aircraft lacked the range to reconnoiter Hawaii from their nearest base in the Marshall Islands, the Japanese formulated a plan for submarines to refuel flying boats in the sheltered waters of the then American-unoccupied atoll. A proving run was conducted on the night of March 4-5, 1942, when Japanese submarines successfully refueled two H8K "Emily" flying boats from Wotje. Following refueling, the "Emilies" attempted a bombing of Oahu on the return to Wotje. Due to cloud cover, one of the aircraft dropped its bombs in the sea, while the other bombed the hills behind Honolulu, breaking windows in the city. On May 31, a second mission cancelled when Japanese submarines found American ships present. The Japanese were thus denied possible vital reconnaissance of the American fleet that could have played a major factor in the Battle of Midway.

Prior to the Battle of Midway, the Navy conceived a plan to establish an air facility at French Frigate Shoals. On August 13, 1942, elements of the 5th Seabee Battalion arrived and commenced work. The development concentrated around Tern Island, a tennis court sized island, at the northwest corner of the reef. Tern Island was chosen because its location offered protection from the swells. Dredging opened a 200-ft. ship channel into the lagoon and created an 8000 x 1000-ft. seaplane runway. Seabees utilized 660,000 cu. yds. of dredged coral, contained by a sheet piling seawall, to create a 3100 x 275-ft. rolled coral runway and parking ramp for 24 single-engine aircraft on Tern Island. Partially buried Quonset hut buildings, including housing for 12 officers and 152 men, were erected and painted white to blend in with the coral. A Marine PBY-5A was the first aircraft to land on the runway.

On March 10, 1943, the high point in the facility's history occurred when the Queen Mary, with escorts and tanker, anchored nearby for refueling. The Navy commissioned French Frigate Shoals a week later as an auxiliary of NAS Pearl Harbor. The station's mission was to provide a refueling and emergency landing strip for air traffic between Midway and Oahu. In addition, the facility also served as an outpost of Pearl Harbor to provide forward airborne, radio, and radar surveillance. A J2F Duck and an SBD were assigned to the station and flew patrols at dawn and dusk. The station was well armed with 90MM, 40MM, 20MM, plus .30 and .50 cal. machine guns.

The complement of 118 men rotated from Pearl Harbor on a three month tour at the facility. The station area totaled 27 acres. With the runway taking up 20 of those acres, only seven acres remained for the rest of the facility and the apron. Duty at the station must have been very routine, although once an unidentified surface target was fired on. During the station's existence, several fighter squadrons transited for refueling to/from Midway. The seawall, built in great haste, required constant maintenance. Although the recreational facilities were limited, swimming and fishing were excellent. With the conclusion of the war, the station's usefulness ended.

The Navy closed it on June 6, 1946, after the island was swept clean by a tidal wave on April 1, 1946.

In 1952, the Coast Guard built a 20-man Loran station at the old Navy facility. The airstrip was used by a weekly mail and supply flight. French Frigate Shoals was incorporated into the State of Hawaii in 1959. The Coast Guard closed the Loran station in 1979. The atoll is a part of the Hawaiian Islands National Wildlife Refuge and no one may enter the refuge without the permission of the U.S. Fish and Wildlife Service. A ranger station now occupies the former Coast Guard facilities.

FRENCH FRIGATE SHOALS   *JULY 1943 NATIONAL ARCHIVES*

NAF Molokai

Molokai, the first island southeast of Oahu, measures 40 miles long and seven to nine miles wide. The island is famous for the 1800's leper colony where Father Damien de Veuster spent his life attending to the spiritual needs of the colony. Father Damien succumbed to leprosy in 1889.

In 1929, the island's first official airport was established on a 205-acre site at a cost of $5,000. Since the airport had been built on land belonging to the Hawaiian Homes Commission, it was named Homestead Field. Inter-Island Airway (later Hawaiian Airlines) began service that year. The Army first used the airport's 1,300-ft. sod runway in 1931, for maneuvers. Four years later, the Army built a headquarters building and barracks to conduct regular training operations. During 1938 and 1939, additional runways were added to the airport, although the main runway remained at 1,300 ft. When Inter-Island Airways began operating the new Sikorsky S-43 in September 1939, operations were suspended due to the short runways. The next year, the Army revealed plans to lengthen the runways and build facilities for 600 men.

In November 1940, the Navy acquired 261 acres on the west coast of the island at Ilio Pt. for a bombing range. In May the following year, the Navy received 14 acres from the Territorial Government to build a facility at the airport to support the bombing range. Little history remains concerning this activity and it is doubtful that the Navy officially commissioned the station; however, the facility was listed as an NAF during 1943, and 1944, in some documentation. At any rate, the station served as an aerial gunnery camp to relieve congestion at other stations. Carrier aircraft would deploy to Molokai for intense gunnery, bombing and FCLP training. An additional target was set up on Mokukooniki Rock off Molokai's eastern end. Utility aircraft from Pearl Harbor were also present for target towing service. Construction on two hard-surfaced runways took place from 1941, to 1943, and when completed were 5400 and 3400-ft. by 200 ft. The Army and the Navy used the base as a joint facility and added underground shelters as well as 40 new buildings and runway lighting during 1944 with a total investment of over $2 million.

Operations wound down rapidly after the war as Hawaiian Air Lines resumed service. In 1947, the airport was returned to the control of the Territory. In 1952, the Navy property was turned over to the Marines from Kaneohe Bay. The Navy retained its 14 acres at the airport until 1977, when the property was returned to the State of Hawaii. Homestead Field remains as the municipal airport of Molokai .

MOLOKAI -- the Navy facilities are the group of buildings in the lower center of the photograph. *DECEMBER 1943 NATIONAL ARCHIVES*

APPENDIX C

Miscellaneous fields leased or owned by Navy, or Navy operations permitted

Abilene, Abilene Air Terminal, Texas - trans-continental blimp stop
Amarillo, AAF, Texas - NATS
Bakersfield, Bakersfield-Kern County, California - NATS
Battle Mountain, FS Site 35, Nebraska
Boulder City, Municipal, Nevada
Burbank, Lockheed Air Terminal, California - BAR Vega
Chadron, Site 15, Nebraska
Chehalis, City-County, Washington
Coolidge, AAF, Arizona - NAFC
Dryden, Dryden Airdrome, Texas
El Paso, Municipal, NATS, NAFC
Harlingen, Laguna Madre AAF, Texas - later NAAS Port Isabel
Hawthorne, Municipal, Nevada - Navy Ammo Depot
Hawthorne, Northrup Field, California
Houston, Ellington AAF, Texas
Houston, Hobby, Texas - NATS
Iowa City, Municipal, Iowa
Kansas City, Grandview, Missouri
Kenosha, Municipal, Wisconsin - BAR Howard
Lewiston, Municipal, Idaho
Little Rock, Adams, Arkansas - NAFC, SFU-3
Long Beach, Daugherty Field, California
Los Angeles, Mines Field, California - BAR Douglas, now LAX
Los Angeles, Van Nuys, California

Madera, AAF, California - AFSU, VRF-3
Medford, AAF, Oregon - NATS, NAFC
Midland, #2 Army, Texas - NAFC
North Platte, Lee Bird, Nebraska
Oklahoma City, Will Rogers AAF, Oklahoma - NATS
Oklahoma City, Tinker AAF, Oklahoma - NAFC
Omaha, Offutt AAF, Nebraska
Paso Robles, Sherwood, California
Portland, AAF, Oregon - NATS, NAFC
Red Bluff, Bidwell, California - NAFC
San Diego, Lindbergh, California
San Benito, Site 2, Texas - ZP-23
Santa Ana, Orange County AAF, California
Santa Maria, AAF, California
Shreveport, Municipal, Louisiana
Shreveport, Barksdale AAF, Louisiana - NAFC
Tacoma, McCord AAF, Washington - Kaiser
Tulsa, Municipal, Oklahoma - NATS, NAFC
Tucson, Oilpin, Arizona
Tucson, Municipal, Arizona - NAFC
Wichita, Municipal, Kansas - NATS
Winslow, Municipal, Arizona - NATS
Yakima, County, Washington - VRF-3
Yucca, AAF, Arizona
Yuma, AAF, Arizona - VRF-3, VRF-3

APPENDIX D

STATION LISTING BY STATE

Alaska

NAS Adak
NAAF Afognak
NAAF Amchitka
NAAF Annette Island
NAAF Atka
NAS Attu
NAAF Cold Bay
NAS Dutch Harbor
NAAF Kiska
NAF Otter Point
NAAF Port Althorp
NAAF Port Armstrong
NAAF Sand Point
NAAF Seward
NAAF Shemya
NAS Sitka
NAAF Tanaga
NAAF Yakutat

Arizona

NAF Litchfield Park

California

NAS Alameda
NAAS Arcata
NAAS Brown Field
NAAS Camp Kearny
NAAS Crows Landing
NAAF Del Mar
NAAF Eureka
NAAS Hollister
NAAS Holtville
NAF Inyokern
NAAS King City
NAS Livermore
NAAF Lompoc

NAAS Los Alamitos
NAAF Mills Field
NAS Moffett Field
NAAS Monterey
NAS Oakland
NAAS Ream Field
NAAS Salton Sea
NAAS San Clemente
NAS San Diego
NAAS San Nicolas
NAS Santa Ana
NAAS Santa Rosa
NAS Terminal Island
NAF Thermal
NAAF Treasure Island
NAAS Twenty Nine Palms
NAAS Watsonville

Hawaii

NAS Barbers Point
NAAF Barking Sands
NAAF French Frigate Shoals
NAS Hilo
NAS Honolulu
NAS Kalului
NAS Kaneohe Bay
NAS Midway Islands
NAAF Molokai
NAS Pearl Harbor
NAS Puunene

Iowa

NAS Ottumwa

Kansas
NAS Hutchinson
NAS Olathe

Louisiana
NAS Houma
NAS New Orleans

Minnesota
NAS Minneapolis

Missouri
NAS St. Louis

Nevada
NAAS Fallon

Oklahoma
NAAF Durant
NAS Clinton
NAS Norman
NAS Shawnee

Oregon
NAS Astoria
NAAS Corvallis
NAS Klamath Falls
NAAF Lakeview
NAAS North Bend
NAS Tillamook

Texas
NAAS Cabaniss Field
NAAS Chase Field
NAAF Conroe
NAS Corpus Christi
NAAS Cuddihy
NAS Dallas
NAS Eagle Mt. Lake
NAS Hitchcock
NAAS Kingsville
NAAF Meacham Field

NAAS Rodd Field
NAAS Waldron Field

Washington
NAAS Arlington
NAAS Quillayute
NAS Pasco
NAAS Shelton
NAS Whidbey Island

BIBLIOGRAPHY

American Airship Bases and Facilities, Shock

Building the Navy's Bases in World War II, U. S. Navy

The Concise Guide to American Aircraft of World War II, Mondey

History of Marine Corps Aviation in World War II, Sherrod

The Illustrated Encyclopedia of Combat Aircraft of World War II, Gunston

Jane's Encyclopedia of Aviation

Japan's WW II Balloon Bomb Attacks on North America, Mikesh

Jane's Fighting Aircraft of World War II

Miracle at Midway, Prange

Sky Ships, Althoff

Squadrons of the Fleet Air Arm, Sturtivant

United States and Marine Corps Bases, Domestic, Coletta

United States Naval Aviation 1910-1980, U.S. Navy

United States Navy Aircraft since 1911, Swanborough and Bowers

U.S. Coast Guard Aviation, Pearcy

U. S. Marine Corps Aviation - 1912 to the Present, Mersky

Wings at the Ready, Turpin and Shipman

Wings of Gold, Newton and Rea

Wings to the Orient, Cohen

World War II Combat Squadrons of the United States Air Force, U.S.A.F. Historical Division

GLOSSARY

AAF - Army Air Field

ABATU- Advance Base Aviation Training Unit - trained men to go into CASUs, ACORNs, and AROUs.

ABTU - Air Bomber Training Unit - trained air crewmen for multi-engine patrol aircraft

ACORN - built and operated advanced airbases

ADDL - Aircraft Dummy Deck Landing (later called FCLP)

ADU - Aircraft Delivery Unit

AE - Piper Cub - ambulance utility - 100 built

ALF - Auxiliary Landing Field

AROU - Aviation Repair and Overhaul Unit

AVR - Aviation Rescue Vessel

B-314 - Boeing seaplane used by Pan American under contract to the Navy

BARONPAC - Barrier Squadron Pacific

BD - Douglas Havoc - twin engine target towplane (Army A-20) - 9 acquired by Navy

BLMPHDRN - Blimp Headquarters Squadron - provided blimp maintenance and other services

BRACC - Base Realinement and Closure Commission

BOQ - Bachelors Officer Quarters

BTD - Douglas Destroyer - single engine torpedo-bomber - 28 built

BTM - Martin Mauler - single engine bomber - built after war as the AM

BUAER - U. S. Navy Bureau of Aeronautics

CAA - Civil Aeronautics Administration

CAA Intermediate Field - CAA emergency airfield on lighted airways

CAG - Carrier Air Group

CAP - Civil Air Patrol

CASU- Carrier Aircraft Service Unit - performed maintenance on squadrons aircraft, provided instrument aircraft, trained squadron's enlisted men, maintained pool of spare aircraft, and towed targets.

CAT II - Catagory II - instrument approach with 1200 ft. visibility

CAT III - Catagory III - instrument approach down to 300 ft. visibility

CO - Commanding Officer

CQ - Carrier Qualification

CQTU - Carrier Qualification Training Unit

CV - Aircraft Carrier or associated with carrier aircraft

CVLG - Carrier Light Group

F2A - Brewster Buffalo - single engine fighter - 503 built

F3A - Brewster Corsair - additional production of F4U - 735 built

F4F - Grumman Wildcat - single engine fighter - 1, 978 built

F4U - Vought Corsair - single engine fighter - 7, 829

F6F - Grumman Hellcat - single engine fighter - 12, 275 built

F7F - Grumman Tigercat - twin engine fighter used mostly by Marines - 364 built

F8F - Grumman Bearcat - single engine fighter - 1266 built, most after the war

FAA - British Fleet Air Arm

FAA - Federal Aviation Administration

FAW - Fleet Air Wing - command unit of scouting and patrol squadrons

FG - Goodyear Corsair - additional production of F4U - 4,006 built

FLCP - Field Carrier Landing Practice

FM - Eastern Wildcat - additional production of F4F - 5,927 built

FPM - feet per minute

FR - Ryan Fireball - fighter with reciprocating and jet engine - 69 built

FSU - Ferry Service Unit - unit of Naval Air Ferry Command

GB - Beech Traveller - utility/transport - 360 built

GH - Howard Nightingale - single engine utility transport - 280 built

HEDRON - Headquarters Squadron - training, command, or maintenance unit

HNS - Sikorsky helicopter - 25 acquired

IFF - Identification Friend or Foe - transmitted an identifiable radar signal

J2F - Grumman Duck - single engine utility amphibian - 546 built

J4F - Grumman Widgeon - twin engine utility amphibian - 156 built

JM - Martin Marauder - twin engine bomber similar to Army B-26 used for target towing - 272 built

JRB - Beech Expeditor - military version of Beech Model 18 transport - 1195 built

JRC - Cessna Bobcat - utility/transport - 67 built

JRF - Grumman Goose - utility amphibian - 257 built

LSO - Landing Signal Officer - pilot who directed carrier landings from aircraft carrier

MAG - Marine Air Group

MLG - Marine Glider Group

NACA - National Advisory Committee for Aeronautics

N2S - Boeing Kaydet or Stearman - primary trainer similar to Army Pt-13 - 4257 built

N2T - Timm Tudor - primary trainer - 262 built

N3N - Naval Aircraft Factory - biplane primary trainer and floatplane - 817 built

NAAF - Naval Auxiliary Air Station

NAAS - Naval Auxiliary Air Station

NACTU - Night Attack Combat Training Unit

NAF - Naval Air Facility

NAFC - Naval Air Ferry Command - an arm of NATS

NAMU - Naval Aircraft Modification Unit

NAS - Naval Air Station

NATS - Naval Air Transport Service

NATTC - Naval Air Technical Training Command

NE - Piper Cub - primary trainer - 250 built

NH - Howard Nightingale - single engine instrument trainer - 205 built

NP - Spartan - primary trainer - 201 built

NPG - Naval Proving Ground

NR - Ryan Recruit - primary trainer similar to Army PT-21 - 100 acquired by Navy

NRAB - Naval Reserve Aviation Base

NTS - Naval Torpedo Station

O in C - Officer in Charge

OLF - Outlying field

OS2N - Naval Aircraft Factory built OS2U Kingfisher

OS2U - Vought Kingfisher - scout/observation/trainer floatplane and landplane - 1218 built

OTU - Operational Training Unit

PB2B - PBY production by Boeing in Canada - 362 built

PB2M - Martin Mars - four engine seaplane used as transport and later produced as JRM - one built

PB2Y - Consolidated Coronado - four engine seaplane/transport - 176 built

PB4Y-1 - Consolidated Liberator - Naval version of B-24 - 977 built

PB4Y-2 - Consolidated Privateer - single-tail version of B-24 - 739 built

PBJ - North American Mitchell - similar to B-25 and primarily used by Marines - 706

PBM - Martin Mariner - twin engine seaplane/patrol bomber - 1366 built

PBN - Naval Aircraft Factory Nomad - improved version of PBY - 155 built

PBO - Lockheed Hudson - twin engine patrol bombers - 20 built

PBY - Consolidated Catalina - twin engine seaplane/patrol bomber with 7 crewmembers - 2,387 built

PV-1 - Lockheed Ventura - twin engine patrol bomber version of Lockheed Model 37 - 1600 built

PV-2 - Lockheed Harpoon - improved version of PV-1 - 535 built

R3D - Douglas DC-5 - twin engine transport - 8 built

R4D - Douglas Skytrain - Navy version of DC-3 - 568 built

R5O - Lockheed Lodestar - twin engine transport - 99 built

RY - Consolidated Liberator - transport version of PB4Y

SB2C - Curtiss Helldiver - single engine dive-bomber with pilot and rear gunner - 5,516 built

SBC - Curtiss Helldiver - single engine scout-bomber with 2 crewmembers - 258 built
SBD - Douglas Dauntless - single engine dive-bomber with pilot and rear gunner - 5,321 built
SBF - Fairchild of Canada Helldiver - additional production of SB2C - 300 built
SBW - Canadian Car and Foundry Helldiver - additional production of SB2C - 894 built
SC - Curtiss Seahawk - single engine observation/scout floatplane - 577 built
SNB - Beech Kansan - military version of Beech Model 18 twin engine trainer - 1613 built
SNC - Curtiss Falcon - basic trainer - 305 built
SNJ - North American Texan - basic trainer similar to Army AT-6 - 4384 built
SNV - Vultee Valiant - basic trainer similar to Army BT-13 - 2000 built
SO3C - Curtiss Seamew - single engine scout/floatplane with 2 crewmembers - 794 built
SOC - Curtiss Seagull - single engine scout/floatplane with 2 crewmembers - 259 built
SOSU - Scout Observation Service Unit - similar to a CASU for scout and observation aircraft
STAG - Special Task Air Group - units of TTF
TBD - Douglas Devastator - single engine torpedo bomber with 3 crewmembers - 130 built
TBF - Grumman Avenger - single engine torpedo-bomber with 3 crewmembers - 2,290 built
TBM - Eastern Avenger - additional production of TBF - 7,546 built
TBY - Consolidated Sea Wolf - single engine torpedo bomber with 3 crewmembers - 180 built
TDC - Culver drone used as target for ship anti-aircraft training - 200 acquired
TD2C - Culver target drone similar to Army PQ-14 - 1201 acquired
TDN - Naval Aircraft Factory TV guided drone
TDR - Interstate Aircraft production model of TDN
TTF - Training Task Force - developed drones, guided missiles, and other secret weapons
VB - Bombing squadron or aircraft
VBF - Fighter/Bomber Squadron
VC - Composite Squadron - squadron that consisted of different types of aircraft
VD - Photographic Squadron or aircraft
VF - Fighter Squadron or aircraft
VFN - Night Fighter Squadron or aircraft
VJ - Utility Squadron or aircraft
VK - Drone Control Squadron
VMB - Marine Bombing Squadron
VMD- Marine Photographic Squadron
VMF - Marine Fighter Squadron
VMJ - Marine Utility Squadron
VML - Marine Glider Squadron
VMR - Marine Transport Squadron
VMSB - Marine Scouting Bombing Squadron
VN - Training Squadron or aircraft*
VOF - Observation/Fighter Squadron
VP - Patrol Squadron or aircraft
VPB - Patrol Bombing Squadron
VPB2 - twin-engine patrol aircraft
VPB4 - four-engine patrol aircraft
VR - Transport Squadron or aircraft
VRE - Hospital Evacuation Squadron
VRF - Ferry Squadron
VRS - Ferry Service Squadron, maintained Ferry Squadron's aircraft
VS - Scouting Squadron or aircraft
VSB - Scout-bombing Squadron
VT - Torpedo Squadron or aircraft
VTB - Torpedo Bombing Squadron
VTN - Night Torpedo Squadron or aircraft
WPA - Works Progress Administration
X - used as prefix to designate experimental unit or aircraft
ZP - Blimp Patrol Squadron

* Training squadrons' designations included the Naval District in which they were located. For example, VN-18 at Corpus Christi was officially VN-18D8 or Training Squadron 18 of the Eighth Naval District. If more than one of the same type of squadron existed in the Naval District, a letter was added at the end. For example, Rodd's VN-18D8C, had a "C" added, since a similar squadron existed at Corpus Christi. In the text, the Author has taken the liberty to shorten the designation.

Index

About the Author

Mel Shettle, a native of Baltimore, Maryland, graduated from the University of Tennessee in 1961, and entered the U.S. Navy's Aviation Officer Candidate Program. He received his wings in February 1963, at Corpus Christi, Texas. Serving with VR-3, the Military Air Transport Service dedicated squadron, at McGuire AFB, New Jersey, he flew the Douglas C-118 Liftmaster and the Lockheed C-130 Hercules -- becoming an Aircraft Commander and Instructor Pilot. In 1966, he joined Delta Air Lines in Atlanta, Georgia while flying the C-54 in the Navy Reserve at NAS Atlanta. Over the years, Delta aircraft flown included the DC-6, DC-7, Convair 880, DC-9, B-747, DC-8, B-727, and L-1011. Mr. Shettle retired in 1997 as Captain on the L-1011, at age 56.